10 May 1994

To

Marilyn Sweet
— who lived through
the formulation of
many of these ideas
and shared in the
vitality of their
expression at CBIS/
BHC

Gratefully,

Jim Ashbrook

HUMANITAS

Twelfth-century Kamakura Scroll, dragon—ship

used by kind permission of Kozan-ji, Kyoto, Japan,
owner of the Kegon Enji, a national treasure

If I have ventured amiss—
very well,
then life helps me by its punishment.

But if I have not ventured at all—
who then helps me? . . .

(to venture in the highest sense
is precisely
to become conscious of oneself).

Faith is:
that the self
in being itself and
in willing to be itself
is grounded
transparently
in God.

Kierkegaard,
Sickness unto Death

HUMANITAS
human becoming & being human

James B. Ashbrook

Nashville · ABINGDON PRESS · New York

HUMANITAS: HUMAN BECOMING AND BEING HUMAN

Copyright © 1973 by Abingdon Press

Library of Congress Cataloging in Publication Data

ASHBROOK, JAMES B. 1925- Humanitas; human becoming and being
human.
Bibliography: p.   1. Man. 2. Christian life. I. Title.
BD450.A77   248'.48'61   73-8840

ISBN 0-687-18030-9

Scripture quotations unless otherwise noted are from the Revised Standard
Version of the Bible, copyrighted 1946, 1952, and 1971 by the Division
of Christian Education, National Council of Churches, and are used
by permission.

Scripture quotations noted NEB are from the New English Bible, copyright © the Delegates of the Oxford University Press and the Syndics of
the Cambridge University Press, 1961, 1970.

The poetry on p. 36 is reprinted by permission of Grove Press Inc.
Copyright © 1967, Grove Press, Inc. and permission of Granada
Publishing Limited, London.

The figures on pp. 46-47 are from *Journal of Experimental Psychology*
55 (1958), 291 (copyright © 1958 by the American Psychological Association) and from *British Journal of Psychology* 49 (1958), 316,
and are reproduced with permission of the association, the British
Psychological Society, and the author.

MANUFACTURED BY THE PARTHENON PRESS AT
NASHVILLE, TENNESSEE, UNITED STATES OF AMERICA

To those who have risked themselves
with me
and
allowed
me
to risk myself
with them

Acknowledgments

The dedication page expresses the deepest appreciation I can acknowledge. In the risking of *human* contact I have been able to give and to receive life beyond anything I could have anticipated.

In discussing my background I allude to some of the many personal and professional relationships that have been part of my becoming. More specifically in terms of this book there are some that I want to single out. Edward E. Thornton urged me to investigate Zen Buddhism and to travel to Japan as part of my work in awareness. I am equally grateful to him for suggesting Abingdon as a possible publisher. Joseph Messineo and Maxine Walaskay each read portions of an earlier and much bulkier manuscript. Both responded to and encouraged the more personal style. I assist Patricia Ashbrook as a consultant in her work as director of a day-care center. She, in turn, assists me. She read next to the final draft with her critical eye for detail and clarity on which I have come to rely so much.

What I owe to Colgate Rochester–Bexley Hall–Crozer is immense. Dean George Brett Hall continues to be a firm, quiet support in the background. On two occasions—the spring and summer of 1969 and the academic year 1971-72—I have been granted time for research and writing. The American Association of Theological Schools provided a faculty fellowship which helped with some of the expenses connected with the latter leave. Both the Mugar Library of Boston University and the Swasey Library of Colgate Rochester have been gracious and efficient in assisting me. The secretarial staff of Colgate Rochester Divinity School–Bexley Hall–Crozer of Karen Evans, and especially Hazel Spaven and Nancy Root, under the ever thoughtful direction of Joanne Oliver struggled with my scratching and scrawling, my fits and starts, with a cheerfulness and a competence for which I am ever grateful. Peter C. Ashbrook, Susan J. Ashbrook, and Barbara Strehlow also typed portions of earlier drafts. Alice Wilson graciously shared not only her proofreading skills but her enthusiasm even more.

I am able to reproduce the dragon/ship segment of the Kegon Enji picture scroll because of the kind permission of Kōzan-ji, Kyoto, Japan, owner of the Kegon Enji, a national treasure. I first became aware of the segment in a work on the art of China, Korea, and Japan which Rose Hall brought to my attention. I would express special appreciation to Masao Abe who put me in personal contact with Kōzan-ji Temple.

I want to say more, yet there is no way I can say enough.

J.B.A.
Rochester, New York

Contents

CONTENTS

Illustrations

CONSIDER

ONE
What Am I About?

Purpose

I am writing to converse with a special kind of person.

The conventional, down-to-earth, everyday individual may not respond. For I will be pressing where many feel life ought to be left alone. I will be tapping the strange and not easily understood and even the bizarre. I will be questioning what is accepted and affirming what is uncomfortable. So, if you want life to stay put, if you prefer things as they are "supposed to be," then what I am about may not be your cup of tea.

I am writing to converse with *the searching person*.

If you have sensed—however dimly—that there is more to life than meets the eye, then perhaps we can sense together.

If you have struggled—however casually—with the meaning of who you are, then perhaps we can struggle together.

If you have longed—however faintly—for a more intimate intensity with others, with yourself, with your world, then perhaps we can long together.

However, in pointing to sensing, struggling, and longing, I may be misleading you. For my intent goes beyond those who search for their own becoming. Clearly and fittingly, such people are looking for that which will illumine and enlighten their individual lives. My exploration, rather, is with those whose personal becoming is linked with the broader issue of humanity's becoming. These people critically explore their lives in the light of the experiences and expressions of people in other times and other places.

So, if you are critical of your own cultural embeddedness—however tentatively—then perhaps we can be critical together.

If you are searching—however flounderingly—for a fuller and truer humanity, then perhaps we can search together.

I am writing to converse with the seeker who questions, *the serious seeker*.

For I am writing to explore and to express the universal that lies within the unique. I am caught up in the mystical and the mythological, yet I am grounded in the dynamics of persons and structures. In short, I am on the meaning trip—but meaning in terms of the configuration of the mystical, the mythological, the psychodynamic, the cultural, the prophetic. For me, genuine humanness opens up the fullness of life itself.

If you lean toward this larger life, then try conversing with me in this book. We may come upon more life than we now know.

At the start of his monumental project, *The Masks of God*, Joseph Campbell described our problem as the opposite of the problem of earlier times. In stabler periods the group carried and confirmed the meanings by which people lived. Today the group no longer bears that orienting and organizing meaning.

In our period the weight of meaning rests upon the individual. "But there," Campbell reminds us, "the meaning is absolutely unconscious. One does not know toward what one moves. One does not know by what one is propelled. The lines of communication between the conscious and the unconscious zones of the human psyche have all been cut, and we have been split in two."

It is that split that I am investigating. We experience the rupture between the unique and the universal, between the potential and the actual, between vitality and intentionality, between our being human and our human becoming. How can the rift be healed?

I am convinced that to become the humanity we are to be, we need "to learn," as Campbell claims, "to recognize the lineaments of God in all of the wonderful modulations of the face of [humanity]." To become a part of that whole, we must participate in the part that we are. To overcome the rupture in our humanity, we must *be* the split that we have become. Then we will be the whole that we are not yet, yet are to be.

I have used the concept of "split" to convey my intent. That is correct, but a little too abstract for what I am about. Let me shift to the more experiential level of an image to get my purpose across.

Pictured in the frontispiece is a section of a Japanese picture scroll. You can see a powerful sea dragon carrying a ship on its back. It comes from the Kamakura Period (A.D. 1185-1392), which was a time of great cultural and social complexity. The scroll depicts the founding of the Kegon sect of Buddhism in Korea.

The founding and authority of the sect derives from the Kegon Sutra. The sutra are sermons given by Buddha immediately after his perfect enlightenment:

> In the higher realm of suchness
> There is neither "self" nor "other." . . .
> In being "not two" all is the same.

He expresses a mystical sense of underlying sameness in all difference and pervading difference within all sameness. Instead of a realm in which all particular objects are absorbed in the all-pervasive All, a spiritual world is postulated where each object holds within itself all other objects. Within the unique we come upon the universal. Throughout the universal we see the unique. Life is whole.

Legend has it that Zemmyo, a nobleman's daughter, falls in love with Gishō, one of the founders of the sect, while he is studying in China. Hearing that he is returning home, she gives chase, only to learn his ship has already sailed. The sequence from the scroll shows that as she throws herself into the sea in pursuit, she is immediately transformed into a sea dragon. The dragon both protects the ship and carries it on her back to Korea where Gishō founds the sect. For my purposes,

(read picture scroll from right to left, bottom to top)

used by kind permission of Kozan-ji, Kyoto, Japan, owner of the Kegon Enji, a national treasure

Zemmyo transformed into sea dragon   Zemmyo leaps into the sea

the Buddhist particulars are secondary to the drama itself.

In the journey from old life to new life it is necessary to cross from one space to another. Always the passage is treacherous, always stormy, always risky, always uncertain. The venture is usually accompanied by a plunge or a fall into the seemingly nonrational. While thought and care and planning may have been present, the actual event is borne by the intuitive initiative of the unconscious.

This vital power of the impersonal depths carries us through the turbulent waters. It comes from the near shore, the site of our being. It drives us forward toward the far shore, the place of our becoming.

Above the waters this conscious intellect directs the vital force. It, too, comes from the near shore, the site of our becoming. Its intention is the place of our being. It charts the course and steers the ship.

The sea dragon—the ship—the shores—these are images of the split in and the search for the human self.

> To be/come aware
> to be/come related
> to be/come whole

that is my purpose—pretentious as it sounds, impossible as it may be, inevitable as it really is.

Now I must ask you about . . .

Contact

Can there be any real contact between you and me in terms of my purpose?

You have picked up this book for reasons I can only surmise and for motives you may only partially sense. How fragile the bridge between us!

The elusive image of humanitas—being human and human becoming—stretches from my pen to your eyes. Can that delicate strand bear the weight of our distance? Can it carry the load of our difference? Can it provide the support for our explorations?

I know I do not write to give you answers to questions you

never ask and about which you care little. Rather, I set forth where I am and what I experience that my life may be strengthened as, I hope, your life may be strengthened.

I need not remind you there are enormous obstacles to such contact between us.

There are the images we hold of each other as well as the images we hold of ourselves.

For myself, I would like to set before you the image of a brilliant and clever man, one who can survey vast reaches of human experience, who by the turn of a phrase or the twist of a word could capture your attention and quicken your imagination. But frankly, I am not that image (as if you even need my pointing that out). I would be wasting my time and yours if I were to try to construct such a fraudulent bridge.

Rather, I am a person who has known hurt and heartache as well as love and life. I have trusted and mistrusted. I have been worthy of trust and unworthy of trust. I endeavor to be real that contact might be genuine.

As I imagine you, I see one who looks both confident and critical. I see you as having lived intensely whether you are younger or older. I suspect you have read widely and thought carefully. And you have probably found handles on your own humanity.

Yet I say to myself, "What you see with your mind's eye is only your image of the reader. It is not the whole story. Behind the image lies a deeper reality, a more complex person, one who hurts and loves even as you hurt and love, one who reaches out in trust and uncertainty even as you reach out in trust and uncertainty, one who hungers and hopes for humanness even as you hunger and hope for humanness."

Yes, the images we have of ourselves and of each other loom as a major obstacle to our connecting.

The language we use and the lives we live raise additional barriers. You have your own special expressions—words and phrases and images—that I cannot know except in vague speculation. In turn, I have my own special expressions—words and phrases and images—that may or may not speak to you. Certainly, until you stay with me awhile and try to get my meanings, what I am seeking to express will remain blurred and of little relevance to you.

If we could be together, then you might be honest enough to say to me, "I don't understand what you're talking about. It does not make sense. It leaves me cold. Get to where I am."

If we were together, then I could respond, "Help me get to where you are. Could you tell me more of what you understand? How do you experience life?"

Perhaps out of our give-and-take we would suddenly find we were no longer talking at each other; instead we would simply be "with" each other. In that moment language and life would be transformed. A barrier would have changed into a bridge. In our speaking and in our listening, in our receiving and in our giving, beyond the words and within the silences, the deep part of your being and the deep part of my being would open to each other. And if that happened, in that moment we would indeed know ourselves to be in the presence of that Reality that is beyond the depth of both of us yet within the depths of each of us, that Reality that is the in-between where I and thou meet.

Background

A black truck driver and I are sitting on the grass in the shade. We have been experiencing the exhilaration that comes as two human beings vibrate with each other. We have met at a conference I am leading on "be/come Community." Suddenly, John crosses the chasm between us. I have not fitted his image(s) of a conventional human being. He wonders why. "Ashbrook, what makes you tick? How did you get the way you are?" In part he was asking to know *me*; in part he was seeking clues for himself and his own becoming. Frankly, I learned as much from him as he did from me.

Be that as it may, my point now is to indicate why I tell you of myself. John was not alone. I find people not only curious, but caring, about the experiences that I have selected to shape me. Students, particularly, press me for my background and my biases. Therefore, let me tell you briefly of my experiences and exposures. For in this ultimately personal area of humanness a more personal style is called for.

My undergraduate work consisted of a broadly conceived interdisciplinary major involving philosophy, history, psychology, and sociology with special studies in labor economics.

In seminary I turned more particularly to philosophical theology and New Testament. An exciting moment came in sensing Paul's meaning in that great seventh chapter of Romans. I glimpsed the split people experience between what they think they want and the way they actually behave.

Between my second and third year of seminary I had my initial exposure to clinical pastoral education. That was the first of a series of ongoing experiences in state hospitals, general hospitals, reformatories, mental health clinics, and counseling centers (both in the community at large and in university settings in particular). I bumped against crippled and crushed humanity. I caught glimpses of the toughness, the resiliency, and the tragedy of humanity. I began to dig into the depth and breadth of my own humanity.

My study of sociology and urban problems quickened my imagination and channeled my activist bent. As a consequence, my first parish nestled in the inner city. For four years I lived and worked, loved and wept, struggled and stumbled, found and fumbled, with what church and ministry and meaning and humanity meant. Those were good years; I experienced the anxiety of responsibility; people risked sharing themselves with me; problems of individuals and problems of society emerged as both more distinguishable and more inseparable than I had anticipated. One could not *not* grow in such a setting.

Perhaps my most significant learning from those first adult years was the painful, yet powerful, discovery that I myself inevitably and invariably affected every situation in which I found myself. My strength fed strength and in turn was fed by strength. My weakness fed weakness and in turn was fed by weakness. While I experienced and expressed wholeness and health, I also experienced and expressed—more often than I cared to—brokenness and unhealth. In fact, my unhealth had an uncanny way of intruding at the most inopportune moments. While disasters fortunately were avoided, disruptions did occur. I came to the realization that *if* I wanted to be more effective rather than less effective, *if* I wanted to grow and use *all* my experiencing for my own and others' becoming, *then* I would have to probe more deeply into my own humanity. And I would have to understand others' humanity systematically.

A year in New York city provided ingredients to draw together professional and personal search. My own intensive personal therapy, work at the William Alanson White Institute of Psychiatry, responsibility as the first pastoral counselor intern at the American Foundation of Religion and Psychiatry, studies at Union Theological Seminary(theology, Old Testament, and preaching), and an interim pastorate of an Italian Baptist Church in the Bronx combined with one additional element to provide an increasingly firm, though flexible, integration of my personal-professional humanity.

That integrating element was this: my family and I lived with my parents. Such intimacy forced me to come to terms more directly with my past—seeking to acquire and make my own what I had inherited from my parents (as Freud directed at the end of his last book, *An Outline of Psychoanalysis*). More particularly, long conversations with my father—a man and a minister, but most of all a sensitive, caring, sometimes limited, though mostly liberating, human being—provided the catalytic encounter enabling me to draw together these widely separate, yet essentially complementary, experiences.

The next five years yielded consolidation and accelerating growth. As a college-town pastor serving the church home of state denominational officials, of missionaries either on furlough or retired, of farmers and business people and professionals, as well as of university students, faculty, and administration, I had my work cut out for me. Every dimension of personal and community life flowed into and out from congregational life and worship. During this period, as a part of my relationship with the out-patient clinic at the Columbus State Hospital, I began conducting group therapy with ministers and, subsequently, with ministers' wives. Cell groups and study groups sprang up within the congregation. They have blossomed and died and reappeared in many forms. If ever I experienced a golden age, those last three years were it.

Sadly, though fortunately, life refuses to let anyone stand still. With the experience of deep tearing—"pulling my blood vessels out," as I experienced it—I moved from, what for me was, direct ministry in the parish to indirect ministry in the seminary. Others believed I had some reality-tested ideas and insights of church and ministry—"biases" I have called them— that should be utilized in the training of potential ministers. Seeing this as an opportunity to spread my biases faster, I moved reluctantly into a teaching role.

Two forces converged during this last decade as a theological professor. First, students and colleagues pressed me and pressed me to be clearer and more systematic in expressing my biases. If it is true that to influence, one must be capable of being influenced, then I confess to the second part especially. I have been influenced—by colleagues and students—so that my growing biases hopefully are broader and deeper and more appropriately applicable than in earlier years.

Second, I have taken—and been taken by—a degree in psychology as an academic discipline. In the process I have had to learn experimental (a little) and empirical (a lot) research; I have had to be more hard-nosed in moving from impressionistic and clinical judgments to controlled and accumulated experimental, empirical evidences. Theological and clinical insights do open up meanings of humanity, but empirical and experimental data are essential in tightening up the content of those meanings.

Throughout these phases my wife and my children have provided a connecting and correcting human relatedness. With Pat I have been forced to deal with the excitement and the ache of intimacy, with the fulfillment and the promise of a freeing relatedness. With our children, Pete, Sue, Martha, and Karin, I have been forced to be responsibly mature in caring for and casting forth bearers of the future. When I have been in danger of becoming lost in my work or my ruminations, the pressure of their presence has brought me back to reality. When I have been in danger of becoming lost in their particularities, my responsibilities and studying have served to bring perspective to us all.

Orientation

Students, especially, are prone to want more handles than I have provided so far. They want names, particular categories, specific books as a way of identifying me and my orientation. At best such labels orient by pointing to parameters of understanding. At worst such labels wall off the life of understanding. For what it is worth and as a witness, let me touch on what has made an impact and to what I have responded.

I could detail persons and reading. Both for their writings and their humanity, I could point to such diverse people as a Paul Tillich, a Rollo May, and a Fritz Perls, among so many. For their writings, I could indicate my excitement with an Augustine, a Martin Luther, an Erich Fromm, a Talcott Parsons, to give but a hint of those who have enlarged my understanding. For their persons, I am inestimably more than I might have been because of a Richard M. Johnson and an Edward M. L. Burchard, to name but two from among two score or more such individuals.

So many names and so many faces crowd before me. They have shared in my humanity either in a personal way of loving and being loved or in a professional way of helping and being helped. Each matters to me. What I want to convey to you, however, is the extent of my intense linkage with others.

For years as a white liberal, I have—for better and worse—been involved, embroiled, and detached in the racial crisis. Nowhere else do the misery and the grandeur of humanity show themselves more damningly or more dramatically. Nowhere else do the implications of our humanity result in such drastic consequences. From my high school days with my initial sensitization to race (and equally to war), triggered by my contact with Bayard Rustin and James Farmer, to this latter period with exposure to Martin Luther King, Jr., and Malcolm X, I have been battered and bruised and bettered in my own humanity and my participation in humanizing.

As I think back on these and similar clues as to who I am and what I understand, my immediate reaction is: what an array of people and influences! But where am *I* in all this? Am I only the accumulated waters of those scattered tributaries?

My considered response is: No. *I am* the recipient of these known and unknown streams. I have let them flow into what is my ocean—me—with its own unique/universal configuration of boundaries and basins, of ebbings and flowings.

My rationale for such personal musing is my desire to set a tone, to convey a stance, to intimate an approach to understanding the humanity of human beings. The role and stance of my being a professor or a clergyman or a psychologist or a husband or a father or a citizen or a companion on the way need to recede into the background. The reality and spirit of my being Jim Ashbrook—a human being endeavoring to seek and to share humanness—need to emerge into the foreground.

A Zen story aptly illustrates the pitfall of role-playing and the possibility of real relating:

Keichu, the great Zen teacher of the Meiji era, was the head of Tofuku, a cathedral in Kyoto. One day the governor of Kyoto called upon him for the first time. His attendant presented the card of the governor, which read: Kitagaki, Governor of Kyoto.

"I have no business with such a fellow," said Keichu to his attendant. "Tell him to get out of here."

"That was my error," said the governor, and with a pencil he scratched out the words Governor of Kyoto. "Ask your teacher again."

"Oh, is that Kitagaki?" exclaimed the teacher when he saw the card. "I want to see that fellow."

Ultimately, the meaning of *human* intertwines with the meaning of *me*, even as the meaning of my *humanity* intertwines with the meaning of *humanity*. As I would contact you, I hope you, in turn, can contact me.

I am setting down ideas, evidences, hunches, conclusions, speculations, hard data, and soft insights* in what I regard as the crucial and critical concern of each and everyone—namely, what does it mean to be and to become human?

Will you join me in the search?

TWO
What Does Humanitas Mean?

I begin our exploration with deep hesitancy. My hesitancy flows from two sources: the one rising from the inappropriateness of the task, the other stemming from its impossibility. Separately, each presents an insurmountable barrier to what I am undertaking. Together they convey a sense of the foolishness of it all.

In the Book of Tao I read: "Whoever knows does not speak; whoever speaks does not know." If I participated fully in my own humanity, I would have no need to speak. I would *be* and I would *let be*. Because I would really know, I would simply live! Because I do not simply live my humanity, I am driven to speak. I try to make sense of my own humanity. I try to stand within your humanity. Not really knowing, I may say a lot that means little. Therein lies the inappropriateness of what I am doing.

A psychiatrist friend is given to asking, "How can you tell anybody what a strawberry tastes like?" The dilemma he presents is self-evidently compelling: if you know what a strawberry tastes like, there is no need to describe it to you; if you do not know, there is no way of telling you. An unambiguous means to convey directly the meaning of humanity does not exist. Therein lies the impossibility of my effort.

In spite of both the inappropriateness and the impossibility of exploring the experience and the demand of humanness, we find ourselves doing it. Experiences of humanity are inescapable. Expressions of humanity are unavoidable. We live and move and have our being-becoming within a world of expressed experience. When what we say is understood, we know we are sharing common experience. As we share common experience, what we express becomes more understandable. Out of such understood expression and shared experience comes the humanness of humanity.

But let's be quite clear as to what we can expect from this exploration. I can neither open up nor wrap up the meaning of humanity—not for myself; not for you. Answers lie in the rightness of questions. I hope that I am asking right questions.

Yet I am mindful that answering grows out of the process of questioning more than the finding of the right question. Ultimately, questions-and-answers reside in the *questioner-*answerer. Personal questioning, or more precisely the questioning person, is basic for meaningful understandings. At best I may be able to hint at my understandings and point toward your understandings. Out of hinting and pointing, your experience of humanity may be more available, as may mine, and your expression of humanity more adequate, as may mine.

Recall Anne Sullivan's efforts to teach deaf, sightless, speechless Helen Keller the meaning of humanity via the means of language. Again and again Anne drummed onto the palm of Helen's hand, letters that represented words that symbolized experience. The finger movements made no sense. That is, they pointed toward and connected with nothing. They hinted at no other referent than themselves. Then, in one moment, as the water from the pump spilled over Helen's hands and as Anne kept up the meaningless movements of her fingers on Helen's palm, the water and the finger movement coalesced. W-A-T-E-R added up to what Helen was experiencing on her hand. Experience found expression. Expression represented experience.

So, we, too, move back and forth between experience and

expression. Experience includes more than its expression. We always know more than we can say. Expression conveys less than the experience. We always say less than we mean. But equally, expression can clarify experience. And clarified experience makes for more meaningful expression. In the end, the meaning of humanity is never simply experience but ever the *experiencer*, never merely expression but always the *expressor*. What finally matters for you and me is *our* experiencing and *our* expressing *our* humanity.

To think as living, real human beings compels our personal participation in the experience and demand of humanness. There can be no proxies. I am human for myself. You are human for yourself. Neither of us can be human for the other, yet both of us can be human with each other.

Meister Eckhart (1260-1327), father of German mysticism, pointed in a right direction when he quoted Augustine to the effect that "there are many people who have sought light and truth, but they look for it outside themselves where it is not . . . they never discover the truth, for truth is at the core of the soul and not outside the man." I am pressing for personal knowledge *of* humanness within and surrounding and beyond the impersonal knowledge *about* humanness. If we fail to move in this universal dimension, for that is in truth what constitutes the core of the personal, we miss humanness no matter how comprehensive our intellectual understanding may be.

Søren Kierkegaard dramatized my point with a parable:

> It is related of a peasant who came cleanly shaven to the Capital, and had made so much money that he could buy himself a pair of shoes and stockings and still had enough left over to get drunk on—it is related that as he was trying in his drunken state to find his way home, he lay down in the middle of the highway and fell asleep. Then along came a wagon, and the driver shouted to him to move or he would run over his legs. Then the drunken peasant awoke, looked at his legs, and since by reasons of the shoes and stockings he didn't recognize them, he said to the driver, "Drive on, they are not my legs."

Every experience provides an occasion to encounter our own humanness and thereby the humanness of others. Yet, like the peasant, we may so abstract ourselves from actual involvement that we, too, respond, "Go on, that's not me." At times such detachment is desirable and even necessary. Many of us too easily overpersonalize experience, confusing what is me with what is not me, to the detriment of both the situation and ourselves. But if what is occasionally desirable turns into the chronically necessary, then, like the peasant, we may lose our capacity to stand and to stand up in our world. We shall find ourselves run over by the ongoingness of experience.

To be run over by the ongoingness of experience, however, *and* to participate in that being run over as happening to us and we in turn happening to it, holds hope for our humanization. So, I want to direct your attention to our full immersion in moment-by-moment meaning.

We need to engage humanitas, yet we tend to avoid it.

So far I have referred to humanitas without saying what I mean by it. While I am unable to capture it, I may be able to suggest it. *Humanitas* is a Latin word meaning "human nature" or "humanity." It is a feminine form while carrying the connotation of mankind or humankind. More particularly, it refers to kindliness, civilization, culture, refinement. For my purposes I intend it to embrace and convey both the reality of being *human* and the expectation of *human* becoming. But more of this as we go along.

Experiences of Humanitas

What comes to mind as you think of the word "human"? What images do I evoke in you when I speak of human nature? What do you make of humanitas?

Here are some of the words and images that come: weak — biased — uptight — cruel — hurting — warm — alive — caring — inadequate — finite — spontaneous —

Immediately I am aware of the mixed character of these associations. Weak, biased, inadequate, uptight, cruel, hurting sound negative; warm, alive, caring, spontaneous come across as positive. Finite seems to be negative or positive, depending upon how we look at it; death of a Biafran child by starvation is negative; individuality by knowing who one is, is positive.

Note further, though, that the sequence of associations runs from the more apparently negative to the more seemingly positive. Our initial "feel" about humanness tends to carry undesirable connotations. Only secondarily and subsequently, do the more positive attributes come through. For whatever reasons, we experience a clear consciousness—really a self-consciousness—of the old Adam. We are all too painfully aware of our limitations. Perplexity over the negative aspect of human beings continues to plague us.

Let me point to some specific, though random, experiences which I believe catch that painful felt-meaning of being human.

In September, 1959, the Museum of Modern Art opened a special exhibition. It bore the title "New Images of Man." Instead of evoking enthusiasm, it sent emotions flaring and set controversy raging. What disturbed and unhinged the public was not so much portrayals of new images of humanity as the proclamation of old images of man.

"Here are human figures," wrote art critic Aline Saarinen, "with bodies distorted, misshapen, mutilated. Sometimes their flesh is decayed and corrupt, sometimes corroded or charred. Here are faceless figures—or figures that seem to have death's

The Cry by Edvard Munch

Oslo Kommunes Kunstsamlinger

heads—looming, leering out of nightmarish nothingness. . . .
Here are figures that seem imprisoned in cagelike spaces and
others incarcerated in spaces 'measureless to man.' If the
exhibit had a sound track," she continued, "it would be a
cacophonous medley of anguished cries and screeches and quiet
sighs and sobs of loneliness and longing."

The Cry by Edvard Munch screeches "the horror of frozen
fear." Ghostlike, agitated, restless, almost unbearable suspense.
But if there are people and moments when shrill screams pierce
empty fullness, there are other people and moments when, as
in Francis Bacon's "Study of Velasquez' Portrait of Pope
Innocent X," with mouths aghast, there is the strain to scream
and yet no sound sounds forth.

A graduate student in clinical psychology sips a cup of
coffee. He is bright, sophisticated, competent, sensitive. He
gives every appearance of having life well in hand. Suddenly
he shifts the conversation from the casual to the intimate.
He opens up to me another side of himself:

I would like to know just who in the hell I am. And irrational as
I know the question is, I would like to know why am I here?
And what am I doing?

The old metaphysical certainties are gone. The logical positivism
of operationalism leaves "me" out of it so that there is no essential difference between me and that table. I think we psychologists
and grad students are really crazy people.

My strength and weakness are that I am clinging to reality and
terrified to let go. I followed Kierkegaard into suffering, went with
him into the abyss, then I pulled back. And the awful thing is
that bastard was held by something that let him down gently. But
if I jumped, I would just keep hurtling into a bottomless pit.

A ninety-two-year-old woman lies in her bed in her daughter's
home. During the last three years, and with rapid acceleration
in the last months, her life and her relationships have grown
deeply disturbing: unrelieved agony, constant confusion, the
indignity of utter helplessness, the aggravation of aggressive
concern to be self-sufficient, cancelled by dangerous inability
to be trusted. In an especially poignant episode, her daughter

34

finds her trying to crawl around her bed searching agitatedly among the covers. When asked what she wanted, she replies, "I'm looking for my lost self."

Not dissimilar from that graduate student, a divorced mother with four children under twelve years of age achingly observes:

I have at least half a dozen friends in various stages of marital break-ups—their behavior constantly reassures me of how sensible I've been. They do really dumb things—chasing rainbows and creating more complications for themselves. Yet in all my good sense I could go somewhere and quietly die. . . . I'm sure in time this will pass. I don't really want to die—I just want to find out why life isn't more meaningful, given what one has.

Coming out of the concentration camps of World War II, Viktor Frankl describes the utter nothingness of the person from whom every*thing*, even one's eyeglasses, had been stripped away. For many in affluent America that ghastly in-humanness stands remote and unreal. However, the unexpected hospitalization of a friend because of an emotional breakdown closes the distance between there-and-then and here-and-now. My friend tries to put on paper something of what it means to her to be "lost in that horror":

Do you know, in that place [one of the less therapeutic state hospitals] there is a law operating unlike any I have ever had to deal with. I guess what has been seared away—and as yet nothing creative has taken the empty place—is a certain innocence or naiveté that I had—that people operated on certain civilized levels —some levels less positive than others—but I was totally un-humanized (no, I don't mean de-humanized, I mean "*un*")!

Do you know that that night, after they took all my things away—my watch, my books [and for her, books help organize meaning], my lipstick (I somehow managed to hang on to my soap—I think it got lost in the shuffle) that they checked my hair for *lice* [for one who is obsessed with cleanliness that was almost the ultimate degradation]! Oh dear heavens—such a stupid little thing, which left me so totally nothing!

I was a trapped, caged animal, sedated and punished for being upset and getting upset—and somehow or other, through the grace of God, when it really counted I was able to re-assert my humanity and escape. But inside I am not the same person I was, and I am not sure what that means.

For a white person such an experience of un-humanness carries the shock of what humanity is meant to be by means of what is stripped away. For a black or brown or red or yellow person experiences of de-humanness carry the shock of what humanity is meant to be by means of what *does* happen. Real as psychic pain is for affluent whites, even more real is the physical-psychic pain that a black poet writes of in "the time of the martyr":

> . . . The white man killed my father
> Because my father was proud
> The white man raped my mother
> Because my mother was beautiful
> The white man wore out my brother
> in the hot sun of the roads
> Because my brother was strong
> Then the white man came to me
> His hands red with blood
> Spat his contempt into my black face
> Out of his tyrant's voice
> "Hey boy, a basin, a towel, water." . . .

Or listen to random voices from the northern urban ghetto:

I have been uncomfortable being a Negro [woman]. I came from the South—Kentucky, on the Ohio River line—and I have had white people spit on me in my Sunday suit.

A lot of times, when I'm working, I become as despondent as hell and I feel like crying. I'm not a man, none of us are men! I don't own anything. I'm not a man enough to own a store; none of us [blacks] are.

"What kinds of changes would you want to make," inquired an interviewer, investigating the problems and pathology of the ghetto, of a little girl, "so you can have a better chance, your sister . . . your brother?" "Well, I just want a chance to do what I can do."

The psychic pain and the societal pain crying through these experiences converge in the overwhelming pain of the quicksand war in southeast Asia. In mid 1969, a graduate student, unaware of what the problem was, but very aware of the symptoms, penned an open letter to Americans:

You should not have allowed the Vietnam War to happen.

What would have been a hesitancy about the military has grown into a repulsion of the mindless system that executes your inhumanity.

What would have been a questioning about this country's ability to halt its racial and social polarizations has resolved into the acceptance that amelioration is impossible within the present structures.

What would have been a disillusionment about the economic priorities of this country has become a rigid anticapitalism.

What would have been a distrust of your "religion" has led to a denial of your "faith."

What would have been a legitimate apprehension about "communism" has changed into a horror for the "American Way."

What would have been a loyalty to your conception of a "democracy" has forced me to become a spiritual expatriate.

What would have been a rather narrow view of America and what it means to be an American has expanded into a preoccupation with what it means to be a man.

It's too late now. You should never have allowed Vietnam to happen.

By early 1970, the student had moved to a more definite portrait of the illness and not the symptoms. At that time he penned a second open letter to Americans:

You are the child of yesterday, the father of today. You have made my heritage, my country, into a whore into which only the rifles of your fear and hatred can penetrate.

You want me to "wait" and "see" how appealing your whore can be to my needs. You want me to become celibate, passive and silent so the whore has the time to infect me with the syphillis that you have not found a cure for. You want me to voluntarily sacrifice my manhood simply on the credentials of tradition and custom and because wiser men for generations have whored with her; and then you are concerned about my sexual "immorality." You expect me to become swollen and pus-ridden so that I will be impotent to threaten or destroy the whore. My reward will be an apolitical, amoral, and aspiritual existence while I wait for a cure for syphillis to be found.

37

I don't know whether to hate you or to love you. Hate—for not telling me that this beautiful woman you have been luring me with for four (or four hundred) years is a whore: love—for at least waiting until now to demand that I submit to her when I can understand and conceive of life in my own frame of reference. Perhaps I have inherited some of your syphillis, and it has rendered me incapable of the distinction between love and hate— the sacrificial lamb can be neither love nor hate.

I only know that I must destroy what you are too ill to destroy. The whore of yesterday and today must be destroyed so that the children of tomorrow can love man and woman and not a whore.

I am the child of today, the father of tomorrow.

The first letter details the rape; the second depicts the whore. But, he goes on to wonder. "What of the love child —the people of my generation? Can the love child, the sacrificial lamb, distinguish between love and hate in relation to his progenitors? Can he make that step from the apathetic, which is pathological, to the transpersonal? My personal liberation had led to hate. How can I make that step to the transpersonal?"

Each of these individuals gives voice to a universal situation. Experiences of humanness screech most poignantly in the negativities—un-human, in-human, de-human. Yet even in their horribleness, I glimpse the demand of human becoming.

Demand of Humanitas

Within each of those painful experiences moves the demand to be more than we are. In piercing the negative we break through to the positive—the affirming, the demanding, the confirming humanness of being human.

Many people left that exhibition of "New Images of Man" shuddering and disgusted. Others responded with excitement and even pleasure. More pointedly, an art critic speculated, "It may even be that when visual beauty transcends horror and ugliness, it gives the work dignity and poignancy which add to its dimension." To say that, however, is not enough. Even beyond transcending beauty, "it can be argued that the

38

very act of making beauty out of ugliness is the artist's means of affirmation and compassion."

That sophisticated grad student in psychology felt the necessity of *his* being directly part of what was happening to him. He realized that to cling frantically to the controllable and the controlled was to miss the vitality of personhood. Even in his inability to let go and be he experienced the ultimatum to become.

The pathetic picture of a deteriorated woman searching among her blankets for her lost self conveys my point. Even in that tragic state of having lost her centeredness, she is enough herself to realize that she is not herself. In sensing she is not herself, she experiences the demand to be what she is—a truly functioning human being.

Or that divorced mother knew that deeper than her despair in wanting to get out of life lay her desire to get into life. She knew there are possibilities beyond the present that call us forth from infantile and illusory pursuits. She longed for more meaning—more connectedness between her inner life and her outer life, between her desires and her satisfactions, between the person she experienced herself to be and the place which she had in existence.

The hospitalized woman felt the removal of her possessions as the rape of her person. We are who we are, in part, through what we surround ourselves with. As these are gone, so we are gone. To lose what expresses us is to lose ourselves. When stripped of *her* humanity, she was forced to reassert her *humanity*.

The inhumanness against blacks and browns and reds and yellows and whites grinds the human spirit into powder and dust. Yet something deep within people refuses to let them remain so crushed. "I want a chance to do what I can" springs spontaneously from human lips. Powder turns into POWDER—dynamite, explosive humanity. People demand dignity. Their passion to be present catalyzes their drive to be competent. From having been kept apart, they want to become a part. From having been no-thing, they respond to the demand to be some-body.

Unexpectedly and imperceptibly, the Vietnam cancer has spread throughout the organism of American life. With convulsive and unnarcotized pain, that student screams of its dehumanizing effects: mindless system, denial of possibilities, expatriate of mankind, sacrificial lamb. Yet he now knows of the rape and the whore precisely because the cancer has reproduced so much so insidiously. He longs to go beyond his bitterness.

Because the victimizer is victimized even as is his victim, the victimizer experiences the victim's demand for human dignity as destructive instead of constructive. He has so deluded himself into thinking that he and his way of life and his kind of people constitute humanity that any question, any contrast, any criticism strikes him as incomprehensible. What has been is thought of as what should be. His world is *the* world. His life is *the* life. His humanity *is* humanity. And by that very distortion he exhausts resources necessary for his humanity; he activates responses in his victims that upset his balance even as they restore their balance.

Writing a College Entrance Examination Board essay, a girl describes being interrupted in her daydreaming by her friends: "They're invaders. They seem to be trying to tear me from that peaceful life and plant me in the dismal reality of the horrid world."

That temperate reaction to crowding in and pushing out by others grew into gargantuan proportions in society at large in the decade of the 1960s. In reaction to disruptions, many whites complained with bewilderment and frustration and dread, "Everything was fine before. Nobody bothered anybody then. Why, all of a sudden, do we have to have so much turmoil, so much agitation, so much confrontation?"

The tragic denouement in the maximum security prison in Attica, New York, in September, 1971, dramatizes forces surging within the larger society. Some 1,280 prisoners (out of 2,245) held thirty-nine hostages during four days of tense negotiating. In the end a no-give stance on either side resulted in the slaying of nine hostages and thirty inmates as the forces of society overwhelmed the forces of the dispossessed.

40

Although a world unto itself, that life-and-death drama ripped open our wider world.

Rural, conservative, honor-America, upstate New York found itself unexpectedly confronted with urban, radical, revolutionary, downstate New York. As one observer noted, "You have Harlem and South Bronx and Bed-Stuy inside the walls, and they're being guarded by farmers who are scared as hell of them."

One inmate whispered to a reporter during the siege, "We're going to get clobbered when this is over. We know it. But we want to be treated like human beings." And their demands reflect that demand for humanness: more objective grievance procedures, more freedom to act politically and to believe and act in diverse religious patterns; more education, rehabilitation, and recreation programs; more provision for black and Spanish-speaking personnel. When a reporter referred to the hostages, a prisoner corrected him by insisting, "They're not hostages. They're human beings." And in the showdown at least one prisoner, reportedly assigned to slit the throat of a guard, murmured as the assault shooting erupted, "I don't have the heart to kill you." With that he shoved the guard to the ground, threw himself on top of him, thereby saving the guard's life. When one inmate yelled to give officials "a pig," meaning to kill one of their hostages, he was shouted down with cries of "No, no; don't do that." The leader took the microphone and said, "That's good." Then, turning, he pointed to the one making the suggestion and said, "That's not good." And the gruesome ending cannot erase those forces for life.

In sharp contrast, those intertwined with established society responded, "The hell with them [inmates], what about the guards?" When she heard a hostage quoted as saying, "We will be better correction officers after living as the prisoners do," the wife of one of the hostages screamed, "There's never been any brutality in there!" When the father of another hostage shouted that if talking to the governor did not work, "then I say blow the whole sonofabitching place up. If it keeps on this way, it'll blow up anyway. Not just this place but the whole prison system."

"We have to get our son back," he continued more quietly and still crying, "or just bomb the hell out of the place. That's all that's left."

The rampant ambiguity was caught most precisely by one prisoner's comment to a reporter. Regardless of charges and countercharges, regardless of miscalculations, regardless of planned exploitation, the underlying truth remains: "They say some of our demands are impractical. I tell you the way we have been living is impractical."

When pushed to extreme, in-human and un-human and de-human treatment reverse themselves. The feared becomes fearful. The strong collapses. The weak rises up. The pushed-around pushes around. The ignored ignores.

The dehumanizing of the whole of society bestirs the re-humanizing of its tenderest parts. Not the muddled frightened middle, but the sensitive hurting forgotten fringes—there is where the spirit of human becoming moves. We have lost humanity that has been given: we are discovering that we *must* seek humanity that is demanded.

What is true of society as a whole is true of individuals as well. The cut-off, the isolated, the alienated forces of ourselves are as basic to our being and becoming as the accepted, the favored, the intended parts. Not the anxious, conscious fixations but the peripheral, moving meanings—there is where the power of new being arises.

Negative human experience forces us to ferret out ways of reclaiming our only sure inheritance. Much as we strangle the voice of humanity, humanity demands to be heard. We are called to become what we truly and genuinely are—*human* beings. Humanity confronts us as task and not as fact.

So, humanity beckons!

THREE
What Do Humans Desire?

Perhaps I should have started our exploration of the meaning of humanitas not from its experience and demand, but from the more personal question, namely: what do *you* want?

Why have you even bothered to pick up the book? What about it intrigues you, stirs your imagination, awakens your interest? What, in short, are you looking for?

Perhaps you are experiencing mostly an idle curiosity. In the face of overwhelming impersonalization and depersonalization, in the presence of unhumanization and dehumanization, people in schools, in suburbs, in ghettos, in business, in churches, in government are wanting to be acknowledged as *human* beings. Maybe you simply feel an intellectual interest in others' insistence upon their humanity.

More likely you are struggling with your own humanity. Whether you are at home or in school or on the job, maybe you feel your*self* consistently overlooked as other people's desires and demands erode your own being. Charles Reich in *The Greening of America* may be describing you as he writes of "The Lost Self." Perhaps your own "unfinished" experiences leave you continually exhausted in trying to come to terms with your past. Perhaps your own fearfulness and uncertainty hobble your attempts to step into the future. Perhaps your own anxiousness drives you into frenzied activity in order to prove you exist as a real person. Perhaps you are painfully preoccupied with your own humanity.

If you are at all like me—and I suspect we are definitely similar by virtue of our being human—what you want combines both insights and experience, both ideas and emotions, both thoughts and feelings. You are not only curious about human becoming, but even more you care very much.

To put the issue of desire simply, I assume you want from this book (1) some ideas about what it means to become human, and (2) some experience of what it feels like to be human.

Obviously, my supply of information/insight will not fill your demand for ideas/experience. Yet that discrepancy between expectation and reality characterizes most transactions. We want more than is possible; we give less than is desirable. Even so, out of such asking-receiving/receiving-asking, we often discover we have received more than we imagined, and we have given beyond what we anticipated. So, *if* you are actively seeking information/insight from this book (me) and *if* I am actively conveying ideas/experience, *then* we both shall be surprised at what is set loose between us and within us in our search for our own and others' humanity.

Let me back away from the immediately personal for a moment. I want to put down some general background about experience and its development and about insight and its usefulness as the handles best available for our understanding.

Handles for Understanding

We seem to be basically curious creatures. We are intrigued by the unfamiliar, the unknown, the dimly perceived. From the young infant's peering at the index finger of his left hand to the advanced scientist's testing Martian soil, we want to find out *what's-there*.

We also seem to have been created with gut reactions. We respond to ideas, to people, to situations with feeling. The emotional response may be cold withdrawal into an impenetrable shell of indifference; but even that is responding with (lack of) feeling. We may become personally involved in situations so that what is going on very much matters to us.

It affects our sense of self-worth and self-esteem. It influences our experience of competency and adequacy. From the young child's crying in response to his mother's scowl of disapproval to the grownup's obsession with where national representatives are to sit at a conference table, we react to the *felt-meaning* of what's-there.

Experience

Initially, everything we know depends upon the body. The body alone is the ultimate instrument of knowing. It is the only reality that we can never really experience as an object outside of and separate from ourselves. Even in schizophrenic splits, we are still responding in terms of our body base.

In exploring experience and the creation of meaning, Eugene Gendlin describes experiencing as "simply feeling, as it concretely exists for us inwardly, and as it accompanies every lived aspect of what we are and mean and perceive. . . . Within experiencing lie the mysteries of all that we are." Experience, thus, is always and ever concrete, complex, and continuous.

By virtue of its concreteness experience simultaneously embraces the many meanings we call upon to order what we know. By virtue of its complexity experience remains open to yet unknown, though not unsuspected, possibilities of expression. Except for somewhat arbitrary distinctions, experience is "a continuous stream of feelings with some few explicit contents."

Let's look at this experiential base of meaning from the viewpoint of development.

With birth an infant finds itself thrown out of a stable, undifferentiated environment—sheer existing—into a booming, buzzing bombardment of fleeting, disconnected, incoherent experience—*startling existence*. The infant begins orienting itself to this massive, mysterious, chaotic environment by touching and tasting and poking and exploring everything within its reach. It initiates responses by generating interest in and manipulating what's there. Gradually, the strange environment takes the shape of a more *known world*.

Nor is such curiosity confined to humans alone. Monkeys have picked things apart, poked fingers into holes, and explored all sorts of situations when such motivators as hunger, fear, sex, and comfort have not been present. In one experiment, for instance, monkeys learned a discrimination problem when the only reward was opening a window permitting them to look out and watch the normal comings and goings at the entrance of the lab.

Sheer inquisitiveness—striving for stimulation, information, knowledge, or understanding—appears universal among primates, and most especially among humans. In fact, the more complex and varied the stimuli, the more attention the stimuli attract.

Human infants, for instance, responded first to the more complex figures on the right rather than the more simple ones on the left.

Simple and Complex Figures by Daniel E. Berlyne

Similarly, when adults were presented with the following pairs of figures, they spent more time looking at the right-hand ones than the simpler or more conventional versions on the left.

Beginning around age two, the child moves into the stage of trying things out. That is, from regarding what one sees as literal, the child begins to demonstrate an ability to think abstractly. One plays with one's world. One makes believe one is a mother or a daddy or a fireman or a racing car or a horse or a dog or an airplane. One finds out whether a spoon makes noise in a glass or food falls to the floor or a cat is soft or a scream brings a parent. But even though the child's

46

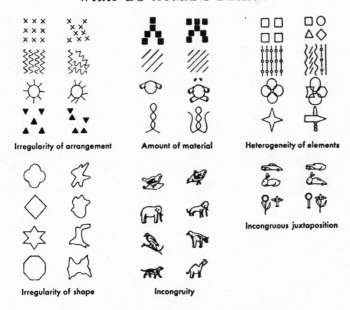

Arrangements of Pairs by Daniel E. Berlyne

rationality appears like an adult's, it merely takes account of one aspect of a situation.

Only later—somewhere around the eleventh year—does the young person enter into the maturer stage of understanding. At this point formal logic appears. By now the individual can think at the totally abstract level. One can create one's own hypothetical universe. One can separate the symbols one uses to express experience from the actual experience itself.

My point in touching briefly upon the development of our ability to think is to underscore the experiential base from which understanding arises.

We seem driven to do what we can do. But what we can do is a process including both the way we organize what's-there *and* the way we adapt to what's-there.

We take in food as well as food for thought. We assimilate what "fits" with us as we are. This makes for continuity. We experience a familiarity and an identity with what we know.

47

Simultaneously, we are confronted with foreign food and strange ideas. These press for attention. They require some accommodation on our part. They make for discontinuity, thereby requiring us to reconstruct what we are by further identification with what we are not.

These two aspects of understanding are inseparable. As we adapt to what's-there, we organize what we know. As we organize what we know, we affect what is there.

So, we increase both adaptation and complexity. We create ever more complex forms. These forms become progressively more suited to the settings in which we find ourselves. In short, we strive to know—to experience felt-meaning and to express what's-there.

Insight

The attractiveness of the puzzling, the unfamiliar, the unknown, and the curious takes on an intensity as we confront that which impinges on us personally. Then the meaning of things in general changes into the meaning of life specifically.

Much of society's current anxiousness surfaces from the break-up of the familiar. No longer can we assume with any confidence that what is there in the world is what we want in the world. When Friedrich Nietzsche proclaimed "God is dead!" he was pointing to the experienced dissolution of Western civilization's "world": the organization and adaptation of society's meaning. Alvin Toffler terms it the crack-up of consensus, while Emile Durkheim and the sociologists label it anomie. The stable structures are gone. People doubt whether there is anything to go on.

Recoiling from the head-on collision with the pressure to live at an ever faster pace, making swifter decisions, adapting more rapidly, making and breaking ties with people and places oftener, people then smash into the equally powerful counter-pressures of novelty and diversity demanding that they process more data, break out of old, carefully honed routines, and examine each situation anew before making a decision.

Instant   change—forced   change—resented   change—demanded change—desired change—planned change—intended change—resisted change—relentless change—continual change —change—change—change—

Juxtaposed with inundating change, people experience overpowering powerlessness. Even more than the rapidity of change, the plague of mindless bureaucracy and the corporate state sweeps through the world mutilating, exploiting, and eventually destroying nature and human nature equally. The insanity of its "reasonableness" explains impoverishment and dehumanization as logical and necessary and sane.

Instant conformity—forced conformity—resented conformity—demanded conformity—desired conformity—planned conformity—intended conformity—resisted conformity—conformity—conformity—

No wonder people feel uptight, frightened, timid, resentful, vindictive, at loose ends, all in pieces. They want certainty and stability.

Saul Alinsky provides a dramatic and pathetic illustration. He had been lecturing at a large university at the very time a marine recruiter had been driven off campus. Upon returning to his hotel around one o'clock in the morning, Alinsky went to the bar for a nightcap. There at the far end of the bar sat a demoralized, crying, very masculine marine master sergeant with a chestful of campaign ribbons and hash marks up to his elbows.

The bartender informed Alinsky that the sergeant had been that way for the previous three hours. Taking his drink, Alinsky sat down next to the sergeant. "Come on, buddy, things can't be that tough."

Soon the marine started talking. His eyes were saturated with confusion, not just from drinking, but more from his afternoon's experience. He kept repeating over and over, "I don't get it, I don't know what's happening. I was at Iwo Jima. I was at Tarawa. I've seen my buddies alongside me getting their guts blown out; they died for these punks. And now I go on a college campus, and you'd think I was a goddamn Nazi, the way they treat me. I just don't understand what's happening to the world."

Like that sergeant, we each must have some rationale for making it in the world. We may reduce the breadth of our humanity by subordinating our existence to a subsection of humanity, a narrow or limited or distorted caricature of what we are capable of being. But then we reduce the genuinely personal to the distortingly subjective. When we are personal, we actively enter into our commitments; when we are subjective, we merely endure our feelings.

In contrast to the merely subjective feelings of, say, that sergeant, the personal focuses on the felt-meaning *of* what's-there. We submit ourselves to requirements acknowledged by ourselves as independent of our own subjective biases. There is a nonmanipulative, a noninterfering, a nonintruding observation and receptivity. Abraham Maslow has termed it taoistic objectivity. We bring our fascination, our interest, our care to what we see and what it means. Rather than obscuring what's-there, such involvement, paradoxically, opens that up.

We come upon clues, hints, hunches, yes, even more, directions and possibilities as we reflect upon our ongoing experience. These dimly perceived realities take on increasing clarity. By making explicit what is implicit, we gain insights that link the various pieces of our world in a meaningful way. Such insights enable us to see and to act, to alter and to create more easily than we otherwise would be able to. They allow us to learn from experience rather than be battered by it. They enable us to approach humanitas with understanding rather than bewilderment. We exercise our humanity over what's-there by ordering experience in terms of its adaptively appropriate felt-meaning.

Insights, however, can never finally hold together what's-there. Insightful expressions may be more or less adequate to experience, but they can only point toward and refer to experiencing; they can never fully organize it. We always know far more than we can ever tell.

I am groping toward expressing the interplay between bodily existence and symbolic expression.

What we do physically, constitutes the most direct and immediate level of knowing. What we image provides living data with which we can express the meanings by which we live. At the most advanced level of comprehension we construct the abstract and the systematic. Here we understand through disciplining the images and the metaphors. We make explicit what is implicit and then tighten their connections.

In action we focus on what's-there. In images we sharpen the felt-meaning of action. In abstraction we use our understanding to move more confidently from the familiar and known into the unfamiliar and unknown.

By a process of tightening experience into expressions we can agree on and, by a process of linking fragments of experience together in recognizable patterns, we develop an orderly and workable way of coming at the world. When our abstraction loses its power to organize experience, as inevitably happens, then we need to shift our attention back to the level of the orienting images. When our images lose their power to awaken experience, as often happens, then we need to shift our attention back to the level of concrete actions. By utilizing all three levels of knowing, we renew our ability to contact the felt-meaning of what's-there. Our ability to respond to life is restored. We know the reconciling of that which has been torn apart.

Without experience all expression remains empty; without expression all experience remains blind.

Consider again what it is we are both wanting in this book. I have touched upon some idea of what's-there and upon some experience of the felt-meaning of what's-there. We are looking for insight into what it means to be human. We are longing for experience of what it feels like to become human. These two very general and overlapping categories have been characterized in various ways. They have been called the intellectual and the emotional, the cognitive and the experiential, mind and body, objective and subjective, outer and inner, universal and unique, knowledge about and knowledge of, facts and feelings, truth and meaning—among many. I have intimated their presence in the image of the ship and the sea dragon. Each of these designations refines our understanding of human desire in suggestive ways.

For instance, knowledge about what's-there enables us to pass on particular, quantifiable, and relatively explicit information that is verifiable by virtue of its being recoverable, given the same conditions. This has been accurately labeled as *inter*subjectivity. Knowledge of the felt-meaning of what's-there conveys a mood, a tone, an attitude, an atmosphere that is primarily an implied seeing-into what is nonquantifiable by virtue of its being immediate. This emphasizes inter*subjectivity*. Similarly, truth implies a firmly established and widely agreed upon denotation of some*thing*. Meaning suggests more fluid and multiple connotations of *some*thing.

You want, I take it, some knowledge about the truth(s) of humanitas and some knowledge of the meaning(s) of humanitas.

These distinctions reflect the perplexity of our human dilemma and point toward the possibility of a human direction. At the moment the words *insight* and *experience* provide convenient handles for the question of human desire.

Wants and Needs

Things have a way of not always *being* what they *seem*. Figure 1 shows two straight, parallel lines. Careful examination

Figure 1. Parallel Lines

with a ruler can establish that if the lines are extended as they are they will never cross. Therefore, by definition and description, they *are* parallel. If we place those "same" lines within contrasting settings, we "see" something else.

Figure 2 shows the two crossing a number of intersecting lines. Only this time the two lines no longer look straight. They appear to curve outward toward the middle and inward toward the ends. If you were to measure their distance from each other at any point along the continuum, you would

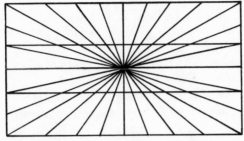

Figure 2. Parallel Lines, Convex

discover that they are in fact straight parallel lines, even though they seem to bend slightly inward.

Figure 3 shows the same two lines crossing a number of other intersecting lines. Again the two lines do not look

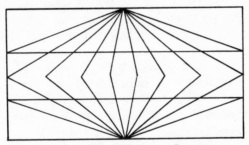

Figure 3. Parallel Lines, Concave

straight. This time they appear to curve inward toward the middle and outward toward the ends. If you were to measure their distance from each other at any point, you would find that they are in fact straight, even though they seem to bend slightly outward.

Intellectually, we conceive of what's-there as two straight parallel lines in three contrasting settings. We experience the felt-meaning of what's-there as (i) two straight parallel lines, (ii) two concave lines, and (iii) two convex lines, even though we "know" those latter sets of lines are straight. If we assume for the moment that reality is outside and independent of us, and *if* we assume for the moment that appearance is inside

53

and dependent on us, *then* we conclude reality and appearance sometimes converge and other times diverge. What is and what seems to be overlap in some instances and differ in other instances.

Now, translate this exercise in perception into the question of human desire.

People *want* a variety of things—love, food, sex, recognition, luxury, challenge, insight, approval, achievements, to be left alone, to be a part of a group, to let go, to live it up, ad infinitum. People *need* a limited number of things, though agreement on what we need differs.

Some authorities emphasize the primary biological needs of hunger, thirst, and sex; others see the psychogenic needs of love and hate, fear and approval, and self-actualization or fulfillment. Most investigators try to embrace both the what's-there and the felt-meaning. Depending upon how specific we wanted to be, we could have a list as long as a million or as short as one. There is no single agreed upon way of classifying motives.

But, and this is my point, whether human needs are two or five or twenty-eight or a million, needs are limited, whereas wants *seem* limitless. Something is to be regarded as a need if being deprived of it or not having it produces disease or deadening or destruction.

In an affluent society, what people regard as necessary expands as the economy expands. With affluence, people's needs are less biological and more individuated. Under such conditions, needs change with relatively high speed. But such necessities have the character of wants, as I have defined want. Eyeglasses are needed to see; the kind of frame relates to wanting to be seen. An automobile provides a way of getting around; the kind of car shows something of the status in which one wants to live. Fad producers prepare for shorter and shorter life cycles for their products. Economic growth has come to depend upon creating new wants long after the most pressing needs of society are met. As one experimental psychologist put it: "need" only means an organism would die without the needed condition. To assume need and want are the same is like assuming that when an automobile gets low on fuel it automatically heads for the closest gasoline station.

Evidence strongly suggests that most of us are unaware of what we want.

One consulting firm concluded a few years ago that to take the word of a customer as to what he wants is "the least reliable index the manufacturer can have on what he ought to do to win customers." Research in customer motivation disclosed, among the subsurface factors that motivate us, we are driven to conformity, we need oral stimulation, and we long for security.

Nevertheless, when I refer to human needs, I am not thinking of expanding necessities or unconscious motivations. Instead, I have in mind that basic what's-there of humanitas, however we refer to it. Similarly, when I refer to human wants, I have in mind that richer felt-meaning of what's-there, however we intimate it. As Reich aptly sees, "today's emerging consciousness seeks a new knowledge of what it means to be human."

To the extent the felt-meaning excludes or distorts what's-there, to that extent humanness proves perplexing. To the degree the felt-meaning confirms and enhances what's-there, to that degree humanness points toward possibilities. Figure 4 suggests the consequences in a diagram.

Exclude or distort

Include and enhance

Figure 4. Diagram of Wants and Needs

When our wants express our needs, we are whole, balanced, together, creative; when our wants distort our needs, we are at-odds, off-balance, fragmented, conflicted.

Thus, by asking the question of human desire in the form of wants instead of needs, I open the door to one expression of our human struggle. For some strange reason, what we want can contradict what we need. We can think one way and react another way. We can say yes and act no. We can say no and act yes. I may be grinding my teeth and clenching my fist at the very moment I say to you, "I like you very much." What we think we want often turns out to be different from what we actually want. Thus, Oscar Wilde could conclude with little exaggeration: "In this world there are only two tragedies. One is not getting what one wants, and the other is getting it. The last is the real tragedy."

Our ingrained ways of interacting often negate what we intend. Consider the following reports from a woman and a man who were unable to maintain satisfactory marriages:

The woman stated: "What I want in a husband is a strong, successful man who will take care of me; but all I seem to attract are penniless artists and passive, dreamy book-worms." Her mothering responses proved so deeply auto-matic that strong men felt "smothered and alienated by the maternal stability to which dependent men are drawn with moth-like fascination."

The man reported: "What I want more than anything else is to marry a dependent, feminine girl, but my three ex-wives were bossy, exploitive tyrants." His distrustful, immobilized and self-effacing behavior was "enough to force the most neutral woman into exasperated activity."

In the moments when we discover "I want what I need," we sense a wholeness—a humanity—that is ours, yet not ours, but a reality in which we participate and of which we are a part.

Generally, we may assume we want—and need—to be in touch with what's-there. That reality of thereness or suchness may be within us or around us. It may be the physical en-vironment or the human world. It may be ourselves or what we give ourselves to. Regardless of the locus, however, we want to know what's-there head-on, face-to-face, without distortion.

Equally, we may assume we want—and need—to determine the felt-meaning(s) of what's-there. That reality of weighted-ness—how much weight to give to what we contact—may apply to what's within us or around us, to the physical environment or the human world, to ourselves or what we care about. Regardless of the focus, however, we want to know the significance of what's-there for ourselves as well as for others.

We want, in short, to make sense of what we bump against and to act on the basis of its significance.

Erich Fromm has characterized such wants as the need for a frame of orientation and the need for a frame of devotion. Our searching eyes—scanning, observing, analyzing—express our need for the security that comes with understanding. Our longing heart—yearning, caring, integrating—reflects our need for the satisfaction that arises from commitment. Such a way of indicating desire, shifts the focus from us as organisms to us as *human* organisms. We are made aware of the fact that even biological needs (except in rare instances) must be understood in light of humanity itself and seldom as primary needs in and of themselves.

Distorted Wants

In exploring the what's-there of *Caste and Class in a Southern Town*, for example, John Dollard found greater sexual and aggressive expressiveness among lower-class blacks in the South and greater sexual and aggressive controlled renunciation among middle-class blacks and whites. He traced this discrepancy to "a kind of intuitive balance operating in the minds of the (slave) masters of the white caste" that allowed and encouraged "impulse freedom" to blacks "as a compensation for deprivation on other scores." Such informalized substitution still operated in the 1940s, only then what had been a concession had become "a means of rebuke." From having been set up to act "loose," blacks were now condemned for "being loose." Even more disturbing, "the evidence is unmistakable that the moral indolence allowed to Negroes is *perceived by them and by their white caste-masters* as a compensating value and gain" [italics mine].

The felt-meaning of what's-there suggests what is valued and valuable. Both black worker and white master view the exchange of human freedom for personal expressiveness as reciprocally desirable. The black is taken care of, while the white acts as caretaker. The white gets economic advantage, while the black gains emotional expression. Really, the world is admirably put together.

From a biological viewpoint, we could conclude that for the black *organism* all was well. Within tolerable limits, hunger, thirst, and shelter needs were met; within wider limits, sexual and aggressive needs were satisfied. With such a thereness one could devote oneself to maintaining and enhancing it without serious reservations.

But for the white and black to place the black in a biological frame of reference and then devote themselves to that illusion proved a serious distortion of want and need. They wanted the *organism;* they needed the *human.* Despite the affair, desire for *humanity* could not be permanently repressed and ignored. Human need struggled against biological want. The *human* frame of reference radically changed what's-there. Devotion to a *human* focus radically altered the felt-meaning.

While whites still are enviously fearful of black expressiveness, the appearance of the freedom movement in the second half of the 1950s and the eruption of the black power movement in the second half of the 1960s have served to reorient the what's-there that Dollard described. Now whites perceive black expressiveness no longer as compensation to be encouraged, but rather as chaos to be channeled or even crushed. Now blacks perceive black expressiveness no longer as compensation to be tolerated, but rather humanness to be affirmed or even flaunted. Chaos feels radically different from humanness. One can give oneself to humanness, even as one would withhold oneself from chaos. If humanity is what's-there, then one devotes oneself to that felt-meaning. If destructiveness is what's-there, then one acts to contain and destroy that felt-meaning.

Today, "it is now generally understood," according to Kenneth B. Clark,

that chronic and remedial social injustices, corrode and damage human personality, thereby robbing it of its effectiveness, of its creativity, if not its actual humanity. No matter how desperately

one seeks to deny it, this simple fact persists and intrudes itself
It is the fuel of protests and revolts. . . . The fact remains that
exclusion, rejection, and a stigmatized status are not desired and
are not voluntary states. Segregation is neither sought nor imposed
by healthy or potentially healthy human beings.

Human Need

Human desires, in other words, find expression in our wanting whatever is in fact the truth and in our acting on the
significance of whatever in effect it means. There is something
deep within us that wants to see what's-there as it actually is,
even when it hurts. We cannot be satisfied with what W. H.
Auden called "a hazy truth" or "a shining lie." Something
deep within us knows that the most painful truth is always
less demoralizing than the most encouraging lie.

So those who work intimately with people—clinicians, coun-
selors, clergymen—assume, as Maslow has claimed, that individuals want "to be fully human rather than . . . to be sick,
pained, or dead." Death wishes, masochistic wishes, self-defeat-
ing behavior are seen as against one's best interest. If a person
ever experiences, however briefly, the wholeness of life, he or
she can never again settle for painful fragmentation.

We want to be human. We want to become the humanity
that has been given us. Being human and human becoming
are basic needs, whether we are considering food, housing, sex,
work, play, technology, or celebration. Identification and individuation, aspiration and inspiration are crucial variables in
our experience of ourselves.

Our being human constitutes what's-there.
Our human becoming constitutes its felt-meaning.

In the end, meaning includes thoughtful commitment and
emotional willing. We need both a ship to navigate and a sea
dragon to carry us.
We want what we need to be-come human!

A HUMAN FOCUS

FOUR
Where Do We Look?

There is a sense, one person commented, in which this approach to human becoming is like being challenged to a dare. The dare consists of exploring a haunted house, alone, in the dark, with the help of a candle. Also, there is a rumor that the house is full of treasure. The dare took the form of a dream.

"I accepted the challenge," he reported, "and advanced bravely toward the house. Yet I felt vaguely uneasy. The fence gate opened; the house appeared bathed in moonlight. It looked friendly but mysterious. My uneasiness increased. I took hold of the knob and the door squeaked open.

"The immediate candle-lit surroundings seemed quite ordinary. The room looked dark, dusty and neglected. I advanced steadily, relieved by the temporary familiarity and slightly disappointed at the lack of spooks. Suddenly I noticed a movement at the end of the long corridor.

"As I advanced, I realized with horror that it was a specter —a light, with a figure behind it moving steadily toward me. There was no retreat; the figure had seen me. I did not dare turn my back to the enemy. So I advanced, mesmerized by the also advancing specter. I was but a few feet from it; then the insane truth dawned on me: The image was a distorted image of myself! I had been advancing toward a hall of mirrors. All around me were distorted images of myself.

"I tried to find the light switch, but there was no light except for the candle."

That man was not relieved by his discovery. He did not say, "There are no spooks here; there are only mirror images." Instead, he realized life demands personal participation. Meaningful engagement invites us, yet it intimidates us. It calls, yet it alarms. In the face of the unknown we find ourselves.

The Demand to Be and the Fear of Becoming

The book of Deuteronomy (30:19) has God Almighty declare, "I have set before you life and death, . . . therefore, choose life." The choice sounds so simple yet proves so difficult.

A woman reports a dream:

I was on a boat in a darling little harbor. There were green meadows all about and the sun was shining on them. We sailed out. The mouth of the harbor was just a little narrow opening. As we started to sail through I saw the ocean with the waves breaking. The wind was blowing and it seemed quite wonderful. All of a sudden I was terrified. There was just the great ocean outside, and the boat was so little. I felt I must get back before we went out. I jumped and landed on the shore; but as I ran back I felt as though the grass was clutching me, and I saw that the land was trying to suck me in. It had all turned to quicksand. I woke shaking with fright. It was a horrible dream."

Having set forth on her journey, she panicked at the sight of stress. Her first reaction was to run for cover. She tried to get back where she came from. Only then, the cover had been transformed into catastrophe.

We can take the step—the risk—of choosing life, of reconciling our being with our becoming, only when, as Maslow put it, "the next step forward is subjectively more delightful, more joyful, more joyous, more intrinsically satisfying than the last." When that takes place, growth supersedes safety, exploration replaces withdrawal, excitement relieves boredom. We climb into our little boats and set sail no matter what. And the stronger the wind the more exciting the venture.

Maslow diagrammed the choice in the following way:

61

enhances the dangers   enhances the attractions

SAFETY $\longleftarrow$ ⟨ persons ⟩ $\longrightarrow$ GROWTH

minimizes the attractions   minimizes the dangers

Such a diagram rests on the assumption that given a free choice, and assuming the chooser is neither too sick nor too frightened to choose, one will choose wisely. One moves toward health and growth more often than not.

But the courage to choose oneself bears some connection with the courage to disclose oneself. The human organism is the only organism capable of being one way on the outside and another way on the inside. To the degree my outside conflicts with my inside, to that degree I confuse others by my responses; to that degree I struggle with my conflict between closeness and distance. To the degree my outside discloses my inside, to that degree others understand me; to that degree I send clear signals as to what I am experiencing and who I am.

The contrast between seeming and being was illustrated in a sequence of associations one man had to a projective picture card. The card is described in the test manual as "a weird picture of cloud formations overhanging a snow-covered cabin in the country." The picture allows a person to express something of his inner world.

When asked to tell what he saw, he reported:

I am reminded of the eerie delightfulness of Halloween with its witches and goblins, its lanterns and laughter, its fun and its festivity.

Such a response links him with people. While elaborated somewhat differently, the Halloween theme often comes up in stories about the card. Halloween is a shared myth, or fantasy, of witches and goblins. Despite its unreality, it is an experience open to all and talked about by all.

We may infer that upon first impression, people see this man as friendly, sociable, fun. His needs are met in being with others. If, however, they believe that what he seems to be is all he is, they are in for some surprises.

62

He will respond unpredictably. His next association sharply contrasts with the first:

I think of Admiral Byrd at his advanced outpost in the Antarctica spending six months *alone* in the 1930s, which was the title of his book. He was out there away from everyone—all by himself.

From a Halloween party to an advanced outpost at the bottom of the world is a giant step. Clearly, this man has more going on inside than is apparent to a casual acquaintance. He withdraws into himself as a solitary explorer of the human continent. While he is often with people, he is often by himself. The advanced outpost is generally beyond the reach of others and can be contacted only occasionally and at stated times.

In contrast to the dependency implicit in the first response, here he presents an image of freedom. He has planned and chosen limits away from the domination of the ordinary cultural routine. All that is demanded is the personal strength sufficient to assure survival in the task of active exploration.

His final association synthesizes his being with others and his being with himself in an unexpected manner:

I imagine a cozy closeness in front of a roaring fire. It is an experience of shared intimacy.

The man does not finally withdraw from human contact, only from casual contact. When the energy invested in his public self runs down, he pulls back into his private self for renewal. That, in turn, enables him to enter deeply and intensely into personal relationships.

The seeming of the very public side of this man and the seeming of his very personal side both are constantly modified by the being of the very private side of him. The pattern suggests an ebbing and flowing from casualness to intimacy, from closeness to distance, from openness to aloofness. The response also enables us to infer a rising and falling from activity to passivity, from getting things done to letting things be, from asserting himself to a waiting upon others. His associations are like a parable of his life-style. They picture the way he moves through his world.

For those around him to understand the balancing between his seeming and his being, he must allow himself to be known. In his public side he must interpret something of the meaning of his intensity. In his personal side he must make clear something of the meaning of his activity. As he discloses himself, the mystery of his behavior and the nuances of his attitudes appear more predictable. They make more sense. As the mystery of his being lessens, he comes to know more clearly where he is and what he wants.

The Courage to Be Known

No one can come to know oneself, and therefore choose oneself, except as an outgrowth of disclosing oneself to others. The courage to be is intimately bound up with the courage to be known. One must intend that another see and hear and understand and respond.

But for most of us the prospect of others seeing us—cutting through our defenses—getting behind our facades—gazing into our depths—can be uncomfortable, and even terrifying. Not only will another see our being behind our seeming, even more, *we ourselves* may see that hidden, uncertain, mysterious being that is uniquely us.

I vividly remember my dream the night after making the appointment to enter psychotherapy. I was on a desert island that was about to be invaded. Fortunately, I had an arsenal at hand; big guns on the edge of the island stood poised to repel attack.

My experience of interpersonal intimacy is not unique. There *is* something threatening about entering into a relationship where one's feared emptiness or feared worthlessness or feared chaos or feared competence will be exposed. I experienced the helper as a destroyer. And destroyer he proved to be. He attacked the patterns by which I avoided anxiety. He exposed the ways by which I kept my life barren of possibility. He undermined my image of myself as an inadequate person. He helped create conditions enabling me to grow. He enhanced the attractiveness of the unknown while minimizing its dangers. In the early stages, notwithstanding, I sought safety because the dangers loomed large and the attractions seemed small.

Dietrich Bonhoeffer rightly pointed to the necessity of respecting each person's right to reticence. Reticence—defense—cautiousness—call it what you will—is not simply negative avoidance. It likewise reveals a way of maintaining as much contact with reality as one can tolerate at any given time.

There are some people who too quickly and easily rush into the life of others. They obscure the hiddenness—the inner depth and privacy—at the core of every person. They know only the closeness accompanying adaptation to the environment. They see only identification with others. They overlook the distance necessary for establishing one's own identity. They brush aside the need for maintaining one's integrity.

Distance—reticence—mystery—gives to life an open quality. We never finish exploring the depths of love as we might a cave. Every disclosure opens a vista for further adventure. In one another's presence we stand on holy ground.

The Dimension of Depth

Depth is a word we usually use in terms of space. We speak of probing the depths of outer space or of exploring the depths of the ocean. Implied in those physical referents is the possibility of learning something more basic, something more fundamental, something more far-reaching than what we know or are aware of at present. The word points toward places that are dark and dangerous. Such places are also filled with the possibility of discovery: physical places as well as personal experiences.

Surface shows the side of reality we first encounter. In looking at it, we come to know what things seem to be. Yet if we act only in terms of what things seem to be, we are often surprised and disappointed. Because we are so often misled by appearances, we try to go more deeply into what is really there.

Depth is a metaphor taken from the realm of space and applied to the realm of spirit. The depths of life are neither shallow nor surface. They bring us close to the permanent.

They take us away from the passing. They touch upon the basic rather than upon the base. They are mysterious and majestic rather than vulgar and commonplace. They foster growth rather than regression. They work for wholeness rather than fragmentation.

Pathological

The Swiss psychiatrist, Eugen Bleuler, first used the word depth in relation to psychology. It referred to the developing insights of Sigmund Freud as specifically expressed in the recognition of infantile wishes and their repression. In *The Psychopathology of Everyday Life* and more especially in *The Interpretation of Dreams*, Freud began to spell out the extent to which unexpected torrents of vitality and feeling determine much of our living.

In that early period of psychoanalysis, the unconscious was regarded as repressed, chaotic, irrational, and irresponsible. The powerful emotions of lust and hate proved unacceptable to the individual and to the culture. Emotions were driven underground. But repression and avoidance did not mean that feelings no longer affected activity and thought. Instead of being in the open, they coursed through the inner world as a fifth column, inner saboteurs, wreaking havoc on every side. They reappeared in the frightening guise of animals and beasts and mad people.

Popular imagination perceived the unconscious as swampy, junglelike, a boiling caldron or a garbage heap. In the *Republic* Plato had claimed that in all of us, even in good men, "there is a lawless, wild-beast nature, which peers out in sleep." One person undergoing psychoanalysis spoke of the unconscious in essentially the same way when he indicated, "The subconscious mind is closer to Neanderthal man than to Emily Post."

Freud himself put it succinctly: normal people are far more immoral than they believe.

With that view of our inner world, little wonder the task of disclosing the depths of one's being looms as threatening, dangerous, and potentially destructive. Better not to look and

66

hope everything will not get out of hand than to look and see how awful everything really is.

Personal

If I were to ask you directly, "who are you?" I might make you feel self-conscious, embarrassed, and even confused. You might feel, "If anyone really knew who I was, they would have nothing to do with me." Perhaps the demand to look at yourself—inside—only evokes from you shivering images such as Eldridge Cleaver used in describing his own becoming:

I was an "outlaw." I had stepped outside of the white man's law, which I repudiated with scorn and self-satisfaction. I became a law unto myself—my own legislature, my own supreme court, my own executive. . . .

I became a rapist. . . . Rape was an insurrectionary act. It delighted me that I was defying and trampling upon the white man's law, upon his system of values, and that I was defiling his women.

But that savage becoming did not turn out to be the last word about Cleaver's becoming. After telling how he ached to slit white throats and rape white women, Cleaver finds another layer—a deeper depth if you will—that called into question his insurrectionary activity:

After I returned to prison, I took a long look at myself and for the first time in my life, admitted that I was wrong, that *I had gone astray*—astray not so much from the white man's law as *from being human*, civilized—for I could not approve the act of rape. Even though I had some insight into my own motivations, I did not feel justified. I lost my self-respect. My pride as a man dissolved and my whole fragile moral structure seemed to collapse, completely shattered. . . .

I had to seek out the truth and unravel the snarled web of my motivations. *I had to find out who I am and what I want to be, what type of man I should be,* and what I could do to become the best of which I was capable. . . .

I was very familiar with the Eldridge who came to prison, but that Eldridge no longer exists. And the one I am now is in some ways a stranger to me [italics mine].

Such breakthroughs prevented depth psychology from stopping with seeing depth only as destructive, a repressed, unconscious churning with irrational sexual and hostile impulses. Somehow the violently sexual aggressiveness turns out to be reaction against thwarted and crippled humanity. Love appears deeper than lust; affirmation deeper than aggression. In the depths we come upon unsuspected sources for being persons in our own right. We tap the personally meaningful ways by which we meet and master the new and unknown. We are carried toward our destination by the sea dragon.

As a consequence of remaining close to clinical data even though developing his metaphysical "speculations," Freud found himself driven to a very reluctant and for him shattering conclusion: "The Ucs. [unconscious] does not coincide with the repressed; it is still true that all that is repressed is Ucs., but not all that is Ucs. is repressed. . . . We find ourselves thus confronted by . . . a third Ucs., which is not repressed." There was no alternative, he concluded, but to realize "that almost all the lines of demarcation we have drawn at the instigation of pathology *related only to the superficial strata of the mental apparatus*—the only one known to us" [italics mine].

Thus, just as Freud concluded people are far more immoral than they believe themselves to be, so he found himself driven to add that people are also far more moral than they know.

The depths of prelogical experience, to avoid the term unconscious, no longer can be seen as merely the territory of purgatory. They somehow touch upon paradise. The inner world contains the seeds of life as well as death, the potential for growth as well as regression. These prelogical processes are rich, crucial, *and* dangerous simply because "being alive has always been dangerous."

Freud's discovery of a nonrepressed, nonrepressing unconscious came late in his career. It undermined the whole structure of his psychoanalytic theory as he had been developing it. Yet he himself could not carry the search for the depths beyond those "superficial strata" of pathology.

Others had to pick up that probing beyond pathology. No

longer can the personal beliefs and meanings of people be restricted or reduced to infantile wishes, obsessive compulsions, and other neurotic symptoms. That pathology is present can never be questioned. That pathology is all there can be much question.

Transpersonal

In the years since the early 1920s evidence and insight into this potentially positive creative depth have continued to mount. The penetration of the deep place of the psyche has brought to light not only personal dynamics, but equally universal meanings. Here we come upon that which is beyond an individual's own psychology.

One does not have to accept all of Jungian theory of inherited archetypal images of the collective unconscious to acknowledge the operation of universal meanings among people. Increasingly, we are seeing into the ultimate nature of life: the nature of humanitas and of cosmos and their interrelatedness. Increasingly, we are rediscovering dynamic potentialities embedded in expressions from the inner world.

The intimate interrelationship of an individual's depth with the ultimate of the cosmos is not a discovery confined to our day nor to depth psychology. Searchers of every age have known this. Within the depths we are confronted with destructive, as well as constructive, forces. Only those who sense that the two forces are somehow fundamentally linked can face the fright, move into the unknown, and come through whole.

The Eskimo shaman Najagneq told anthropologist Rasmussen that this inner Reality is "the inhabitant or soul (*inua*) of the universe. . . . All we know is that it has a gentle voice like a woman, a voice 'so fine and gentle that even children cannot become afraid.' What it says is: *sila ersinarsinivdluge*, 'be not afraid of the universe.' "

Depth psychology has given us new tools with which to penetrate truth that transcends the limitations of space and time. Ways open to move from the surface and the superficial into the deep and the meaningful. We are freed from the fixedness of literal space and literal time to participate in the fluidity of personal space and personal time. From the experience that little is related and relatable, we now find much is related and relatable.

The more our world hangs together—makes sense—is understandable—the more we are whole. And the more we are whole, the more humanity abounds.

The Gospel According to Thomas, an apocryphal gnostic document of the second century from Egypt, described the process:

Let him who seeks, not cease seeking until he finds, and when he finds, he will be troubled, and when he has been troubled, he will marvel and he will reign over the All.

Once we start searching for humanity we must not stop. But once started the experience can prove upsetting, troubling, disrupting. As the demon-possessed people cried out to Jesus when they experienced their brokenness in confrontation with his wholeness, "For God's sake, stop torturing us."

If we stay with the troubling, however, we come to the experience of marveling, as Eldridge Cleaver has detailed. We *are* "fearfully and wonderfully made." We *do* rule our own lives. We *become* our own persons.

But the way clearly leads through the depths, as Thomas stated:

The Kingdom is within you and it is without you. If you (will) know yourselves, then you will be known and you will know that you are the sons of the Living Father.

The depths are inner and outer. The depths are knowing and disclosing what is in me as much as they are discovering and sharing what is in you and in others. The depths uncover our common humanity as grounded in a truer humanity than anyone of us manifests.

The Path Through Ourselves

In his *Institutes on Christian Religion*, John Calvin pointed out that "our wisdom . . . consists almost entirely of two parts:

70

the knowledge of God and of ourselves. But as these are connected together by many ties, it is not easy to determine which of the two precedes, and gives birth to the other."

For me, Kierkegaard put the issue more pointedly.

> The more conception of God, the more self;
> the more self, the more conception of God.

In another place he expressed the necessity of coming to himself "in a deeper sense, by coming closer to God in the understanding of myself."

What this suggests is that true humanity and real humanity are reciprocally intertwined. Humanitas can be understood, as Gardner Murphy put it, as "a universe in miniature." The more I experience my own humanity the more I am transparent to universal humanity. The more universal humanity confronts me the more my personal humanity becomes apparent.

So, Origen, the great Christian writer and teacher of Alexandria in the third century, could speak of the mystical marriage between the Logos and the soul. In some mysterious way the structure of the universe shows itself in the structure of human beings, even as the structure of humanitas provides the clue to the structure of the universe.

It was Augustine, pivotal theologian for both Roman Catholics and Protestants, who spelled out his understanding in the famous words:

> I wish to know God and the soul.
> Nothing else?
> Nothing at all.

God and the soul. True humanity and lived humanity. The being of becoming and the becoming of being. Reality appears to us in the soul, in the centered self. So Augustine sought to know his soul because only there could his destiny be known, only there and in no other place.

Tillich interpreted this passage of Augustine's to mean: "God is seen in the soul. He is in the center of [humanitas], before the split into subjectivity and objectivity. He is not a strange being, whose existence or non-existence one might discuss. Rather He is our own *a priori*." Truth in the inward being is the immediacy of contact with humanity.

Usually, we regard that which is outside of us as foreign and alien and repulsive. We feel that which is inside of us as of ourselves and therefore desirable. Saliva in one's mouth, for instance, tastes warm, lubricating, and necessary. It is an intimate part of one's self. When one spits it out, however, saliva turns cold, disgusting, and hateful.

Behind the Hebrew injunction to welcome the stranger at the gate lies this truth. The stranger is a (br)other. The stranger portrays aspects of one's self that one either has not yet discovered or, having seen, has become frightened of and has rejected. Because the Hebrews once journeyed as strangers in Egypt, so they now are to take the stranger in. You, who are other than I, are an expression of me. And I, who am other than you, am an expression of you. And our interaction expresses humanity. To reject the stranger is to reject oneself. To accept the stranger is to accept oneself.

The path through ourselves may begin with awareness and end in disclosure. It may begin with action and end in reflection. Either way we come to a "heightened sense of 'I-ness'" —a sharpened experience of being an active agent, capable of initiating, persisting, completing, and evaluating. Instead of simply knowing oneself, which can so easily result in an obsessive preoccupation with endless analysis, we choose ourselves, as Kierkegaard put it in *Either/Or*. Consciousness of one's own centered reality looms as a decisive criterion of one's humanity.

Let me point toward that experience by means of an account of a black student and a white student who were randomly assigned to each other in an exercise in interpersonal relationships. In detailing their interaction I am depicting the experience of most of us. They were required to meet twice weekly for eight weeks for half an hour each time. They were to try to understand each other, get inside each other's experienced world, learn to give and receive in such a way that some kind of relationship evolved.

Further instructions insisted: "No matter how difficult your relationship might become, continue the twice weekly meetings. Since a common reaction to difficulty or uncomfortableness is to withdraw, the requirement to continue meeting will prevent your withdrawing, thereby forcing new ways of relating."

At the completion of the sixteen meetings each had to describe the world as experienced by the other, show the description to the partner, secure his written reaction, and then write a reaction to the reaction.

The black student, Ed, pours out more description of his own experienced world than that of his partner. Yet Ed's musings ignite the flame of fearful light illuminating the darkness between them.

Ed's description:

No-Exit what? He must be kidding! Why in the name
of God should I expose myself to someone I don't even know?
What difference does it make? I'll probably get one of
the brothers. Then we can bullshit for a half hour twice
a week. That could be fun.
    Professor Ashbrook said that the name of our partners
would be in our boxes today. I wonder who mine will be.
Len! Who in the hell is Len! He's probably some
liberal ass "honky" from the north that wants to tell
me how many black friends he has or how unprejudiced he
is. Well, it doesn't make any difference. I'll just
talk about football or baseball or some junk that really isn't
important. We don't have to meet but sixteen times
for a half hour each. I won't "bug" him if he won't "bug" me!
    That's about how I felt. I have hang-ups like anyone
else and even though I'm not always bragging or complaining,
I, too, have been hurt as a black man in a white society,
and I was in no hurry to talk about myself to someone
who probably could care less. Believe it or not, *I was
also afraid* [emphasis added]; afraid that if I got
to know this Len I might like him and expose too much
of my past, present, or future and be left wide open.
    With all this in mind, I conveniently arranged to postpone
our first two meetings. But then ever so swiftly, our
time of meeting rolled around again. I didn't want to go
but I knew I had to. Ever so reluctantly, I walked
over to his apartment. I knocked hoping that he would not
be there and yet feeling the inevitability of that initial
encounter. Before I could turn to run or think of something

73

witty to say, the door opened and a rather tall, lean Virginian opened the door.

That first meeting lasted about an hour; surprisingly it flew. Most of the preliminaries were gone. At the end of the hour, however, I knew that we would not be talking about football!

The next meeting lasted for an hour and a half; this time we talked about our families and our in-laws; the ice was beginning to break.

I now looked forward to those weekly meetings. I felt that we might get down to the real basics, but some-how for me somewhere between the fourth and fifth week, I blew the deal.

I "kinda" liked Len, but he was white. I kept wanting to ask him about his racial views. I had played basketball with him; I had shared some personal things with him; I respected him but I had to know whether he respected me as a man, a black man! I wanted to know but I couldn't ask him, and I began to withdraw. From then on we engaged in trivialities each showing politeness and attention to the other's words but never again achieving any real depth in our relationship.

I am glad that I could write about our experience because it allows me to say what has "bugged" me these last weeks. Maybe now we can really have a no-exit relation in the best sense of the term.

Before turning to Len's reaction, set along side Ed's out-pouring Len's more descriptive expression of Ed's experienced world. Len, too, however, touches upon their wariness of each other with his own musings.

Len's description:

Describing the experienced world of one's partner presupposes being that partner: knowing his thoughts, fears, hates, joys, and prejudices. Such an empathetic state was not achieved to a significant extent in my no-exit relationship. Yet from our encounter outside of the no-exit realm I was able to cull some observations on Ed's perspective and why our relationship wasn't dug deeper than it was. Ed is intelligent, witty, talkative, athletic, extrovertish, and dynamic. In the face of these attributes one expects condescension but gets only confidence, however. Not the confidence of superiority

over the *hoi polloi* that seems widespread,
but the confidence in one's ability to execute tasks
and to be oneself.
This personal confidence appears to be broadened
in his interpersonal outlook and relations. His
view of man is neither pessimism in the Voltaire tradition
nor optimism in the Leibnitzian sense.
I would place it somewhere between. Perhaps tempered
optimism that can be restrictively pessimistic
would suffice as an adequate summarization. According
to my interpretation of Ed's views, man is a cherished
being with an infinite potential for goodness and
for badness. But the stress is on the former. Ed is
not one to expect or to anticipate one's ugliness.
If he finds ugly traits, he more often than not
overlooks them. For instance, on the basketball
court Ed has one of the coolest heads. Even infringements
upon his personal rights do not elicit the outbursts
and rebuttals one expects. Ed's emphasis is on the need
for men to understand, cooperate, and communicate with
each other, allowing little room for bickering. This is
manifested in both his racial views and in his personal
example.
Ed is also a man of faith with a passion for
righteousness. His religion is buttressed by a deeply
grounded belief and trust in God, and in God's destiny
for mankind. Fate and fortune have little place in Ed's
vocabulary. Accompanying this firm trust is the
aforementioned passion for righteousness. Ed does have
a temper, and here is where it fits in. In the presence
of justice he is ebullient and effervescent, whistling
or singing while he walks; yet in the presence of injustice
Ed is angry and aggravated, stalking as he waits for the
proper time to attack the injustice or its perpetrator.
In spite of a few moments of revelation, our relationship
made little headway. I do not conceive myself as
easy to understand or easy to know, but even after I had
established a basic sense of trust in Ed, and let down
some of my defense mechanisms, superficiality crept
back into our discussions. We had not successfully taken
that frightening "leap" of becoming the other [emphasis
added]. I now ask the question "why?"
I do not know why, to be sure, but I do have
hunches. Perhaps my personality was such that Ed
was repulsed. It did not appear so overtly, but maybe
it was covert. Maybe I appeared as if I did not

75

want to expose myself to Ed? Even the place of our
meeting, in my apartment, might have exerted some
causative influence. The answer, however, is probably
more complex than these simplistic explanations,
and conceivably is the fact of my whiteness and Ed's
blackness. My approach to Ed's blackness was nil.
I had no approach. I was convinced that Ed could
sense my views without my having to state "I accept you
Ed, not because of or in spite of your blackness. I just
accept and respect *you!*" There was so much
to talk about, I felt, that we really did not need
to talk about the black problem except in general
terms. Perhaps this is where I failed. Had I given Ed
no reason to trust in me? I had not confronted
his blackness because it did not matter, but did he know
this? Was he aware of my respect for him as a black man?
Had I taken too much for granted, Ed?

With these two viewings before us we can now turn to their
reactions to each other's perception. Len continues:

I refrained from reading [Ed's description of me]
until after I had written mine, so much of my response
is already in my initial description. But I feel compelled
here to explain some of my actions.
First, I feel that I should write the paper over again,
at least the part about Ed's belief in the need to
communicate and understand. As he says in the paper "I
kinda liked Len, *but* he is white!!" [emphasis added] I
had misjudged Ed. It was not only a matter of my
lack of ability to convey respect for him
as a black man; it was also my lack of ability to transcend
my whiteness. I underestimated the inhibitive
influence that my color generated toward Ed.
My second reaction is directed toward Ed. Why
was he unable to ascertain my respect and unable to
confront me with his dilemma? Fear of hurt?
Perhaps, but it is hard for me to grasp that hurt
could be the reason.
I had told Ed that I trusted him, the first male
in my life I ever admitted this to. I shared with him
some of my most hidden thoughts, such as a high
school incident which has haunted me, where I was
unable to stand for my belief. Maybe these
"revelations" appeared as trite, but for me they
were immense.

76

WHERE DO WE LOOK?

Why does communication, deep communication, appear
so difficult? Was I afraid unconsciously to handle Ed's
blackness and thereby failed in conveying my respect?
Was Ed afraid unconsciously of rejection and failed
to communicate his dilemma to me?

Obviously, Len experiences confusion as to what has tran-
spired between them. If we were to turn his closing questions
into statements, some of the painful complications would be
more explicit: he *was* fearful of Ed's blackness; he *did* fail to
convey his respect; Ed *was* fearful of rejection; Ed *did* fail to
communicate his dilemma.

The pain of their paths intersecting stabs more sharply in
Ed's response to Len's description.

So close and yet so far apart and yet we somehow
felt the reason for our separation. It's not
very easy to sit down and really talk to each other
over such trying conditions. I refer to the condition
of our backgrounds and our prejudices. I would
like to blame America for all the hell that is in my
background and I would like to say that she is the
real cause of our hesitancy, but if I am to be
honest, I can't. *We failed because of ourselves*
[emphasis added]. Oddly enough, I trusted Len with
some things that were so personal that they had
remained thoughts, only for the rare moments of
complete solitude. Yet he is correct in saying
we didn't take the "leap."
I only wish I were all, or could be all, that
Len has seen within me. However, I believe that the
reason we did not make the leap was because of race
alone. We were unable to escape the dreaded sickness.
We became victims, perpetuators, and supporters
of the sickness that separates men from each other.
I failed Len and he failed me. We failed each other
because we did not help the other become
more human. We now realize what we missed by not
venturing beyond the known and niceties. But our failure
was not complete because we now have faced
each other (if in reality only through a paper)
as a black man and a white man and hopefully
can now become men to each other.

77

Having seen more clearly—each into the other's experienced world—each discovers new sources of courage and compassion. The possibilities of growth stretch forward in exciting ways; evidences of growth have continued to mature through the years that have followed.

Race loomed as a prominent and primary barrier to their meeting. Beyond that Len tended to be an introvert, intuitive, reflective, and somewhat passive. Ed, in contrast, tended to be an extrovert, becoming aware of the world through the data he received from his five senses, and he was definitely active in his orientation to life. Quite different patterns!

Here are the responses of each to the other's reaction to their original perceptions. First Len's, then Ed's:

Len:

Even if we had accomplished nothing during all
our meetings, the time spent on our no-exit assignment
was worth it in the face of these responses.
Indirect communication succeeded where direct
communication failed. But if we have really learned
something valuable out of this experience, our future
direct encounters between ourselves and others
will improve immensely.
I cannot escape the haunting feeling that if
two educated people, trying to communicate deeply,
failed, due to the color barrier, what hope can
there be? We were forced to write responses,
and found each other through these papers. But
what of the majority who is never asked to write
papers, much less attempts to really communicate?
I trust that both our problems are unique, not
general. If general, then perhaps a great deal
more tension must come before true understanding
can begin.

Ed:

Len and I talked today for a while when I
returned his paper to him. It was so ironic. We had
been able to do in a paper what we had been unable
to do for eight weeks. We had a confrontation: a
confrontation with the truth. Somehow from that
confrontation came a new birth. We talked so

much freer today!
Len had been unable to transcend his whiteness
and I had been unable to transcend my blackness.
Maybe we were *both afraid* [emphasis added] of
being hurt or rejected. But today after rereading
Len's response I thought of something very strange.
Perhaps, just maybe, we were *afraid of really becoming*
[emphasis added] the other! It's so much easier
sometimes to be content with viewing the world (no
matter how good or bad it may seem) from only your
point of view with your "hangups" and misunder-
standings rather than to attempt to view it from
another's perspective. If you find a black or a white
who is genuine, who really means what he says,
who deals honestly and openly with you, you can
no longer say that *they* don't understand or that *they*
don't care, without footnoting that I once met one
that did (if not consciously admitting to others,
it must be admitted to one's self).
The similarity of our papers shows that there
was a moment of truth for both of us. We both
told each other that we were tempted to write
both our papers and reactions over, but we didn't,
and in that we found strength. Perhaps this is
what the whole no-exit relationship was about. Maybe,
like Jung says, we found the other within ourselves
and exposed him for what he was: weakness
and prejudice. Now that he has been exposed,
perhaps we can now have some sort of meaningful
relationship.
No man is an island!

That both could come through to themselves and to each
other as sensitively as they did is beautiful and hopeful. Each
is so different yet so real. Clearly, though, the structured necessity that initially put them together, kept them together, required them to expose their perceptions and get feedback,
proved not only helpful, but necessary. The demand to be and
their fear of becoming required courage. They had to explore
the depths of each other and of themselves.

The more aware I am,
the more humanity I have;
the more humanity I have,

79

the more capable I am of human becoming;
the more capable I am of human becoming,
the more humanity I have
for the purpose of being truly human.

The way to humanity lies through human beings becoming human with one another.

Rather than start at some point removed from our own experiencing, in the following chapter I shall ask the basic question, where are you? By attempting to answer that question we ought to experience a solid enough base within ourselves that we can then look at humanitas without losing touch with real humanity.

FIVE
Where Are You?

A woman agonized over a possible divorce. Because her own being was disturbed, her becoming was also disturbed. In a human potential workshop, she agreed to embark on a guided fantasy into her inner life.

She was asked to imagine that she was very small and was then to enter her body wherever she wished. After some anxious avoidance, she closed her eyes (the artificiality of the exercise quickly faded) and started down her trachea: "Suddenly, I saw my heart. It was floating in my chest cavity with no attachments—just suspended in nothingness. I was frightened by the detachment."

She sought a way to get to her heart. As an earthquake rumbled, a plank bridge swayed precariously. Despite her efforts to make the bridge more secure, both ends disappeared, shrouded in fog, obscuring the places where it was connected.

Help appeared in the form of the Jolly Green Giant who offered her "a can of peas for a heart." She thanked him and sadly told him, "I want a human heart."

After the roof caved in and the heart faded away, she found the heart "in a bird's nest, all shriveled up very small. It terrified me and I cried out again. It was like a little chicken liver."

As she tried feeding it to make it grow, it suddenly ballooned, filling every part of her body. With caution, she managed to regulate its growth. Next, it turned into a little yellow canary singing happily, only from somewhere a yellow-and-black bee swooped in and stung her.

When asked if she could find something valuable or pleasant about her heart, she saw it "with a glacier through the middle, but the snow was pleasant, bright and warm."

Her fantasy guide had taken as his task that of helping her "integrate her heart with the rest of her being. . . . If she could build sound bridges from her heart to the rest of her body perhaps her love feelings [which had been causing her so much difficulty] could be handled more realistically in relation to herself."

Levels of Meaning

I have cited this journey into self as a way of dramatizing our need to integrate our being with our becoming.

The woman had gone on growing as an organism without grounding in her humanness. The consequences erupted in the unpredictability and turmoil of her *human* reactions. These surfaced as either too much feeling or too little feeling, as either too hot or too cold, as either too cutoff or too connected, as either too isolated or too encapsulated. She acted as an older woman one moment and a giggly young girl the next. As she reestablished connections between her heart and her body, her life began taking on more centeredness, more satisfaction, more effectiveness.

I have also cited this fantasy excursion for another reason. In our highly rational technological orientation, people too easily restrict life to one-dimensional meaning. Against the tendency to make one thing many things, or even everything, Gertrude Stein protested, "Rose is a rose is a rose is a rose." But to stop with such concreteness somehow drains life of its vitality. A rose is a rose *and* also symbolizes a relationship. A rose is a flower *and* also expresses flowering. A rose is a rose *and* also manifests a green thumb.

I am trying to relate the inner meaning of words with their

outer images. I want to connect the personal with the physical. The image of humanity opens up many meanings. These meanings grow in power as they are linked with concrete experiences.

Much of our alienation finds expression in the way we distance ourselves from objects. We cut ourselves off from our surroundings, believing that what is inside the skin is me, and what is outside the skin is not me. In contrast, I am pressing to recover the continuity between ourselves and the world, yes, and the cosmos itself.

With Gardner Murphy, I am convinced that human fulfillment quite literally depends on the truth that "there are no sharp boundaries" between what we are and what the universe is. Initially, we believe we are gazing through a window; suddenly we recognize we are actually looking in a mirror. As one American ex-businessman expressed it in a diary entry while seeking enlightenment in Japan, "Yesterday skipped my meditation because of a headache and [Mount] Fuji looked somber and lifeless. . . . Today after a couple of hours of good meditation in a chair it's grand and soaring again. A remarkable discovery: *I* have the power of life and death over Fuji!

The gestalt approach to dreams provides a way of sensing that continuity. Every aspect of the dream—people as well as objects—is regarded as purposeful, disclosing parts of the dreamer that have been disowned and projected outward. Thus, the dreamer is asked to play at being the objects as well as the people in the dream. By means of such identification one reestablishes the bond between oneself and one's surroundings. Every "it" becomes an "I"; every noun becomes a verb.

Two of Fritz Perls's favorite examples of this interaction came from the same man:

In one dream, he leaves my office, crosses the street into Central Park, and walks over the bridle path. I ask him to play the bridle path, and he answers, "What! And let everybody tramp and shit on me?" In another dream, he left his attaché case on the stairs. I asked him to be the attaché case. He said, "Well, I've got a thick hide, in a thick skin. I've got secrets and nobody is supposed to get to my secrets. I keep them absolutely safe."

Perls then summarized his point: "See how much he tells me about himself by playing, identifying with the objects in his dreams?"

We are jarred to attention whenever anyone suddenly asks us, "Where are you?" They sense we are elsewhere, not with it, lost to the immediate scene. When I ask people that question, they often become flustered. I have confronted them with the demand of there-ness and here-ness. Did I mean where were they literally? Did I mean where were they in thought and imagination? Did I mean where were they in their lives? What did I intend by "where"? The simple question lays open a complex process.

According to the creation story in Genesis (3:9), the question of where one is, is the first question God addresses to humanitas. The confrontation startles us into a painful consciousness of ourselves-in-relationship. We are forced to look at the truth of our situation.

Despite all the talk and truth of the question "Who am I?" the issue of identity first requires a sharpened awareness of "Where am I?" Location precedes locomotion; becoming depends on being. Personal reality grows from physical reality.

In asking the question "Where am I?" we must avoid the danger of literalizing the quest. In the sultan's palace in Istanbul, Turkey, I stood between two giant mirrors facing each other in a small alcove. I was fascinated by the infinite regressive mirroring of my presence. But no fresh viewing could come from such a closed process: only an infinite re-presentation of the same limited data. The same applies to a self-conscious observing of one's self, observing one's self introspectively. All introspectionism rapidly dries up because it turns into an endless process of my looking at my looking at where I am.

Instead, to say where I am activates a dynamic process. I grow sensitively aware of my place in a field of inner and outer forces playing upon one another. I become the centering focuser and directing organizer. Myself-in-a-setting and my-setting-in-a-self destroy any arbitrary and absolute separation of self-from-setting, even while retaining a clear differentiation.

WHERE ARE YOU?

Awareness

The key is awareness: what one contacts, what one senses, what excites one, what one sees in terms of the interplay between pattern and elements, between the background context and the foreground focus. Think of awareness in terms of light.

The flashlight approach to introspection—an outer light piercing inner darkness—evaluates, controls, and interferes with what's-there. It prevents an immediate and intimate knowledge of where and who one is.

Contrast that with the glow of burning coal—an inner light illuminating outer darkness. It shows forth what is without distortion or disguise.

A further analogy is the contrast between central and peripheral vision in terms of a spotlight and a floodlight. Central vision, like a spotlight, focuses on a small area, taking in one thing at a time. Peripheral vision, like a floodlight, shines less intensely, less specifically, less directedly, taking in many things simultaneously. Peripheral vision becomes important at night—in the dark—when we need to notice objects and movements that we do not recognize immediately.

I believe we need to cultivate peripheral, free-floating awareness without losing central vision. I believe we need to see with the light that glows from within, without forgetting the light that pierces. The point is a spontaneous experiencing instead of a forced concentration.

Such with-ness is strikingly simple, yet astonishingly complex. That can be sensed in an early dialogue of the Buddha himself:

> In what is seen there must be just the seen;
> in what is heard there must be just the heard:
> in what is sensed (as smell, taste or touch)
>   there must be just what is sensed;
> in what is thought there must be just the thought.

Open, receptive awareness differs from staring *at* or looking *for* something. We are not trying to impose our individual ideas, thoughts, desires, labels upon what's-there. We simply try to allow what's-there to speak for itself. We reject all pressure to make it something other than is there.

Here-and-Now

Rather than begin abstractly, let me direct your attention to your own immediate experience.

Where are you?
Where are you in relation to *space?*

What is around you?
What are the distances?
What are the boundaries?
What is the setting?

What, in short, is your oriented space—
that which is measurable and objective?

But do not stop by describing only the external and physical aspects of your situation.

Where are you in terms of your *life-space?*
What is your standing-ground?

Do you have personal breathing space?
Do you feel free to move around?
Are you boxed-in?
How do you experience your world:
Is it comfortable or uncomfortable?
Does it feel full of life or drained of life?
Is it chaotic or creative?

How, in short, are you attuned to your
space—that which is intangible and felt?

Consider architecture as one way to feel the meaning of space. For the Romans, space was expansive, vast, audacious; yet it had definite limits in its solid walls. One senses something static in all that massiveness. In America, for instance, the

Roman style found expression in the interiors of great banks
and the immense marble halls of railroad stations. One is always
impressed by their size, yet uninspired by their coldness. Roman
space is experienced as impersonal. One does not feel at home.

Wide World Photos

Interior of dome of Hagia Sophia

In contrast, Byzantine space conveys a more expansive
quality. Look at the inside of the Hagia Sofia in Constanti-
nople. There is a dynamic, a vitality, that emanates from the
shining planes and vast luminous surfaces. Contradictory
tendencies balance each other. Byzantine culture offers people
a sense of new and inspired self-confidence, combined with
a sense of spiritual universality. Here we experience quickened
and expanding space.

By the Gothic period, architecture had transformed expanding space into exalted space. The dimensional forces of the
vertical and the horizontal were contrasted. In the cathedral
at Amiens, one feels the contradictory forces. The overwhelm-
ingness of height conflicts with the pull of length. One feels
unbalanced, exalted, yet humbled.

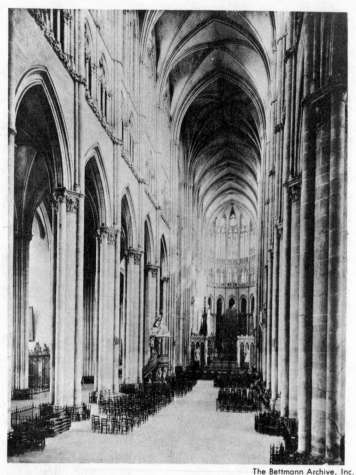

Interior of nave and choir, Cathedral of Amiens

Predictably, by the Renaissance, people sought to reestablish control over their world. Measured space replaced infinite space. The laws of architecture were made for humans, not humans for the laws of architecture. Thus, the dynamic energies inherent in axes began to be controlled. Whenever the pattern of the Greek cross was utilized in a church, the structure did *not culminate* in the center. Instead it spread out from the center under the dome by means of radiating aisles. Height and depth were once again in hand.

Space provides that meeting point between what's-there and felt-meaning. It "is not merely a cavity, or void, or 'negation of solidity,'" suggests one architectural analyst. "It is alive and positive. It is not merely a visual fact; it is in every sense, and especially in a human and integrated sense, a reality which we live."

Turn again to your own immediate experience.

Where are you?
Where are you in relation to *time?*

What time of day is it?
What day of what month is it?
What is your age in years?

What, in short, is your clock-time—that which is measurable and objective?

But do not stop by telling me what time it is.

Where are you in terms of your *personal time?*
What is it for *you?*

Where are you in the meaning of your moments?
Are you between a hopeful beginning and an
uncertain end?
Are you fulfilling or frustrating your dimly
understood goals?
Is your past accessible to you?
Do you value it or reject it?
Is it open to changing meaning, or is it fixed
permanently?
Do you feel time running out? standing still?
dragging its heels? racing ahead? pregnant
with possibility?

How, in short, are you attuned to your time—
that which is intangible and felt?

Look around you. What do you see? Attend first to some object. Can you describe its shape, its color, its uses, its texture, its setting?

Close your eyes. Withdraw into yourself. Allow the images waiting offstage to come out and show themselves.

Where are you?
What is taking place?

Give yourself to your spontaneous action as it unfolds.

What is going on?
What are you experiencing?
What is happening in your body? your jaws?
   your legs? your arms? your neck? your breathing?
What do you feel—pleasure? bewilderment?
   anger? embarrassment? uncertainty? elation?
   tension? boredom? frustration?

What prevents your being here-and-now? When in your imagination you leave this place in this moment, where do you go? What occurs? Are you rehashing what has happened in the past? Are you rehearsing what you anticipate may happen in the future? What difficulties do you encounter in being in the present? What unfinished situations clamor for your attention and pull you away from what is? When you go from here-and-now to there-and-then search in the there-and-then for the clue to what is missing in the here-and-now.

Behind this brief exercise in heightening your sensitivity, lies the assumption that what is self and what is setting are never fixed and absolute, but ever fluid and relative. What I experience as "of me" or "self" is familiar, desirable, close, and reliable. What I experience as "not me" or "environment" is foreign, undesirable, distant, and suspicious. At the boundary we find our conflict—the impasse between here-and-now and there-and-then—the narrows of anxiety—stage fright—"the intermediate zone of fantasy," as Perls described it, that prevents our being in touch with either ourselves or our world.

Someone once asked Perls whether, when a person is at the impasse level of experiencing, one is afraid of seeing the world for what it is. "No," he replied, "there is more to it." Then he illustrated his point:

The impasse occurs every time you are not ready or willing to use your own resources (including your eyes) and when environmental support is not forthcoming. The extreme example of the impasse is the blue baby. The blue baby cannot provide its own oxygen, and the mother doesn't provide oxygen any more. The blue baby is at an impasse of breathing, and he has to find a way to breathe or die.

To break the impasse requires our becoming fully aware of the impasse—telling it like it is—meaning the experience. We ask: What am I doing? What is going on? When we can do that, then the barrier collapses. We begin breathing again, and the crisis ebbs.

To the degree we are cut off from our here-and-now, the attempt to experience what *is* makes us anxious. The anxiety may be disguised as uncertainty, uncomfortableness, awkwardness, fatigue, boredom, annoyance, anger. Whatever specifically arouses our anxiety will be the disowned and lost parts of our personality which we use to throttle and prevent full experience.

As we become aware of and attend to what in truth *is*, we center down and thereby become more authentic and real. We recover our capacity to feel—to see and to sense, to act and to evaluate. We reintegrate that which has been segregated. We reclaim our lost inheritance—the gift of life itself. We relearn our ability to act.

At this point I am not trying to probe the depths. I am only seeking to discover and heighten the obvious. We are simply to reflect the here-and-now without caressing it or cultivating it. In Chuang-tzu's words, "The perfect man employs his mind as a mirror. It grasps nothing; it refuses nothing. It receives, but does not keep."

Thus, the application of the awareness continuum—the "how" of experiencing—is remarkably simple, yet initially difficult. We are to attend to and speak of what we are experiencing in the here-and-now. One exchange between therapist and patient suggests the process:

T.: What are you aware of now?

P.: Now I am aware of talking to you. I see the others in the room. I'm aware of John squirming. I can feel the tension in my shoulders. I'm aware that I get anxious as I say this.

T.: How do you experience the anxiety?

P.: I hear my voice quiver. My mouth feels dry. I talk in a very halting way.

T.: Are you aware of what your eyes are doing?

P.: Well, now I realize that my eyes keep looking away—

T.: Can you take responsibility for that?

P.: —that I keep looking away from you.

T.: Can you be your eyes now? Write the dialogue for them.

P.: I am Mary's eyes. I find it hard to gaze steadily. I keep jumping and darting about.

What-Is-Not–Yet-Is

In contacting what *is*, we especially need to be in touch with what seemingly is *not*. For it is often in the polar opposite that we discover the lost parts of ourselves. And it is in the recovery of what is lost that we regain our vitality. Life's richness and dynamic depend, in the end, upon attaining and maintaining a healthy balance among the various forces playing in us and upon us.

Despite the fact that consciousness is the defining attribute of human beings, we have constricted it to a narrow intellectualism. Those of us privileged with extensive education often find ourselves thinking more while feeling less. We achieve a mind but lose a body. Spontaneity, vitality, and inspiration atrophy.

The revolt against sterile intellectualism has gathered momentum over the past two decades. The cry for human warmth has risen within religion as well as psychology. Surprising as the idea first seemed to me, I believe the "soul" and "spirit" movements in the churches and the humanistic movement in psychology are similar. They are responses to *human* starvation. The disgrace of our overworked intellect is preparing the way for the grace of our undercultivated emotions.

Think of a healthy equilibrium in terms of the constant rebalancing of the bicycle rider. When one first launches out, one wobbles back and forth. One falls to the left, then to the right. One overcompensates and undercompensates. My back is still sore from running down the sidewalk holding onto the seat as I tried to teach my children how to ride. Skill involves the sense of proper compensation, leaning this way before that way goes too far, leaning that way before this way goes too far. The real fun, then, comes with the artistry of riding no-handed. By appreciating and acting upon differences—analogous to the bicycle rider—we experience opposing forces and the satisfaction of moving through the world with excitement and confidence.

To get this point across, Perls set up an exercise designed to heighten awareness of opposing forces: "Think of some pairs of opposites in which neither member could exist were it not for the real or implied existence of its opposite." In doing the exercise we are to be aware of the ignored continuity between the pairs of opposites. There is middle ground between, say, beginning-and-end, desire-and-aversion, trust-and-mistrust, sound-and-silence, light-and-dark, white-and-black, death-and-life.

More importantly, we are to allow each side to be sensed with its own legitimacy. We are to remain neutrally between the opposites. Perls called this "creative pre-commitment"—a condition in which we feel the beckonings to action but are not yet committed to either side. This is not the shaking-exhausting-conflicting "rest" similar to an airplane gunning its engines at the end of an airstrip prior to takeoff. Nor is it the chronic indecisiveness of the fence-sitter. Rather, it is the taking into account of all factors in a situation as prelude to mobilizing one's energies to act as one chooses. It is turning *re*sistance into *as*sistance, *dis*traction into *at*traction—the harnessing of counter forces for healthy equilibrium.

The next step, according to Perls, is to consider what we take as ordinary, as the precise opposite:

Consider some everyday life-situations, objects or activities as if they were *precisely the opposite* of what you customarily take them to be. Imagine yourself in a situation the reverse of your own, where you have inclinations and wishes exactly contrary to your usual ones. Observe objects, images and thoughts as if their function or meaning were the antithesis of what you habitually take them to be. Furthermore, confronting them thus, hold in abeyance your standard evaluations of good or bad, desirable or repugnant, sensible or silly, possible or impossible. Be satisfied to stand between them—or, rather, above them—at the zero-point, interested in both sides of the opposition but not siding with either.

Perls was pressing our ability to take hold of an impersonal and controlling environment and transform it into a personal and centered world. Instead of being victims of external forces, we are to be the center and organizer of these forces. *We* act as the judge, the evaluator, the decider. *We* direct our bicycle where it goes. *We* determine how fast it goes. The playful attitude engendered by the exercise serves the serious nature of the undertaking. The impersonal environment is almost infinite in possibilities as soon as it becomes a *human* world.

As one student commented after the exercise,

The experience was one of release—quite the opposite of the hemmed in feeling of the actuality experiment. First I imagined snow floating up instead of down, people walking on their hands, raucous behavior in chapel, getting up at night and sleeping during the day, putting ice in the stove and cooking in the refrigerator, and water flowing up instead of down. Then I began to think of myself as loud, boisterous and rough, which I had a little trouble doing.

In doing the same exercise a forty-year-old mother chanced to see the family television set. She utilized that as part of her content:

Primarily it is considered a source of entertainment in our family and secondarily a source of education and information. To reverse its role and see it spewing forth boring material and misinformation makes it a monster. Standing as a judge, I can see it as a useful baby-sitter at times, an occasional entertainer and informer, often boring, an innocuous past-time, a thief of time with the children, a deterrent to homework, and an object that I'm glad I can control with a knob or pulling of the plug.

More personally, the father of a fourteen-year-old daughter had complained about her monopolizing suppertime conversation, creating a scene if she felt interrupted. He often became annoyed to the point of "parental remonstrance or even sarcasm." "Now suppose," he playfully considered,

I was actually more interested in what she had to say. . . . Suppose that I was truly loving as she combed her hair near the table, and expressed appreciation only, or mainly. Suppose that I invited her verbal expressions, instead of quelling them, which only results in setting up a pattern for arguments, in which she quite naturally is probably testing out herself and "acceptance" on the "society image" of a father.

Suppose that I looked forward to letting the children talk because I wanted to hear what they felt, experienced, with all the proper dimension of a loving father, himself well enough adjusted that he didn't need to "let off verbal steam."

This experiment is so intriguing with possibilities I am resolving that I must try it out! It will call for a new awareness of myself and what causes within me evoke my daughter's desire to dominate the conversation. (Incidentally, my wife has suggested that a part of my blindness to what produces the tensions is that my daughter is so like her father.)

Exaggerated attitudes and behaviors are reversals of original tendencies. Excessive modesty hides greed. Excessive cockiness masks uncertainty. Excessive shyness covers inner expansiveness. Below the surface we discover the opposite of what apparently is. What we are not, we often really are!

It is not surprising, therefore, for some to become anxious or frustrated in experiencing the human freedom to reconstruct every interpretation of reality by recovering opposing forces. One student expressed both fear and fascination in response to the exercise.

As I pushed these concepts to their extremities, I sense a feeling of frustration. I don't dare touch another thing because fear is building. Nothing is reacting the way it should or is expected to react. On the other hand, I have a sense of adventure and am gripped with a sense of inquisitiveness to see what will happen next.

There is a feeling of surprise and fear repelling me from action, while there is an attraction toward action through a sense of inquisitiveness. I sense a feeling: if I don't react, I'll not know what will happen; if I do react, I will be surprised. So I am caught up in inaction.

Inevitably, to encounter opposites is to meet oneself. As another student put it, "This exercise has pushed me to an honesty that brings relief. Now I can at least recognize the forces which pull on my being—stretching or squashing me into the shape I am." But that student, like each of us, needs to take a further step. He must translate his experience of himself as object (forces which pull on my being) into *himself as subject* (forces which I *allow* to pull on my being). At least at that point, he had begun to experience his own vitality in a new and liberating way.

My balancing of opposing forces means centering and centeredness. I find my equilibrium, a creative interplay between myself and my world, between inner and outer. You can experience that immediately. Simply perform the following experiment:

> Stand equally on both feet;
> now shift your balance from
> foot to foot;
> just as physical balance centers,
> so does psychic balance.

Context

The seeming paradox of here-and-now, on the one hand, and of what-is-not–yet-is, on the other, can be understood via the way we organize the meaning of any experience.

The character of the organization is always the consequence of the relationship of the part to the whole. Technically, the relationship is known as the gestalt, or the figure/ground relationship. We tend to see situations as wholes or patterns or configurations and seldom as isolated atoms or parts or pieces. What constitutes a situation results from the interplay of what we focus on and what we ignore. Some parts are prominent; other parts are vague.

The context in which something appears is called the background, or ground, for short. The ground provides that which sets up the overall sense of a situation. This is its frame of reference.

Suppose, for instance, I tell you I am thinking of the word "fresh." Of what am I thinking? flowers? eggs? a man's character? lumber? air?

Unless we know the context we cannot know clear content.

The focus of attention and interest is called the foreground, or figure, for short. The figure constitutes that which is in front, or the center of a situation.

The classic way of conveying the figure/ground relationship is shown below. When you look at it, what do you see?

Faces and Chalice

If you see the white space in the middle as the center of attention—its figure, in other words—then you undoubtedly see some kind of goblet or chalice. On the other hand, if you focus on the dark spaces on either side as the center of attention—its figure—then you undoubtedly see two faces facing each other. If you allow the white area to reemerge into the figure and the black area to move back into the ground, the nonexistent solidity of the white becomes the existing solidity of the goblet.

The picture is an old Danish design utilized by Rubins to isolate some of the properties of the figure/ground relationship. There is an old story connected with this design that dramatizes its impact. Supposedly, two Danish princes were banished from the kingdom. A decree made it a crime for anyone to have or to make a picture of them. One of their loyal followers cleverly drew this design. When stopped by the authorities, they could claim they only saw the vase; when desired by the followers, they could readily see the princes.

Situations alter depending on what is figure and what is ground. What may threaten me may not threaten you. What encourages you may discourage me. Illustrations abound:

> In looking at progress in civil rights, blacks
> see the bottle as half-empty, while whites see
> it as half-full. The consequences for behavior
> are far-reaching. Blacks see how far there is to
> go. Whites see how much has already happened.

> At Pentecost the Christians were amazed and
> astonished. Each believed he heard the
> apostles talking in his own language.
> "Others said contemptuously, 'They have been
> drinking!'" (See Acts 2:5-13 NEB)

> When the scouts Moses had sent out to
> survey the land of Canaan returned,
> Caleb reported, "Let us go up at once and occupy
> the country; we are well able to
> conquer it." However, the ten other men who
> had scouted with him answered, "No, we
> cannot attack these people;
> they are stronger than we are. . . .
> All the people we saw there are men of gigantic
> size. When we set eyes on [them] . . .
> we felt no bigger than grasshoppers, and that is how
> we looked to them." (See Numbers 13:27-33 NEB)

We move through life in terms of meanings. That which we experience, we make sense of in terms of the world we are aware of and in which we live. Meanings are always the result of the relationship of figure to ground. The quality of a situation—happy, tragic, attractive, or repellent—depends upon the context. The gestalt, in short, is the grasp we have of our situation—the felt-meaning of what's-there.

The human drama, thereby, turns out to be intimately tied in with where we are. Physical reality grounds personal reality, even as personal reality goes beyond physical reality. We establish and enhance connections by becoming aware of our here-and-now and of what-is-not–yet-is. The character of our drama depends upon the way we relate the elements of life with the pattern of life. Only as we organize and order what's-there in some centered way, do we live out the human drama.

Perhaps one of the 112 ways (found in the Sanskrit of a four-thousand-year-old teaching) to open the invisible door of consciousness is appropriate here-and-now:

> Sweethearted one, meditate on knowing
> and not-knowing, existing and non-
> existing. Then leave both aside that
> you may *be*.

SIX
Some Human Tools

While I have been focusing on the personal, I hope it is clear that I am dealing with the universal as well. By looking at ourselves, we discover something about humanitas.

In reflecting on who he was, Carl Rogers came upon what he called "a learning." He put it this way: "What is most personal is most general."

What we find within is more universal than we have suspected. Even though that "most general" is *in* us, that does not come *from* us in a private sense. As we intentionally converse with what we are only dimly aware of, we grow toward wholeness, *and* simultaneously we recover our relatedness with one another.

But what are some tools by which we can carry on a conversation between the personal and the universal? How are we to bridge where we are with what we are? How do we relate what's-there with its felt-meaning? What links the microcosm of humanitas with the macrocosm of the universe? How can a sea dragon carry a ship to a place of being-in-becoming?

I propose that in symbol, myth, and dream, we find our most powerful tool of understanding.

SOME HUMAN TOOLS

Symbol and Myth

Symbols catch up and objectify the most deeply personal and, therefore, the most broadly universal. They portray our human world of meaning.

Through symbols we tie together fragments of experience. Such concrete representations awaken our imagination. They stir our depths. The mysteries of life are made more intelligible. Symbols are the "essence *and* image of psychic energy." Rather than meaning's being precisely detailed and defined, it is implied. That very open-endedness requires a personal response for the symbols to come alive.

Such an approach, however, contradicts what has until recently been our conventional Western approach. Self-conscious Western man has thought that his conscious thought was all of thought. For some time now, this has been recognized to be erroneous. The human person is more, and much more, than immediate awareness.

Wu Li, the sixth and finest of the great masters of Chinese painting (1643-1708), put his finger on the contrast. After studying certain Western paintings he remarked:

I find Western paintings quite different from mine. They emphasize form, light and perspective in an effort to secure exact likeness. But we do not care for conventional style and outward form. What we try to express is inner rhythm and freedom. We are more interested in the spiritual content than in the bodily likeness.

We in the West have narrowed our focus of awareness. We have concentrated so hard on the parts that we have missed the awesomeness of the pattern. We have missed the meaning beyond the moment and below the surface.

Jung reported a patient's dream that illustrates the disruptive presence of this exaggerated consciousness:

The dreamer is going on a railway journey, and by standing in front of the window he blocks the view for his fellow passengers. He must get out of their way.

From that report Jung saw that the process of inner search had indeed been activated within his patient. The dreamer

101

discovered that he himself kept the light from those who stood *behind* him, namely, the unconscious aspects of his personality. Jung rightly pointed out that "we have no eyes behind us; consequently 'behind' is the region of the unseen, the unconscious." If the dreamer stopped blocking the window (consciousness), then the unconscious material could be seen and understood.

In the history of psychology, behaviorism and empiricism have shoved aside the rich inner world of imagery and symbol and dream that initially dominated the field. But the ostracized has reemerged. We come upon it in the appearance of such practical problems as radar operators' attention, motor vehicle drivers' "highway hypnosis," pseudohallucinatory imagery of prisoners of war, and in such diverse investigations as sensory and perceptual deprivation, hallucinogenic drugs, dreaming, electroencephalography, direct stimulation of the brain, and alpha brain waves.

Focal consciousness can no longer be regarded as the necessary, defining attribute of cognitive processes. We cannot live safely in the literal. Distrust of imagination seriously cripples our understanding of ourselves and of reality. At last, declares Robert Holt, we do not have to make the impossible choice between abstract thought and rich fantasy, between reality testing and what Freudians term regression in the service of the ego. We need both our peripheral vision and our central vision. We draw on both illumination from within and inquiry from without.

So Maurice Maeterlinck (1862-1949), Belgian man of letters, set over against each other what he labeled the "Western lobe" and the "Eastern lobe" of the human brain. From the Western lobe comes reason, science, consciousness—the ship, if you will. From the Eastern lobe springs intuition, religion, the subconscious—the sea dragon, in other words. By virtue of its expansiveness, the Western lobe has paralyzed and virtually annihilated the Eastern lobe. While we owe extraordinary progress to its development of the sciences, we also reel from its catastrophes. The time has come, he declared, "to awaken the paralysed Eastern lobe." The intuitive, the prelogical, the experiential, the integrating, the inclusive are needed now.

The symbolic always performs an integrating and unifying function. By means of its figurative and imaginative quality, it unites vitality and intentionality, the sea dragon and the ship, power and meaning, as well as the personal and the universal, the immediate and the overall. A symbol bridges the gap between what's-there in the outer realm and felt-meaning in the inner realm. Symbols, as Bachofen wrote, carry us "beyond the finite world of becoming, into the realm of infinite being."

When a symbol loses its integrating power, therefore, it deteriorates into a mere sign. We can sense that deterioration by comparing the references in the King James Version (Job 40:15-41:1) to Behemoth and Leviathan, the great monsters of the deep, with those of the New English Bible where they have become crocodile and whale. We need only glance at the powerful and dynamic force portrayed in the winged chimera (a mythological fire-breathing monster) and think of a "real" beast to experience the difference.

Similarly, when a myth loses its power to demand a personal response from us, it turns into a legend. We see that by contrasting the experience of the quest for the Holy Grail as a symbol of our search for inner wholeness with the view of it as a tale of restless and irresponsible soldiers aimlessly wandering through Europe.

Humanness requires both halves of our humanity. The concrete, the specific, the focused, the conceptualized, the narrow represent the one side. The imaginative, the intuitive, the undifferentiated, the symbolic, the broad express the other side. Only as what's-there intermingles with felt-meaning and felt-meaning combines with what's-there do we experience full humanness.

In his studies of comparative religions, Mircea Eliade has probed the special character of symbols. He argues they are not mere reflections of objective reality. Instead they reveal "something more profound and more basic."

Symbols, especially religious symbols, go beyond the level

Winged Chimera

of immediate and ordinary experience. They are thereby capable of revealing a profound structure of the world as *"a living totality."* Because symbols point toward something real they are always, at least for primitive peoples, religious. "For on the archaic levels of culture, the *real*—that is, the powerful, the meaningful, the living—is equivalent to the *sacred*."

Such symbols, consequently, suggest many dimensions. That is, they simultaneously express a variety of meanings, the connections between them not being immediately evident. The effect of multiple meanings is the symbol's ability to disclose an integrated perspective, drawing together diverse realities into a coherent whole.

104

More importantly, according to Eliade, religious symbolism displays the ability to express paradox. This may be seen in transition experiences in which one passes from one mode of existence to another. Transitional experiences have been symbolized by passing between two rocks or two mountains or the jaws of a monster or crossing a river or sailing from one country to another.

Clearly, it was one of the most crucial discoveries of the human spirit when, through certain religious symbols, people experienced that what seemed so contradictory and opposite was actually in harmony. Because of that the disruptive aspects of life have come to be integral to all reality.

This is to say, then, that religious symbolism carries existential impact. In symbols we find ourselves confronted by Reality. Both personal and universal engagement are demanded. The human and the cosmic are translated into each other. We no longer feel isolated in the cosmos. Instead, we experience ourselves opening out to a world that is supportive. The symbol enables us to rise from our own subjective privacy into the realm of the objectively personal and universal.

Just as the sunrise parallels the awakening of consciousness and the bull the blind impetuousness of psychic behavior, so everything in creation can symbolize basic human qualities. Finding themselves in a universe full of uncertainty, people have utilized myth as a way of reducing their anxiety. By it they have introduced the human factor into an otherwise non-human milieu. So, clouds, sunlight, storms, seasons, and every other-than-human element have lost their power to terrify whenever people have been able to give them the sensibility, the intentions, and the motivations that individuals experience daily.*

While some people make the mistake of reading too much meaning into a situation, others read too little meaning from a situation. Robert Frost caught the meaningful trend latent in all experience when he observed about poetic creation: "Always, always a larger significance. A little thing launches a larger thing." Metaphor, the figurative, the legendary, the mythological, the symbolic, the gestural, the poetic, the picturesque always bear intimations of the larger meanings of humanitas.

We are not independent observers—not of ourselves nor of our settings. Rather, we are inevitably and inextricably bound in the bundle of life. Knowledge, therefore, cannot be a factual, impersonal description of that which is detached from us. Both modern art and modern science recognize that what is observed and the act of observing make up one complex whole. We cannot look at a situation without altering the situation by our very act of looking.

Alan Watts lays out the issue of participating knowledge:

Human beings are aware of a world because, and only because, it is the sort of world that breeds knowing organisms. Humanity is not one thing and the world another. . . . An intelligent [human being] argues . . . an intelligent universe.

According to Campbell, dreams and myths are now understood as serving four essential functions:

(1) eliciting and supporting a sense of awe in the presence of the mystery of life;

(2) rendering a cosmology, an image of the universe that supports and is supported by "this sense of awe before the mystery of a presence and the presence of a mystery";

(3) supporting the social order, integrating the individual into the group;

(4) initiating the individual into the reality of one's own psyche, guiding one toward one's own spiritual enrichment and realization.

These functions sharpen the interconnections of various levels of meaning.

A cosmology provides the most inclusive organization of reality. It rises from the undifferentiated ground that by virtue of its very groundedness elicits from us a sense of awe in the presence of the mysterious power of life itself. Such organization orients us toward a social order in which meaning is maintained, nurtured, and enhanced. But since the social order is supported by the shared commitment and involvement of individuals, the orientation also drives toward initiating individuals into the reality of their own psychic structures.

But to point to the presence and power of symbols and myths is not the same as understanding them. We may experience something of their awesomeness while still floundering over their meaning. Some way of getting from seeing the symbol from afar to living in the symbol needs to be found.

Those investigators of comparative religions such as Eliade have given us powerful historical tools for our understanding. Yet I confess I do not find these quickening my own experience. They provide context yet lack dynamics. I turn to them for a sense of perspective, yet it is from the dream I gain a feel of the process.

The Dream

For myself, I have found in depth psychology the single most powerful tool for getting inside religious symbolism and mythological expression. That tool is the dream and its decoding.

Experientially, the dream bridges the subjective inner world and the objective outer world. With and in the dream symbol, the dreamer attempts to reconcile and reunite that which has been overlooked or neglected or alienated or disowned or not yet perceived within one's experience.

In asserting this, I do not intend to collapse the meaning of symbol and myth into the meaning of dreams. Eliade rightly argues against reducing myth to a process of the unconscious. Instead, I am suggesting that in getting a feel for the dynamics of the dream we have an experiential interpretive tool with which to get a feel for the meaning of symbol and myth. As Eliade himself acknowledges: "There is no mythic motive or scenario of initiation which is not also presented, in one way or another, in dreams and in the working of the imagination."

Perspective

In considering the dream, I would remind you that in biblical and postbiblical times people regarded dreams and visions as manifestations of the holy, revelations of and by and from God.

Primitive people paid close attention to their dreams. Egyptians believed in their revelatory character. Assyrians used them for therapeutic purposes. Muhammad himself placed great importance on their significance. He would ask his disciples each morning to report their dreams, which he would interpret and then go on to share his own dreams—a practice also followed by the Senoi tribe of Central Malaya.

Dreams have always played a prominent role in the creative process. Descartes' passion for truth arose directly out of a dream resolving his inner turmoil and pointing a direction for his energy. One of Poincaré's famous mathematical solutions came to him as he was half dreaming on a bus. Kekule discovered the structure for the benzene ring from a vision in which he saw six snakes in a ring, each swallowing the tail of the one ahead. Instances of this kind are so numerous in the history of science and ideas that many believe dreams reveal "the hidden creative and inspirational potential in human beings."

Synesius of Cyrene, like other medieval Christian thinkers, conceived of the universe as a unity. He likewise believed the dream to be the best expression of that meaning. For him the dream disclosed both rational consciousness and the sense experience of the world around. He held that myth was based on dream and that an understanding of mythology aided an understanding of dreams, even as an understanding of dreams assisted an understanding of mythology. As he put it:

I even think that myths take their authority from dreams, as those in which peacock, fox, and sea hold converse . . . for these men to whom the myth is the beginning of their art, the dream ought to be its appropriate end.

Regardless of particulars, the similarities between dreams and myths suggest four conclusions:
(1) The dream is not only common in human experience, it also conforms to definite patterns.
(2) Such patterns are more closely related to the structures of the human mind and to certain fundamental rela-

tionships and experiences than to specific cultural limitations.

(3) The dream is always valued whether the dream is feared or sought.

(4) Virtually every society sees some connection between dreaming and waking life.

The evidence is overwhelming. In the unconscious or prelogical, lie the springs of humanitas. There we are linked with the organic and the universal.

I view the dream as the vehicle of that centeredness within us that works on our becoming whole.*

Dreams are personal expressions of the symbolic. As such, they touch upon what is regarded as ultimate. They provide a way in which we feel and enter into the mysteries of existence. In penetrating our dreams we move invariably from the merely personal to the more mythological. By understanding dreams we find clues to understanding the symbols and myths which express our wider human engagement.

Turn with me, therefore, to a closer analysis of dreams and their meanings. In doing so, I am partially aware of the danger of such a step. For popular interest in the mysterious, the esoteric, the superstitious, and the bizarre can easily latch onto my discussion of the dream as an end in itself rather than seeing it as I intend it: namely, as a means of meaning and a way to meaning.

Dynamics

The dream is not only "the royal road to the unconscious," as Freud knew and demonstrated so persuasively, but it is also "the royal road to *integration*," as Perls communicated so powerfully. As such, I regard the dream as a royal road to the personal/universal disclosed under the various guises of myth, legend, saga, literature, poetry, imagination, and fantasy, as well as history.

We need not accept the wish fulfillment and sexual reductionism of Freudian theory to appreciate and to appropriate the dynamic characteristics of the dream process. Behind various theoretical approaches to dream interpretation—Freudian, Jungian, Adlerian, Rankian, Sullivanian, Frommian, gestalt—I find an approach to meaning that can assist us in our search for our own becoming, our own wholeness, and, thereby, others' wholeness simultaneously.

The dream communicates the most intrinsically personal response of which we are capable. By it we project and objectify the deep currents of our prelogical, and usually nonconscious, mental activity. Consequently, the dream is ever and always symbolic.

The content may be succinct and compact or elaborate and complicated. It never merely reports about what's-there. It allows us to exhibit ourselves in a profound way, to say something about our way of life and about our concept of ourselves as human beings. It expresses the world as we experience it. It is our own existential message to ourselves.

By virtue of that fundamentally human quality, dreams generally have "greater scope and deeper meaning as *personal acts*" than our acts in the outer world. In our dreams we respond completely out of our own individuality. The more the felt-meaning of what's-there is present, the more intense our involvement and the more extensive the referents of the dream material itself. Precisely because dreams are so highly individualized, the symbol cannot be finalized and pigeonholed. In interpreting them, we must always take into account the dreamer and his or her immediate life situation.

Many meanings are present; single meanings are absent. We go beyond the conventional, the ordinary, the everyday. We disclose the disturbing, the alluring, and the enduring dimensions of our becoming. We discover our deepest selves. We reveal our most creative power. Think of the dream as a moving picture-puzzle.

In a television interview a few years ago, Ingmar Bergman, producer of so many significant motion pictures, linked his professional work with his personal dream life:

I have understood later . . . that all my pictures are dreams,
The dream is never intellectual. But when you have dreamt, it can start your intellect. . . . It can give you new thoughts. It can give you a new way of thinking, of feeling. . . . It can

give you a new light for your inner landscape. And it can give you suddenly a little bit of a new way of handling your life.

In commenting on that interview, Ira Progoff pointed out that Bergman's pattern demonstrated the cohesion of each creative act: the turning inward for the orienting imagery, the turning outward for the organizing artwork, and unified in the dream that "brings forth a living myth."

As a visual image, the dream instantaneously presents a vast amount of personally relevant material. Even more than a picture, though, the dream, as Bergman informed us, is a drama. The dreamer himself or herself is the author, the actors, the scenery, the props, the animals, the objects, and the audience simultaneously and separately. Through the pictorial drama, the dreamer projects his or her inner world of meanings and values and conflicts into a semi-outer world of people and phenomena and events.

Research on sleeping and dreaming discloses the activity of our eyes during periods of greatest dreaming. The activity is known as rapid eye movement (REM). We follow the dream action as if we were actually looking at real visual objects. We see what we dream.

Through such symbolic activity, we expand our awareness and uncover a greater sense of our participation in and our oneness with the whole universe.

The Senoi people in the Central Mountain Range of the Malay Peninsula, for instance, exhibit a high degree of psychological integration and emotional maturity. They demonstrate remarkable social facility in promoting creative interpersonal relationships. Observers attribute this to the dream expression and interpretation practice that provides the focusing organization of their social structure.

The Senoi believe that people reproduce images and features of the external world in their own minds as an adaptive process. When these features are avoided or ignored or neglected, the dream beings remain against them, as the environment is against them, or else become dissociated and invested in enervating and wasteful tensions. With the aid of the socializing process of sharing and interpreting dreams with the family at breakfast and later with the community at council meetings, "these psychological replicas of the socio-physical environment can be redirected and reorganized and again become useful to the major personality."

In its more primitive form this Senoian practice is what Perls labels re-identification. That is, by playing the various parts of the dream, we achieve an identification with the dream as a whole through its individual parts. "We *become* the part until we begin to recognize it as a bit of ourselves—and then it becomes our own again." When that begins to happen, growth and maturity are activated. We gain back part of our human potential.

Suppose, for instance, you experience the world as cold and bleak. You might dramatize that felt-meaning by dreaming of a rocky coast in freezing weather. Or suppose *your* world feels full of agitation and turmoil. You might dream of thunderstorms, electrifying lightning, raging seas or ferocious battles, milling crowds and maddening traffic jams. You need only look at this painting by Jackson Pollock to experience the feel

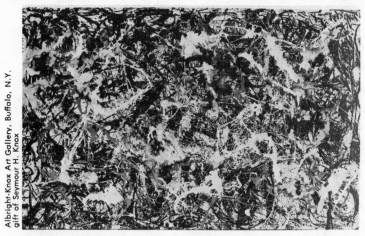

Albright-Knox Art Gallery, Buffalo, N.Y. gift of Seymour H. Knox

Convergence by Jackson Pollock

of such turmoil. In it we are confronted by powerful emotional energy. With their lack of logical structure, Pollock's paintings

112

are almost chaotic, a kaleidoscope of color, lines, and space. They picture, as one interpreter expressed it, "the nothing that is everything—that is the unconscious itself."

If, in contrast, you sense *your* world as settled or serene, you might dream of a quiet pastoral setting in which everything has a place and everything is in its place and all's well with the world.

Prohibitions can take the form of any object or encounter that stops forward movement—walls, curbs, locked doors, putting one's foot on the car brakes, or, the appearance of a policeman or customs agent.

In a dreamwork seminar, Perls asked May, a woman participant, to play the wall which she had experienced in her numbness:

> May: I will not let you come in contact with anyone.
> Perls: Say this to me. You're the wall and I'm May.
> May: May, I will not let you contact anyone completely. You can know them and you can see them but you can never fully come in contact with them as a human being, as a person. . . . You are—you are in front of me, wall, and behind you I am safe.
>
> And the wall says, Yes, and you will never be able to get through me. If you do, then you will be vulnerable and people can come in. And this wall keeps people out.
> Perls: [Say] I keep people out. . . .
> May: I keep people out with this wall. I keep people out.

In contrast, freedom and liberation can be expressed by dancing or jumping or flying or in several ways of getting to the same destination, as in the image of twelve gates into the City of Hallelujah (Rev. 21:23).

Whatever makes up the pictorial images of the dream drama, the qualities, the feelings, the attributes, the experiences, the strivings, the fears, and the hopes of one's own are expressed and conveyed in the objects, the people, and the experiences on the dream stage. The dream simultaneously reflects the ways we attempt to formulate conflicts and provides one of the means by which we attempt to work them through.

Obviously, formal laws of logic do not apply to these personal dramas imaging the felt-meaning of our lives. That does not, however, imply there is no pattern. People mistakenly conclude that dreams are nonsense and myths are more so. There is clearly a law of inner human logic, the recognition of which was Freud's great contribution, even though he rigidified that logic. In the dream, we have flashes of meaning without the ordinary connections of waking life. There is no *"if* this, *then* that,"* no "and" or "but." All is present immediately, inter-mingled, simultaneously.

Dreamlike material never merely depicts what's-there. It always declares the felt-meaning—the impact and the import —of what's-there. Because it springs from the uniquely per-sonal, its meanings can never be rigid. They ought never to be torn finally out of their cultural and personal contexts. They ought not to be given unqualified general meaning. For the material is more figurative than physical, more metaphorical than actual, more true at the subjective level of synthesis than at the objective level of analysis. It can never be linked abso-lutely to the permanent nor left utterly in the passing. We per-sonally participate in the creation and interpretation of every symbol.

Any symbol, combining as it does the intensely private and the extensively public, requires an exploration of its felt-meaning for each particular person. No standard guidebook can outline its human meaning without taking into account its human maker. Reliable inferences can be made of symbols, but in the end their validity depends upon individual confirmation.

Insights into the deeper human meaning require attention to the forces or power, the direction or progression, the con-flict or tension, the equilibrium or compromises of whatever comes to the surface. The impact a situation has on an individ-ual can be sensed from the forces the symbol releases.

The "A cannot be both A and not-A" of formal logic breaks down in the logic of the inner world. For in the symbol, A can be both A *and* not-A, even as B can be both B *and* not-B. Denials are often affirmations, while affirmations may be denials. "I *don't* want to . . ." may mean "I . . . want to . . ." Elements can stand for their opposites. Being clothed may serve as a disguise for nakedness; nakedness a disguise for closedness. The symbolic may compensate for what we experience, because for the inner world it is always a question of equilibrium and disequilibrium. When we have consciously cultivated one aspect of ourselves, we regain our balance through the counterbalance of another aspect of ourselves in the inner world.

Jung enunciated the principle of psychic compensation and complementarity. Whenever a process goes too far, compensation is inevitably called forth. Therefore, in interpreting a dream, it is helpful to ask: for what conscious situation is it compensating? In other words, the dream makes up for the deficiency in our intended activity. It gives voice to that which we have overlooked or undervalued, ignored or neglected. It exposes to consciousness shifts in the vital balance.

If the role we intend to play when we are awake—our persona —the mask through which we sound forth who we are—is too forced, exaggerated, and discrepant from what we are, then our vital forces come back to haunt us—our shadow, in other words. For that which is unacceptable and rejected peers back at us through what we project on and read into others.

The symbol-myth heals because it performs a dual function. On the one hand, its power resides in its calling forth into awareness the deeper human urges and longings—repressed, unconscious, universal. On the other, it discloses the goal, the purpose, the direction with undisguised clarity, thereby resolving perplexity on a higher level of integration. The dream counterbalances conscious disequilibrium by reestablishing inner centeredness. Here the personal merges with the universal in self-transcending awareness.

In analyzing the dream process as providing a tool for opening up the human meaning of symbolic material, I have described one approach. I am less interested in a specialized understanding of dream interpretation per se and more interested in a generalized "sense" of how one can approach the figurative, the picturesque, the metaphoric, the symbolic. For such material always carries deeply personal and broadly universal meanings.

Below the surface of the conventional and the cliché, we come upon powerful forces. Clearly, some of them are infantile and destructive. These, however, seem primarily related to the more superficial strata of our inner world. As we gain courage to confront these, we move beyond the pathological into the more personal realm of growth and creativity. In pressing further, we come upon that which lies beyond even the personal —ultimate depths of meaning as to the nature of humankind itself, the nature of the cosmos as a whole, and the intimate interpretation of the two as *the* interface of one transcending Reality.

I concur with Jung's assessment of the limitations of major approaches to meaning currently vying for dominance.

The Buddhist discards the world of unconscious fantasies as useless illusions; the Christian puts his Church and his Bible between himself and his unconscious; and the rational intellectual does not yet know that his consciousness is not his total psyche.

Obviously, that does not apply to every Buddhist, every Christian, or every rational intellectual. It does apply, however, to everyone who rejects prelogical experience as secondary, extraneous, or nonessential to human becoming. To see the ship and dismiss the sea dragon is not only foolish, but dangerous.

To touch upon felt-meaning frees reason from its bondage to the achievement of more and more, as in the pragmatic West, or to negation by less and less, as in the pneumatic East. To grasp what's-there frees emotion from its bondage to the chaos of everything or to the crush of anything. The symbolic manifests the misery and the grandeur of humanity. It exposes the unbalancing and the rebalancing of life forces. Within the realm of mystery, the symbolic lights up the possibility of wholeness, for there we stand in the presence of the holy of holies. Intuition and intelligence join forces.

The sea dragon carries the ship. From the depths of the prelogical comes the power of the logical.

The ship is steered toward its proper destination. From the heights of the logical comes the purpose of the prelogical.

We are made for making human beings human.

116

SEVEN
More Focused Insights

So far I have been trying to elicit your experiencing of humanitas. To that end I have been somewhat vague in my use of terms. I have chosen to use words in ways that open up a number of ideas simultaneously. I have avoided tying down meanings more precisely. While I shall continue to move at the experiential level, I can no longer postpone sharpening the focus of our endeavor.

Since human beings first appeared, they have tried to make sense of their experience. They have sought to manage the mystery confronting them by turning the random into the regular, the unexpected into the predictable, fragments into patterns. By linking a "this" with a "that," they have created a sense of stability. With a sense of stable meaning, they have learned how to tap the forces of the universe for human purposes.

Symbols of Humanitas

Two images have appeared in widely separate cultures to make sense of the world. They are the circle and the square. By means of these, people have expressed the meaning of their existence.

117

In Hindu thought, the circle symbolizes the Absolute—no end, no beginning; greater than the great, smaller than the small. The term *mandala* denotes a magic circle that is among the oldest religious symbols. It stands for unity and universality. Usually, a flower or a cross or a wheel conveys the mandala form. Always, there is a definite tendency toward a structure divided into four parts. As a symbol the circle includes every concentrically organized figure. Other expressions of the image are the womb and the earth and the sun.

The image of the circle elicits feelings of wholeness, of centeredness, of completeness, of balance. Its perfect form, the absence of angles, its self-enclosure, and its lack of a resting point have all led people to think of the circle as the perfect symbol of Heaven. In it we find our psychic centeredness represented. The circle expresses the *whole* self.

Because of its firm symmetry, its solidity and definition, the square, in contrast, has served as a basic symbol of concrete reality. Earth, with its stable characteristics of four seasons, four elements (earth, air, fire, and water), and four parts of the compass, has been depicted as a square. Because of its axes, a square gives coherent meaning to the circle. In it we find our psychic parts represented. The square expresses the *varied aspects* of the self.

Taken together, a circle and a square combine the perfection of the whole with the individuality of the parts. Thus, people have tried to square the circle. They have sought to get the area of the Earth-square to conform to the area of the Heaven-circle. By means of such symbolic activity they have worked to overcome the split between existence and essence, the everyday and the eternal, humanity and divinity. They have grasped humanitas: what's-there and its felt-meaning.

Not only have images of the circle and the square been prominent historically, they likewise have shown themselves in the dynamics of individuals.

Two dreams, one from a man and another from a woman, suggest my point.

The man reported the following dream:

I am on board ship. I am busying myself with a new method of taking my bearings. Sometimes I am too far away and sometimes I am too near: the right spot is in the middle. There is a chart on which a circle is drawn with its center.

The task of finding the right spot, the center of the circle, is plain. In writing the dream down, he remembered an earlier dream of target shooting: sometimes he shot too high, sometimes too low. The correct aim lay in the center. He took both dreams to be highly significant. A target is a circle with a bull's-eye in the center. At sea getting one's bearings depends upon the movement of the stars and an accurate knowledge of that movement.

The woman described an analogous dream:

I am making a ground plan, perhaps of a house and garden, in which several pieces have to be fitted into a given space. They will go in quite well, only first it is necessary to draw the circle showing the points of the compass, to give the orientation. I look for something with which to draw the circle.

Without going deeply into the dynamics of her dream, it is immediately obvious she is dealing with the basic "plan" of her life. She is working on her personality. How is she going to arrange the parts—the different drives and trends—to fit into her life-space appropriately and satisfactorily?

Deep within her is the confident trust that all "will go in quite well." The contrasts and opposites, in the end, constitute a living whole. Yet for that to take place she requires some kind of compass: a frame of orientation to show what's-there and a frame of devotion to suggest what-it-means. A compass will include all that matters in her human growth.

Squares and circles go together. Intuitively, they open up insight into humanitas. Intellectually, they focus that insight more exactly. Combined, the wholeness of the circle and the opposites of the square enable us to develop the concept of humanitas in more detail.

Remember, I am using humanitas to convey multiple meanings. On the personal level, it points toward the fulfilling of our inner drive with respect to ourselves and our relationships.

On the social level, it points toward justice, which is the fulfilling of the inner drive of human groups and their mutual relationships. Beyond inner and outer fulfillment, I use humanitas to convey the universal dimension, the oneness of individuals and groups, the wholeness of the world and its parts.

I find that all-inclusive meaning in an intuition of the great German mystic Jacob Boehme (1575-1624). In wondering why the world was made, he concluded that God wanted to show himself: the Reality that is the will-to-be is also the Reality that is the will-to-be-manifested. In other words, ultimate Reality can be understood in terms of being, or "the will-to-be," and in terms of becoming, or "the will-to-be-manifested."

The face of humanitas discloses the countenance of the cosmos.

Let's turn our attention now to the difficult task of elaborating the meaning of humanitas more precisely. The concept of being and the concept of becoming seem to be ideas that are at once most general and yet capable of being most specific. They can give us the parts that go to make up the pattern.

Being and Vitality

Consider first the perspective of being. The being of humanitas constitutes our core, our essence, our basic quality and character.

I am using the term as a way of conveying constancy. Apart from being, we are ungrounded, unanchored, and therefore not present. Here is the structure-maintaining expression of existence. Being human designates the what's-there of humanitas. Life maintains itself.

Think of the perspective as a horizontal plane. It sets forth a continuum from the pole of the unique on the left to the pole of the universal on the right. It embraces the accommodation of conformity and the idiosyncrasy of deviance. As suggested by Figure 5, being stretches between the individuality of the part and identification with the whole, between the unique and the universal, between distinctiveness and commonality, between distance and closeness.

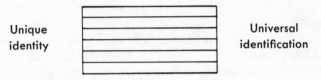

Unique
identity

Universal
identification

Figure 5. The Polarity of Being

As I look at the horizontal lines stretching across the page, I experience a slight dizziness. There is almost an endless openness to the perspective. We could be carried in either direction without interruption. We could become lost in the idiosyncratic, ending up with only ourselves and nothing but ourselves. Or we could become lost in conformity, ending up with only the world and nothing but the world.

In pursuing too much of the unique, we lose the universal and so end up, as Perls saw, growing more preoccupied with ourselves. Surprisingly, the more self-centered we grow, the less we are our real selves, because then we are open to every kind of destructive invasion from the outside. Conversely, in seeking too much of the universal, we lose the unique and so end up growing more preoccupied with where others are and what others think. Now we find, the more other-centered we grow, the less we are concerned with others for their own sakes, and the more vulnerable the situation becomes to the destructive intrusion of our own selfishness.

With the polarity of the universal and the unique, life holds together. Then being proclaims being.

Only by being part of the whole, of others, of the world, can we be ourselves. Only by being ourselves, distinct and separate, can we be part of the whole. As we affirm our humanity, we must aid others by confirming their humanity. As we affirm others' humanity, we confirm our own humanity. There cannot be the one without the other.

Loss of the unique/universal polarity results in the loss of vitality. Instead of a rich diversity of human experience, we find an oppressive sameness. When other people and things cease to be objects in their own right, the world shrivels into simply an extension of ourselves. Similarly, when we lose the sense of being a subject with our own unique integrity, the world stamps us into its own mold.

Let me illustrate the process from the field of art.

Louis Wain was a prominent British painter in the early 1920s. Despite prolonged psychiatric care, his ability to distinguish what was himself from what was his world disintegrated. His loss of contact with the environment can be traced by means of the pictures of his pet cats he continued to paint throughout the years of his illness. In a real sense the pictures are self-portraits. They depict the tragic odyssey of his impaired ability to cope with life.

Here we see a somewhat soft, gentle pussycat. Only the hint of wildness in the eyes suggests anything unusual. While the cat is unique, it clearly shows characteristics of cats generally. The picture combines the imaginative originality of the artist with the distinctive otherness of the object.

Five Cats by Louis Wain

© Guttmann Maclay Collection
Institute of Psychiatry, London

In this second painting we can still see the cat as an experienced object in its own right. But now the soft gentleness has dissolved. In its stead, we see a wild aggressiveness. The electrifying quality of the lines signals evil consequences. We experience the object coming apart and disintegrating. What has happened is that the internal drives of the artist are over-powering the inner integrity of the cat.

By the time of the third portrait the evil, sinister quality has

moved into the foreground. Simultaneously, the wild aggressiveness has dissolved. Only a florid mask of impotence remains. The otherness of the cat as an independent object has broken up. Its distinctiveness has faded into the background.

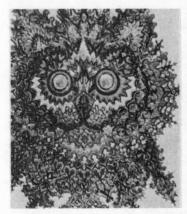 

With the loss of the polar tension between himself and the other, the fantasy of the artist runs wild, yet with increasing rigidity. By now the evil traces have disappeared. All we see is a stupid, staring, inoffensive owl. The artist's aggressiveness has died. With that the clarity of the cat is gone.

In the last portrait we can detect neither the artist as a unique subject nor the cat as a universal object. Vanished is the animal's personality; lost is the artist's originality. Only a charming design remains, carefully balanced to as to neutralize every part. The result comes across as a static whole. The mutual interaction of portrayed and portrayer no longer sparks with life. Controlled emptiness replaces living reality. As the environment has taken possession of the person, so the person has obliterated the environment. Consequently, neither the person nor the world remains.

The Chinese Taoist philosopher Chuang Chou stated the universal/unique polarity back in the third and fourth century B.C.: "Without a *that* there would be no I; without an I there would be nothing to take hold of [the *that*]." Tillich put it similarly: no spiritual life without mature self-relatedness; no spiritual life without objective world-relatedness.

Without the polarity of the unique on the one side and the universal on the other, there can be no constancy. Then being ceases to be.

In contrast, when we interact we come alive. Give-and-take generates excitement. Life mobilizes life. Real mutuality means real vitality. And vitality, said Tillich, is "the power of creating beyond oneself without losing onself." The more we have the power to express something beyond us, the more alive we are.

The ritual disposition of Chinese painting conveys that interaction with terse brilliance. Among the Six Essentials and the Six Qualities, cited from an early eleventh-century work, are:

Third Essential: Originality should not disregard the *li* ["universal principle" or "essential spirit"] of things.

Fifth Essential: The brush should be handled with *tzu-jan* ["spontaneity"].

Sixth Essential: Learn from the masters but avoid their faults.

First Quality: To display brushstroke power with good brushwork control.

Fourth Quality: To exhibit originality, even to the point of eccentricity, without violating the *li* of things.

There is vitality: risk originality, even to the point of eccentricity, without doing violence to the essential character of what's-there.

In explaining the method of painting tree trunks and main

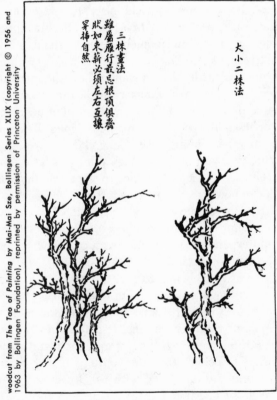

Tree Trunks and Main Branches

branches, Li Yü, writer of the 1679 edition of the *Mustard Seed Garden Manual of Painting*, pointed out the reciprocal relationship between each object in the picture in order to create the effect of the whole. Despite the fact trees may stand in a row, like swallows in flight, the artist must avoid making them the same. If treetops and tree roots are at the same level, the viewer will see only a bundle of firewood. Consequently, "They should be painted so as to seem to yield place to one another and to stand together naturally (*tzŭ-jan*)."

Thus, each tree trunk and branch expresses its own uniqueness while allowing every other tree trunk and branch its own uniqueness. Each seems to yield place to the other. At the same time, each discloses all tree trunks and branches. Somehow, every tree trunk and branch seems to stand forth as the universal tree trunk and branch.

Even more pointedly, Li Yü showed how the originality and spontaneity of the artist interacts with the essence (*li*) of pine trees to produce a breathtaking portrayal of being in which pine trees resemble people of high principles. Their manner discloses an inner power. Like young dragons coiled in deep gorges, pine trees and people of high principles have "an attractive, graceful air, yet one trembles to approach them for fear of the hidden power ready to spring forth."

What remains of the affirmed self/affirmed world is an extraordinary, effortless fullness. The world expresses the person. The person experiences the world. As a consequence, both the person and the world stand forth clearly.

The perspective of being, to pull this together, consists of a horizontal view in which everything rests upon the same plane. The continuum sweeps between the pole of the most general and the pole of the most specific. It emphasizes the personal, the linking, the integrating, the intrinsic, the maintenance concerns of human beings. It is the continuum that connects us with our world and our world with us. Because of it, we constantly weigh the questions:

How much of the world *can* we take in
without destroying our unique integrity?

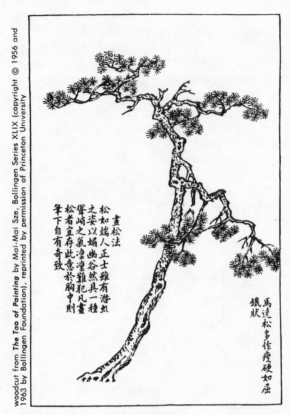

Pine Tree

What of the world *must* we take in
    if we are to avoid an empty identity?

Adapting a famous phrase of William James, I conceive being as a continuum from the "tender" pole of adaptive relatedness to the "tough" pole of integrated independence.

Becoming and Intentionality

Just as humanitas can be seen in terms of being, so it can be viewed in terms of becoming. The becoming of humanitas consists of our direction, our existence, our developing characteristics.

I am using the term as a way of conveying change. Apart from becoming we do not move, we do not grow, and therefore we do not develop. Here is the structure-elaborating and structure-modifying expression of existence. Human becoming designates the felt-meaning of humanitas. Life transforms itself.

Consider the perspective as a vertical plane. It consists of a continuum from the pole of potentiality on the bottom to the pole of actuality on the top. It depicts the disorder of passivity and the control of activity.

Actual form

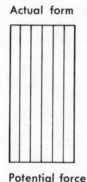

Figure 6. The Polarity of Becoming

Potential force

As suggested by Figure 6, becoming rises and falls between potential force and actual form, between motivating intentionality and meaningful intention, between wishing and willing, between dreaming and doing.

As I look at the vertical lines, I experience a sense of height and depth. There is a soaring to the perspective. My eyes move up and down and down and up. It would be hard to keep them on top with its accomplishment. It would be equally difficult to focus them on the bottom with its possibility.

If we constantly assert ourselves for the sake of achievement, we burn up our resources. If we constantly remain passive for the sake of security, we fail to invest in anything. Either we hang on so tightly we lose out on other possibilities, or we let go and lose even that which we already have.

Loss of the polarity between potentiality and actuality results in the loss of the intentionality in becoming. Instead of adaptation, we find an increasingly empty rigidity. Without renewing purposes we fall victim to inactivity and indecision.

Let me illustrate the process from the field of architecture.

In prehistoric times people apparently lacked orientation. They looked randomly in every direction. With the dawn of consciousness, which means the dawn of history, a radical revolution took place. Instead of glancing every which way, people looked primarily in one direction: namely, perpendicularly. They stood up. Now relationships began to be restricted to that single, upright position. Once the vertical perspective achieved supremacy over the horizontal, architecture appeared. The right angle, the axis, and symmetry stood out.

We cannot help but see ourselves and our world implicitly in terms of the gravitational field. Because of our upright posture, the vertical view dominates our orientation. The human spine symbolizes that perspective. It provides us with our sense of balance. Everything is located in reference to this axis.

Without realizing it, we usually organize the world in terms of the vertical. Styles of life change; the vertical continues. The vertical moves up and down. In its downward movement it directs us to the ground, to the earth, to the solid. In its upward movement it directs us to the sky, to the heavens, to the cosmos. As the vertical became dominant, therefore, that visual revolution enabled people to rise above their world for perspective and to dig into their world for profundity.

Pyramids and monoliths symbolize that thrust of powerful intention. In the Mayan temple, shown below, we see the steep flight of ceremonial stairs reaching upward in a hypnotic, vertical rhythm. Like the Egyptians, the Maya probably sought to touch the unattainable, to enter into the realm of the gods. Here in architectural form, we can sense the meaning of the Tower of Babel (Gen. 11:1-9). Humanity reaches so high above its environment that eventually its achievement collapses from exaggerated extension. Technology has progressed to the point where we are destroying ourselves with our own productivity.

The Castillo, Chichén Itzá

Environmental disaster—a plundered planet, polluted air, silent spring—within a generation.

Affluence now threatens us as "the fifth horseman of the apocalypse." In a recent interview, nutritionist Jean Mayer of Harvard observed:

It's the rich—in a relative sense, the people less likely to starve—who wreck the environment. Rich people occupy much more space, consume more of each natural resource, disturb the ecology more, litter the landscape with bottles and papers, and pollute more land, air and water with chemical, thermal and radio-active waste. . . . It's the spread of wealth that threatens the environment.

Not only are we endangered by the extravagance of our productivity, but also we find ourselves rendered impotent by our power. An inescapable expression of the turbulence is the loss of our ability to think through possibilities, weigh alternatives, and then act decisively. "Ironically if not tragically," Rollo May observes, "it is exactly in this portentous age, when power has grown so tremendously and decisions are so necessary and so fateful, that we find ourselves lacking any new basis for will."

The proud tower of Western Civilization has indeed collapsed.

Without the polarity of potentiality on the one end and of

actuality on the other, there can be no change. Then becoming ceases to become.

In contrast, when we invest ourselves in doing something, we increase our desire to do more. Mastery generates significance. Success brings satisfaction. Real investment means real intention. And intentionality, as Tillich defined it, is "being directed toward meaningful contents." As such, it combines wishing with willing. In wishing, we imaginatively play with various possibilities that might take place. In willing, we mobilize ourselves to move in a certain direction or to act in some particular way.

Greek temples uniquely embody that polarity. The potential force of the setting is taken up into the purposeful form of the architecture. In the view of the Second Temple of Hera, shown here, we can experience just such a reciprocal relationship. The temple stands, as that culture imagined its temples to stand, at the moment in time when the deep fears and joys and inspirations of the past harmonized with the hard challenges of a new and liberated thought. In those moments the human person and the objects outside the person were both experienced as objective realities.

If you look at the picture more closely, you can sense complementary elements. Conflict is conspicuously absent. Instead, you see the columns rising, swelling, contacting, cushioning out in an upward thrusting. Solid as that upper slab appears to be, it does not press down upon the columns unnecessarily. Nor do the columns overdramatize their support. Although conflict has been removed, variation remains.

The architect so constructed the temple that one feels that what it is, is what it must inevitably have had to become. Both the weight and the support are experienced as a single reality. The whole building rises out of the ground. The stepped base itself swells upward in such a way that one single powerful force is moving through the entire structure. At the same time —and this is its centered polarity—the vital force that pushes upward and inward and outward still exerts solid pressure against the ground. In the interaction between its purpose and its place, the temple comes across as simultaneously closed

The Second Temple of Hera

from The Earth, the Temple, and the Gods by Vincent Scully. (Yale University Press, 1962)

yet open. It discloses its own self-contained integrity, yet can carry our viewing far beyond itself into the surrounding setting.

In the Greek temple, we experience powerful actuality resting upon limitless possibility. The active height emanates from the passive depth. The passive depth grounds the active height. As a result, both height and depth stand forth clearly.

With the polarity of actuality and potentiality, life expresses itself. Then becoming becomes.

The perspective of becoming, to summarize, consists of a vertical view in which people or things rise above or fall below the level of other people or things. The continuum flows up and down between the ordering aim of willing and the pregnant ground of wishing. It emphasizes the impersonal, the task, the achievement, the enhancing concerns of humanitas. It is the continuum that connects potential force with meaningful form. Because of it, we constantly struggle with the questions:

When do we *sacrifice* what is actual and known
for what is potential and unknown?
When do we *risk* what is possible and desirable
for what is intended and real?

I conceive of becoming as a continuum between the chaotic ground of possibility and the shaping focus of activity.

Balancing the Forces

Now that I have spelled out the polarity of being and becoming, the question comes: How do these work in a person? What is their dynamic interaction? For they are related. They do presuppose each other. Only for analytical purposes can we separate them.

You will recall the ancient emblem symbolizing the yin-yang principles. *T'ai-chi-tu* means "the great map of the poles." As such, the image demonstrates the idea of a stationary flux enlivened by the yin-yang polarity. These are the two antagonistic, yet balanced, forces whose interaction constitutes the dynamics within the indivisible unity of the supreme One. By virtue of its roundness, the emblem contains all aspects of existence, for it is without beginning or end.

While prior to the historical process, the circle also represents the perfected state of the historical process in which the opposites unite. In the beginning the opposites have not yet separated. In the end they have once again united. All is rest; all is harmony. Heraclitus observed that in the circle the beginning and the end are common. Augustine asserted that the nature of God may be comparable to a circle whose center is everywhere and whose circumference is nowhere.

As a one-dimensional figure, the *T'ai-chi-tu* portrays the cyclical return of the same. Understood in this way, the forward

Yang-Yin Symbol

Poon-cu, the first man on earth, as portrayed in China. In his hands is the Ty-hih, a mystical instrument, which is thought to be a symbol of the creation of the world.

movement of historical time gives way to the endless cycle of natural time—winter, spring, summer, fall.

As a two-dimensional disk, however, we see an area spreading out from a center evenly in all directions. The area is at once contained, yet balanced. At the boundary, each point is the same distance from the center as every other point. Forces move toward and away from a center. Resistance to "being" swallowing up "becoming" encounters resistance to "becoming" devouring "being." The sea dragon does swim toward the ship's destination. Equally, the ship's navigator utilizes the sea

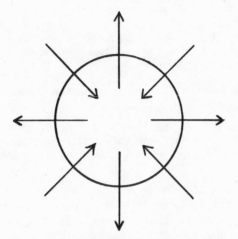

Figure 7. A Centrically Symmetrical Circle

dragon's power. The effect is a coordinated, integrated, dynamic vitality and decisive intentionality.

In everyday experience the closest analogy might be the automatic washing machine. We dump in a load of wash and distribute it evenly around the center. Occasionally, during a cycle, some heavy pieces such as towels or sheets begin to overbalance the load. As the spinning increases, the load pulls more and more to one side, generating a violent off-balancing of the machine. When such a condition occurs, most washers automatically stop. By redistributing the load, we reestablish the proper balance. Then the washing can continue.

Such is a picture of the balancing forces within our personalities. Every part of us is necessary for continuous and constructive functioning. When every part is fitted in and fitting properly, all goes well. When any part gets out of place or is left out, trouble follows.

A woman in her mid-forties illustrates my point. She is facing the transition between her children's leaving home and finding new ways of becoming/being a person herself. She reports the following series of dreams that gives a sense of that process:

I was going to the train station with the children. As we were getting on the train I suddenly realized my wallet and keys were back in the car. In going back for them, I became separated from the children. The two girls had gone off on one train. I tried very hard to find John [her son] who had gone off on another train. I was very confused and uncertain.

We will want to know more about this woman before we can be confident in understanding her dynamics. Even so, the pattern is apparent. Her children are leaving home; they are going off on their own. She herself also experiences the inner movement of venturing forth into a wider world. But her identification still remains closely tied to her regular way of getting around. It prevents an easy transition from the source of being into the search of becoming.

The fragment of a second dream gives further insight into her unbalancing:

I don't know whether I was at school or church or where, but I was at a folk dance. Everyone was dancing and having a good time.

I was standing on the sidelines with one or two other people. The woman in charge commanded us to join the dancers, which we did.

Next, I realized the Christmas party was over. All the children had been sent home to their mothers. There were lots of cookie crumbs all over the floor. I got a broom and started to sweep them up.

My husband was somewhere on the sidelines.

The context of her life appears here. Her world consists of school with her children and of church with her husband. Her conscientious struggle to build a good family life, however, fails to allow her to get into the swing of things. She is unable to enjoy the folk dance. She does not feel free to participate until told to join the dancers by the woman in charge. What ought to have been a natural responsiveness has been transformed into a forced obligation. In the end she is left to clean up alone, without children or husband or friends.

The prospect of her journey into selfhood in the first dream combines with the freedom and enjoyment of the second dream to portray the direction of resolution showing itself in a third dream. In the first dream she herself was the source of the confusion and mix-up. In the second dream an unknown

136

woman in charge commands her to get into the dance, even though in the end her role of homemaker-turned-housekeeper reasserts itself. In the following dream her consciously intended self is confronted by her neglected vital self:

I was on top of a tall, thin tower. There was a woman at the bottom of the tower by the ladder that reached to the top. She wanted to climb up, and I told her not to. She did anyway.

When she got to the top, the tower collapsed. Instead of crashing to the ground, somehow the bricks came together and formed a new structure that was more of a rectangle, lower and broader. We landed safely on the new building without any harm.

Her investment of herself as a mother has grown constant and rigid over the years. She has neglected herself as an independent person with needs and desires of her own. Now the vital side of her personality—the woman at the bottom of the ladder—insists upon being taken into account as much as the intended side of her personality—herself at the top of the tower.

The old form cannot stand the strain of the new life force. She feels herself coming apart. Her pattern collapses under the conflict between the mother-role from the past and the person-need in the present. But, and this is my point, *all the elements of her personality are reassembled and used again.* The new building is lower and more stable than the old tower. In the midst of the change, she knows the continuity of herself.

That is the centeredness, the wholeness, the relatedness, the awareness that finds expression in humanitas. Sea dragon and ship's navigator are united in seeking the distant shore of being-in-becoming, even as they are connected in meeting on the near shore of becoming-in-being. In such moments one experiences oneself touching all one's edges.

But the puzzlement persists: Why don't we touch all our edges all the time, or at least most of the time? What interferes with our being ourselves? How can we account for our lack of balance? What upsets our equilibrium? What is there in our being human that messes us up?

It is to this concern with the perplexity of humanitas that we turn in the next section.

137

BEING HUMAN

EIGHT
What Makes Humans Human?

What makes humans human? I ask the question this way because, as we have seen, the balance of forces within humanitas are so often unbalanced. Instead of *having* problems, we discover we *are* the problem. Somehow, to be human is to be conflicted. How can that be?

Historically, the single most significant clue to understanding humanitas can be found in the way people have perceived ultimate mystery. Creation myths show people's attempts to make sense of their experience. At the same time, these suggest the assumptions people felt about themselves as the experiencers.

Myths take up that intermediate zone between prelogical and logical understanding. Their imagery has oriented and organized humanitas' experience of itself. Their rich metaphors and pictorial language have been the source from which humankind has drawn its more formal and systematic ideas. Thus, by means of myths humanitas has expressed the felt-meaning of what's-there.

Frankly, I find little sense in talking about God as though he were a reality divorced from human reality. God is understandable to me primarily as the universal expression of the intentional vitality of which humanitas is the key manifestation.

WHAT MAKES HUMANS HUMAN?

In putting the issue this way, I do not intend to collapse theological meaning into only sociological or merely psychological categories. Neither do I want to divorce religious essence from human essence. For every doctrine, every idea, every ideal, every myth arises within human history, and so must be understood in terms of its historical setting, which means, therefore, its human origin.

Whatever its focus, cultural discovery is simultaneously human discovery. New dimensions of culture equal new dimensions of the human. Behind the idea of revelation lies the reality of humanitas' ability to discover and respond to latent dimensions of itself. A people's view of God discloses their view of themselves.

Images of God and Images of Humanitas

Let us look briefly at ways people have tried to make sense of the human condition in terms of the sense they have made of mystery. What have been the effects of those meanings on their lives? For as is one's god, so is one's humanity; as is one's humanity, so is one's god.

In trying to answer that question, we are at the point where we can apply our understanding of dreams to our understanding of mythology. The outer drama portrays our inner experience. In the drama we play many parts, yet every part expresses some part of us. In the "without" of myth we find the "within" of meaning.

Hellenistic: Divided

In Hellenistic religion, the gods were polarized. Apollo and Dionysus each epitomized the conflict. In them we see the strength and the stress of that culture.

Apollo summed up the Hellenic spirit. He exemplified beauty of every kind: artistic, musical, poetic, youthful. He represented all that was sane and moderate. Even though he was a latecomer in the Olympian pantheon, nevertheless, he became its most typical representative. In his activity is found the basis of law and order, supported by light and reason. The key admonitions were: "Know thyself" and "Nothing too much." A great gulf separated man and god, mortal and immortal. Man kept his distance and let the gods go their way.

Dionysus confronts us with a sharp contrast. He is at once joyful and bountiful, grim and gruesome, mad and calm, ecstatic and still. He is the giver of all good gifts and the tearer of man and eater of raw flesh. Like Apollo, Dionysus was also a latecomer on the scene, but he was viewed as a foreign god, *barbaron*, since for the Greeks sanity, self-consciouness, and limits clearly distinguished them from the surrounding barbarians. Nevertheless, a basic kinship existed between man and god, human and divine. Man closed the distance by becoming one with God.

Whether humanitas believed itself inferior to the gods, as reflected in Apollo, or linked with them, as reflected in Dionysus, the divorce within humanitas' experience of itself was sharp. A cleavage split body from soul, mortal from immortal, being from becoming. Such contradiction in understanding God disclosed confusion in understanding humanitas. People felt themselves to be split, divided, everlastingly at war with themselves and with one another. They depreciated the body while elevating the soul. Fulfillment lay in liberating the "good" immortal soul from the "bad" prison house of the body. Thus, the submerged body turned into a saboteur in the body politic. In the orgiastic rites, we can glimpse the rejected side of humanitas reasserting itself.

In Hellenistic experience we find humanity divided.

Oriental: Undifferentiated

Among Oriental religions, we come on a variation of that polarization of the gods. In Hindu culture, Brahma expresses an extreme asceticism, while Shiva manifests an extreme sensuality. Like a coin, Shiva, the Destroyer of Illusion, is understood as simply the opposite face of the Creator, Brahma. Thus, the dance of Shiva, encircled in fire and destroying the universe at the close of each cycle, changes with his turning into the remaking of all things under the guise of destruction.

bronze, from the von der Heydt collection, Rietberg Museum, Zurich.
Photograph by Zoe Binswanger.

Shiva as Nataraja, King of the Dance

Among the names Shiva bears is that of Nataraja, Lord of
Dancers. Here you can see Shiva's dance as Nataraja, represent-
ing a clear image of the activity of God. In the forest of
Taragam, Shiva confronts the forces that would destroy him.
The picture portrays the third attack upon him. His right

foot presses upon and breaks the back of this last monster, shaped like a malignant dwarf, representing ignorance. With the destruction of ignorance come true wisdom and release from the bondage to illusion. His raised left foot, pointed out by one of his left hands, gives release and grants eternal bliss.

The deepest significance of the dance is experienced when one realizes it takes place within oneself:

> The dancing foot, the sound of the tinkling bells,
> The songs that are sung and the varying steps,
> The form assumed by our Dancing Gurupara—
> Find these within yourself,
>   then shall your fetters fall away.

At every level—divine, human, animal—life's perplexity is the same: an eternal giving-in to the temptation of losing control of the situation, of trusting oneself to capricious chance. Fulfillment here, however, comes not from a separation of a good soul from a bad body. Rather, liberation comes in the complete loss of distinguishable selfhood. There is to be a complete withdrawal from the cosmic game—maya—the great round of birth-and-death. By awakening to one's true identity with the transcendent Buddha-consciousness, one attains nirvana. Thought no longer divides the universe into distinguishable fragments known as things and events. The individual self merges with the all-pervasive All. One loses an identity that is meaningless at worst and inferior at best.

Only with the erasing of personality can truth emerge. The individual ego is to be wiped out. No desire and no yearning are to remain: only nirvana—nothingness. To be truly human is another way of saying to be Buddha. Self-nature and Buddha-nature are synonymous. Thus, for someone to ask about seeking and finding the Buddha-nature, according to Po-chang (A.D 720-814), is like riding an ox in search of the ox itself.

In Oriental experience, we find humanitas dissolved. Humanitas' perplexity is conceived of as illusion. Because of exaggerated individuality, humanitas denies its identity with Buddha-nature. For such denial, its desires are never satisfied.

Thus, humanitas must be negated, transcended, and transformed into the all of nothingness and the nothingness of all.

Near Eastern: Chaotic

In Babylonian and Canaanite mythology, we find similar conflict, yet with a more basic pessimism. The Mesopotamian mythical poem, *Enuma elish*, is so called from the first two words "When on high." It begins with the initial separation of order out of chaos. It culminates in the creation of the ancient Babylonian cosmology.

In its earliest form, Babylonian mythology depicted a nondualistic state prior to creation. The triad of the father (Apsu), the mother (Tiamat), and the son (Mummu) were indistinguishable. But with the later development of the great gods, we come upon a universal dualism.

Conflict arose over the boisterous activity of the new gods and the inert quietness of the old gods. These primordial gods, symbolized by Tiamat, the mother of the gods, threatened the assembly of the gods, personified by Marduk, the god of order. From the resulting cosmic conflict came the creation of the world and of humankind.

Instead of a dualism within humanitas, as in Hellenistic experience, or a negation of humanitas, as in Oriental experience, here we find a subjugation of humanitas. Humans were to perform menial chores for the gods. They had to labor on tasks the gods found too burdensome. Thus, humanitas experienced itself as a slave.

The war of the gods dramatizes humanitas' struggle to juxtapose light with its rational order and darkness with its irrational chaos. Mastery conquers mystery, and so humanitas becomes the workhorse of the universe. The victory of Marduk over Tiamat portrays the ruthless and unassailable supremacy of order over the vulnerable creativity of chaos. The depths are finally conquered. Humankind, thus, experienced itself at the mercy of an order unrelated to its being. Somehow both chaos and order went against the grain of existence.

Chaos was crushed, but in the crushing, humanitas itself was obliterated.

Hebraic: Whole

The Old Testament writers took over, yet transformed, Mesopotamian thought. While molded from clay, humanitas' function was that of ruling creation.

In Hebraic experience, for the first time in a persisting religion, we come upon an unambiguous declaration of the unity of God:

"Hear, O Israel: The LORD our God is one Lord" (Deut. 6:4).

Creator and Sustainer are manifestations of the same power of being. He created the inner world of the human, even as he created the outer realm of nature. The human and the nonhuman disclose a shared ground. Out of one came all.

With the discovery of the oneness of ultimacy the Hebrews could sense the potential oneness of humanitas. Humanitas, thus, experienced itself as a "kingly steward," serving God in history. Beyond anything else, humanitas is now the bearer of responsibility. It is entrusted with dominion and power for the purpose of love and service.

In Hebraic thought humanitas' perplexity is not because of its revolt against impersonal fate, as with the Greeks, nor because of its denial of identity with Being, as with the Orientals, nor because of its explosive worthlessness, as with the Babylonians. Humanitas' perplexity comes from its assertion against the will of the good God. Unlike other primitive myths which affirmed life, the Hebrews understood perplexity as the result of its own revolt against its humanity, being against Being. The Hebrews affirmed life, but from a critical standpoint.

Qualities of Humanitas

I want to explore the experience of the Hebrews in more detail. For me, it holds the most fruitful insight into our human predicament. For it proclaims human life to be good, even as it portrays human beings messing up their humanity.

144

Hebrew experience is expressed in the intuitive narratives of creation in Genesis 1:1–2:4a and 2:4b–3:24. In these two accounts we have dreamlike material. Each portrays a different aspect of the human condition, so they belong together. They are finally intelligible only when taken together.*

From the account in Genesis 1 we get a sense of what is. Here is the context in which humanitas finds itself.

Life is purposeful. It is going somewhere, and not just in circles. Creation sets in motion both direction and hope. People can trust life's meaning because everything unfolds within the purpose of God. *Humanitas stands at the pinnacle of the creation pyramid.*

But such height is connected with depth. Always and ever, within the midst of the world we experience chaos—the constant threat to everything that is. Chaos, however, is different from nothingness. And the affirmation that order comes out of disorder points to the perpetual miracle of creation. From the abyss God shapes a world.

Here we are given a natural view of humanitas. It emphasizes the victory of order over randomness and centeredness over fragmentation. It may be understood as the perspective of being that I have elaborated above. Creation is a meaningful process for the creation of meaning.

Never in the narrative is creation depreciated. There is no forbidden tree; there is no tragic fall. While being is never the last word, it is always necessary. While creation is never the greatest good, it is ever the very good (Gen. 1:31). Even the terrifying monsters of the deep (Gen. 1:21) are known as good. The natural order may be chaotic, but for the liberated, that order is neither cancelled nor rejected.*

Creation, we discover, comes from division. To create requires us to divide. Yet, we can divide precisely because we can trust that life is whole.

The primary separation is the division of light from darkness, seeing from not seeing, consciousness from lack of consciousness. The first act of creating is not earth or heaven, but when "God said, 'Let there be light'; and there was light" (Gen. 1:3). That implies the first activity of God was the creation of illumination. Awareness of earth and sky, water and land, fish and birds, sun and moon, plants and animals followed initial consciousness. Thus, at the moment of dawn— consciousness—humanitas appeared.*

Whereas humanitas is regarded as the pinnacle of the evolutionary pyramid in Genesis 1, in Genesis 2 (and 3), it is perceived as the *center of things*. This is the world which God establishes around humanitas, around man. The primary theme of the entire narrative deals with *'adam* ("man") and *'adama* ("man-earth"). In this anthropocentric universe, humanitas is at the center of the circle.

Here we are given a historical view of humanitas. It emphasizes life as process—changing patterns and patterned change. It may be understood as the perspective of becoming that I have elaborated above.

Astonishing as the idea may be, the narrative contains the experience of being human and the human becoming of each of us. As individuals, we are at once ourselves and humanitas, "in such wise that the whole race has part in the individual and the individual has part in the whole race." By analogy, Kierkegaard contended, Adam "is himself and the race. Therefore, what explains Adam explains the race, and vice versa."

The word *Adam* does not mean a particular man, such as James Ashbrook. The Revised Standard Version translates the word more accurately as "man," which means "humankind, generic humanity." I am Adam. You are Adam.

And the word *Eve* does not refer to a particular woman so much as it does to "living, life, the mother of every living thing." I am living. You are living. The story of Adam and Eve is the story of every human being-in-becoming.

Now if the drama of Adam and Eve portrays the drama of humanitas, what is actually depicted? What are the basics? What makes up our human quality?

Immediacy

Remember, the Garden of Eden is not a specific place. Therefore we have to ask: What can the symbol represent? What inner realm is projected onto outer reality?

146

WHAT MAKES HUMANS HUMAN?

Let your imagination go. What images come up as you contemplate a garden? Peacefulness . . . growth . . . quietness . . . loveliness. A garden conveys a sense of security and serenity. Everything necessary for life is immediately at hand. All is taken care of.

Within the harmony of the garden we experience no waves, no roughness, no reactions. There is no toil, no struggle, no conflict, no guilt, no anxiety, no turmoil, no strain, no stress. Such paradise, however, does not mean no involvement. For humanitas was placed there to make something of it. But instead of work's being "work," at that point *work was being* and *being was work.*

Now then, I have contended that symbol is always grounded in something concrete. It relates to what's-there apart from the felt-meaning of what's-there. Consequently, what can the myth of the garden symbolize? What inner realm of meaning is set forth as the outer realm of nature?

The only time (and the only place) we work without messing up what we are by what we do is during the prenatal period. In the womb we are involved in a condition of un-broken immediacy. We experience nothing consciously: no awareness, no separation, no complications, no complexity. We express everything directly, immediately, fittingly. All is harmonious. All is one. One is all.

The womb of the mother prepares us for the womb of the world. We are held by that which is other than we. Nothing is initially of ourselves; everything is of the world. We are sheltered and nurtured. We lie contained within the wholeness of the womb of the world. Thus, we ought not be surprised to see a fifteenth-century painting portraying the explusion of Adam and Eve from a walled and womb-like Garden of Eden.

From that primary experience of at-one-ment, people in every culture have read inner meaning into outer events. The dawn of history and the dawn of selfhood coincide in the drama of beginning. Just as the garden with the four rivers flowing into it was thought to stand at the center of the

147

Adam and Eve chased from the Garden of Eden from TRÈS RICHES HEURES of Jean, Duke of Berry

world, so humanitas was experienced as the center of the garden/womb/world.

The experience of the womb marks the time which Tillich spoke of as "dreaming innocence." Innocence implies untested involvement—fresh naiveté. One has not yet wrestled with the real. That, clearly, is existence in the womb. We are not yet responsible for what we do. We live, yet it is not our choosing.*

That dreamlike condition may be likened to the delicate

transition between sleeping and waking. We are half awake, yet not aware. Suddenly, we realize we have been awake, we have been dreaming, yet we only become conscious of the fact *in the midst of the fact* itself. Such may be the dreamlike quality of the innocence of the womb. In that state we anticipate the actual by awaking to the possible. Thus, our innocence is both unreal and real.

We find ourselves caught between two powerful forces.

On the one hand, we are afraid of what is possible. That causes us to hang back and to hold on to what we are. We hesitate to do anything. We fail to make a move. Thus, we weaken who we are by not using what we have. *We simply do nothing.* This is Kierkegaard's despair at not willing to be oneself. It is present in every pattern of passivity and withdrawal.

On the other hand, we are afraid of what actually is. That results in our giving up who we are and going on to try something else. We rush to do anything. We are frantic to be everything. Thus, we weaken who we are by burning up what we have. *We simply try everything.* This is Kierkegaard's despair at willing to be oneself defiantly. It is present in every pattern of frenzy and aggression.

Unless the birth of selfhood and the birth of humanitas involve some such experience of unbroken immediacy, the drama of human creation makes little historical sense, much less personal sense. World and womb, humanitas and human being, Adam-Eve and I-you constitute the felt-meaning of what's-there. We are one in the spirit; we are one in the flesh.

Power

Rather than the garden/womb's being paradise, the Hebrews thought of it as the human situation. The possibility of being-in-becoming requires work. We must preserve life from disruption. We must act to enhance the given.

So God created the animals and led them before Adam. He was to name each creature and the name he gave it was to be its name. This interaction signals the most dramatic expression of human dominion over the created world. Adam assumed responsibility for creation (Gen. 2:20). By giving him this autonomy, God made humankind creator also.

To give something a name is to give order to chaos. Such an act focuses what is random by distinguishing one object from all other objects. The giving of a name—cow, hippopotamus, dog—is less significant than the presence of language itself. For it is language that provides the tool for naming.* The first step out of mindlessness comes with the act of naming. The first sign of the growth of consciousness is our ability to distinguish and to differentiate.

In other words, initially, I experience the world as one. There is no differentiation. The world is I; I am the world. With the leap into self-awareness—conscious of my consciousness—making the center in myself—there appears that which is other than I as well as that which is I. Now there is the world *and* I; I *and* the world.

To be conscious is to distinguish, to separate, to divide, to experience that which was of my essence as now passing out from my essence. It now exists in its own right. It now possesses a substance of its own. It now shows itself in my seeing it, in my calling it forth, in my naming it.

By means of language we create—*bārā*—order and meaning. Language enables us to transcend the specific through the creation of the general. We ask questions. We deliberate and decide. We imagine all kinds of structures that are not present in fact at the time. We respond to both moral and logical imperatives. We go beyond what is by creating something that is not yet.

The active principle of language, according to linguist C. K. Ogden, arises from the perception of opposition. That is, we distinguish what is being said, *significantly* from other things that might be said instead.

The experience of opposition comes from our experience of space with particular reference to our bodies. We know opposite sides, right and left, as well as opposite extremes, head and feet. But there is a third characteristic. Our bodies are symmetrical in terms of sides and ends, yet they are asymmetrical in terms of direction. We face only one way.

Thus, when I see myself in a mirror, mirrored back, or when I face another person, or when I am confronted by the enemy, that experience of over-againstness may be taken as the basic opposite from which the nuances of the metaphor derive. In other words, from otherness and opposition every differentiation arises. To be the same or to be different depends upon facing—a this with a that, me with the world.

In place of our lost environment (garden/womb), humanitas faces the necessity of building a world out of its own mental constructions. We pattern the picture. We organize the experience. We determine the direction. Divine being does not hand to us the meaning of creation. God makes possible a future, as Harvey Cox contends, but we are inescapably responsible for that future. The future is for us to determine. No one decides its shape but ourselves.

From the beginning humanitas has been invested with autonomy. It alone has the power to say what is.

Awareness

As I have noted, the dreamlike drama overthrows the rules of formal logic. It portrays sequentially that which is instantaneous. The power of naming that accompanies the opening of one's eyes represents just such a confusion. Without awareness no naming of experience could occur. In the garden this quality of humanness does not appear decisively until later, although a preliminary hint comes in the prohibition not to eat of the fruit (Gen. 2:18).

Mythically, we have found light linked with the breaking-in of consciousness. The same applies to the tree of knowing everything immediately and intimately.* We are dealing with the breaking-in of awareness.

The serpent expresses life's vitality. Despite the fact that serpents and dragons symbolize the human struggle with demonic power, here the narration minimizes objectifying evil as "a power coming from outside" humanitas itself. We know from the inner logic of dreams that an object such as a serpent discloses part of the forces of our inner world of felt-meaning. So the serpent dramatizes the inner division within each of us.

The dialogue in the account suggests the growing separation in the inner world. The ego, or centering awareness, detaches itself from the primordial nonconsciousness of the body. A less-than-fully-human part of us points the way to selfhood: "Your eyes will be opened, and you will be like God, knowing good and evil" (Gen. 3:5).

In powerful, straightforward, and tragic fashion the drama lays out the human predicament (Gen. 3:6-8):

> they ate of the fruit
> their eyes were opened
> they knew they were naked
> so they hid themselves.*

With physical maturation, a split develops between the organism and its functioning. The human organism wakes up to discover itself to be an experiencing organism. Experiencing refers to our feeling of *having* experience. We distinguish specific people and objects and events.

Psychiatrist Lawrence Kubie finds in the *startle pattern* the first indication of a gap between the organism and its environment. The fetus cannot startle because there is no interval between the stimulus and the response; there is only continuity. Toward the end of pregnancy, however, and decisively with birth, we come upon the distance between the stimulus and the response. With a loud noise the individual jumps. Increasingly, the infant *experiences* waiting, postponement, and frustration. From the gap, anxiety arises. With anxiety, we discover the origin of thought. For anxiety bridges the startle pattern and the dawn of all processes of thinking.

The connection between the stimulus-response interval and later symbolization is clear. With the interaction we create meaning (*bārā*). We order our world. We label events. We name what's-there.* Beginning with our first startle response, we link what's-there with a felt-meaning.

As time passes, the individual separates more and more from the surroundings. Previously, there was simply an impersonal environment. Now a complicated personal world takes shape. The process moves from the actual separation of birth through the development of distinguishing objects and people and events. It culminates in the sense of personal identity and integrity.

My self as a finite center of understanding has emerged. Every statement ultimately rests on that individual base: *my* point of view, *your* point of view, *our* point of view. There is a kind of objectivity to what we see and what we say, yet, finally, it is still we who say and we who see. Knowledge is personal.

Anxiety is the crucial factor. The English word derives from the German *Angst* and the Latin *angustiae*. *Angustiae* means narrowness. Literally, it refers to the narrowness of space or a narrow place. It can also refer to physical restriction, as in shortness of breath. We can picture it as follows:

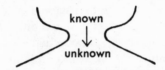

Figure 8. The Anxiety Experience

In its most acute form, anxiety combines our active imagination with which we imagine all kinds of frightening possibilities, our absolute aloneness in which we feel completely cut-off from others, and our total helplessness because of which we are powerless to act.

When anxious, we find ourselves caught between a known present and an unknown future. The woman's dream of setting sail from the safe harbor of the tropical lagoon and finding herself overwhelmed by the stormy sea suggests the felt-meaning of anxiety. She has given up, let go, lost the security of the familiar. She is confronted by the uncertainty of the unfamiliar. The "narrows," separating what is sure from what is unsure, constitutes the bind of anxiety. Here we cling to the past. We constrict who we are in panic at what we might be (come). We dread the new and the unknown.

153

The first and basic separation comes with birth. The fetus pushes out of the immediacy of the womb into the remoteness of the world. The birth canal itself is the physical prototype of the narrows making up anxiety. Within the immediate we feel safe. Looking ahead, we feel dread. Threat comes from everywhere and nowhere.

With birth, the development of the human qualities begins. Now, when the infant requires nourishment, it must cry in order to be fed. Before, nourishment came automatically. Now, when the infant requires warmth, it must cry in order to let the world know it is uncomfortable. Before, warmth came automatically. Now, when taking in and letting out, the infant must participate in the processes. Before, transactions with the environment occurred automatically.

The quality of awareness is symbolized by the tree. The knowledge of good and evil is a formal way of saying the colorless word "everything." Yet the symbol does convey expanding experience. In it we find sensual differentiation in the fruit as "good for food," aesthetic discrimination in the fruit as "a delight to the eyes," intellectual development in the fruit as making humans wise. In effect, in the tree we encounter the self-centered "I." For the infant is the center of the (its) world. What lies beyond its experience does not exist. What enters its orbit becomes something in reality.

The infant's relation with breast/bottle/mother provides the foundation of all experience. Here is the primary closeness and there is the primary distance. To be in touch is to be connected. To be out of touch is to be disconnected. At first breast/bottle/mother are simply there—present—without calling, without demanding, without seeking. Rapidly, they are not always there—absent—and so must be called, must be demanded, must be sought.

Now, there is an I and a not-I. Now, there is a me and a not-me. Now, there is a subject and an object. Now, there is a self and a world.

Every act of separation—the infant from the mother, the adolescent from the family, the individual from the group—marks the distancing process of independent existence. To become aware is to become conscious of oneself as distinct from all else. To become conscious of oneself begins with saying no to the not-me. "I am *not* that; I *am* this." Just as other beings are created by naming, so I am created by naming. Each of us is called forth from randomness. Each of us experiences personal existence by being named some-body. Each of us learns who she or he is by being addressed.

Parents are fascinated by discovering the power of the name for the child. I recall playing a game with our third youngster during her third year. It revolved around her name. I would place my hands on her head and repeat her name—Martha Lee Ashbrook—as though fitting her name to her body (existence). Then I would try to fit other names to her head. Some names like Marth Lee Angelo fit better than Calamity Claire Blockbuster, but only *her* name fit *her* properly.

During those years of three and four, every child engages in fantasy role-playing. They try out a wide assortment of people and things. In rapid succession Martha would "be" Cheyenne, Dale Evans, dust-on-the-prairie, Lucy, or mother. One day she had been wandering far from her existence by an extended period of role-playing. She began to need to recover and re-experience herself as herself. At the same time I kept insisting she "was" Cheyenne or Dale Evans *et al.* The more I insisted, the more upset she became.

"I am *not* Cheyenne! *I am Martha!*"

The inner reality of herself needed the outer reality of her name to insure her *being* at that point. Name and self were synonymous. To say her name was to be her self. To be her self required her to say her name.

No name, no existence. Only a number, only a nothing.

I *am* James Barbour Ashbrook; James Barbour Ashbrook is my I.

Eventually, the individual arrives at a harmonious integrity. Beyond coping with conflict, the person reconciles opposites within oneself and with one's world. One nourishes diversity. One achieves individuality. At the most mature stage, conflict is not only met but embraced. Awareness ultimately differentiates and simultaneously unites.

Relatedness

Awareness is created by, and prepares the way for, the appearance of Eve, the truly other.

Despite the presence of other life in the garden/womb, humankind had no counterpart. Despite Adam's naming all other reality, no other reality could name Adam. Without a counterpart Adam was only potentially human, not actually human.

The tool of dream interpretation enables us to combine the seeming difference in human relatedness in the two creation stories. In Genesis 1, humanitas is singular, a unity, a human being. In Genesis 2, humanitas is divided, separated, male and female. While humanitas is made up of separate sexes, every human being is made up of both functions: the masculine and the feminine principle.

For men, the feminine principle is the inspiriting, enlivening quality of being.

For women, the masculine principle is the inspiriting, enlivening quality of becoming.

So, the Genesis 2 narrative must be read at two levels. There is the intrapsychic realm of each individual. There is the interpersonal realm of two human beings together constituting humanitas.

In having emphasized the autonomy that goes with language, I neglected to stress its dependency. For language itself discloses our dependence upon others as much as our independence. Martin Buber appropriately reminded us that language is first and foremost relational. That is, it is living communication *between* persons.

Our interdependence shows itself in God's observation after Adam has named every part of creation: "It is not good that [Adam] should be alone" (Gen. 2:18).

Here is the first and only aspect of original creation that is not considered good, loneliness. It may well be that of all anxiety we experience none is more terrifying, none is more painful, none is more destructive than loneliness. It is not good to be without a counterpart. It is not possible to be human without another human being.

The necessary counterpart appears in the encounter of Eve with Adam or Clara with Henry. Animals may encourage us, but they cannot be the mirror in which we recognize ourselves. Only another human being can call forth and name a human being. Without another we are not ourselves.

While the truly other is needed for humanness, an inner division is its concomitant. Genesis 2 dramatizes the process. Adam and Eve symbolize the two aspects of each of us. Inner life arises from the separation of the masculine and feminine functioning within the psyche. God forms from the being of Adam—from the structure, the rib—the counterpart needed to make up *human* life—*human* process—*human* becoming. Adam waxes poetical:

This one *at last* is bone of my bones and flesh of my flesh; this one shall be called woman [*ishshah*] for this one was taken from man [*ish*, a literal rendering of the Hebrew].

There is a going out from the self and a taking back into the self. We initiate *and* we receive. Eve and Adam complement each other. It is not a matter of the separate sexes. It is humankind becoming genuinely human.

Regardless of whether we are male or female, these psychic forces interact in a similar way. The masculine force makes up consciousness, hence its association with light and day. The feminine force makes up unconsciousness, hence its association with darkness and night. Consciousness always depends upon unconsciousness, the logical on the prelogical.

The serpent itself symbolizes the primordial wholeness of the masculine and feminine forces.

Every culture has portrayed the great womb of the world as a ring-snake. From the serpent design on a brass shield from Bengin, Nigeria, to a Mexican calendar stone with an encircling serpent, to the snake as the companion of Eve, we can sense the dynamic of differentiation: the fertilizing phallus and the fertilized earth. In its most primitive form the snake symbolizes the mother goddess, the mistress of the earth, of the depths, of the unconscious. In its more advanced form it symbolizes the father god, the phallus of heaven, of the heights, of consciousness. Together these strands of the serpent symbol embrace nonconscious and conscious, potential and actual, intuition and intelligence.

Those divisions between psychic forces and between distinct individuals mark the awakening of human relatedness. Masculine knowing—*logos*—encounters feminine relating—*eros*—with the result that the two halves become one whole. Reciprocity and mutuality are the essence. Because of potential individuality within wholeness itself, we struggle toward wholeness within our own individuality.

The Alchemical Concept of the Squared Circle

We saw earlier that the circle expresses wholeness. Here you can see a portrayal of the symbolic alchemical concept of the squared circle. It shows the presence of the male and the female figures as the union of opposites. It communicates the sense of a center of personality. It suggests a point within ourselves to which everything is related and by which everything is arranged.

The garden/womb shows us what we are and what we are up against: the human quality of human beings. Here is humanitas' awakening—the leap into self-awareness. The possibility of freedom stands out as "the alarming possibility of being able" to act.

NINE
What Are We Up Against?

Life compels us to transform potential wholeness into actual wholeness. While one contains the many, the many are expressions of one. One is to be(come) one.

All shall be what is. None shall be what is not. Ultimate one shall be wholly one.

The garden/womb, centered wholeness, the New City, the squared-circle only quicken us to what can be. Their reality calls us to what is meant to be. It commands us to do what is to be done—live genuinely and fully—be and become human.

Yet, we know what we are up against. We discover a gap—by whatever name we label it—between our potential humanness and our actual humanness. This is the focus—the thread—the issue—which I have tried to come at, walk around, look at, open up, explore, and touch on in various ways. But before going further, I feel it desirable to look back and pull together those several strands of experience and expression. I want you to see quite clearly the tapestry of humanitas that I am weaving.

The Constellation Human

Initially, we looked at what we find and what we want. We realized humanness can be painful and destructive. Yet within that pain we also experienced the demand to be human —to be more human than we are. We discovered humanity beckoning.

As we examined what we wanted more closely, we found a double desire. We both wanted *and* needed experience and insight, emotion and understanding, love and will. That is, we would hold together the what's-there of our being human with the felt-meaning of our human becoming.

In a human focus, I looked at our own situation. We experience the demand to be ourselves, yet we fear becoming ourselves. Part of our ambivalence arises from the necessity to explore the depths of one another as well as our own depths. Knowledge of who-we-are and of what-we-are-meant-to-be is intertwined. If we are to be(come) truly human, we have no choice but to turn inward and to seek outward. The path runs directly through ourselves.

We then focused more closely on where we are and what is happening. Awareness constitutes the key to our human perplexity *and* to our human possibility. As the door of perception widens, we discover a continuity between ourselves and the rest of creation. In sharpening our here-and-now, we saw that in touching what *is* we need particularly to be in contact with what supposedly is *not*. The impact or meaning of any particular experience depends upon the context in which we place it and other experiences to which we relate it.

I suggested that symbols portray most fully the *human* world of *meaning*. Because symbolic material conveys multiple meanings in highly figurative ways, I turned to dreams as one of our most powerful tools for understanding myth and meaning. The dream bridges the deeply personal and the broadly universal. By means of it, we can hold together the intuition of prelogical experience—the sea dragon—and the intellect of conscious expression—the ship.

Having pointed toward that experiential background, I then tried to sharpen the meaning of humanitas. From both cultural and personal expressions the circle and the square have emerged as symbols of our being and our becoming. Human wholeness, while always a constellation that is more than the sum of its parts, nevertheless, can be understood from two perspectives.

From the one angle there is being, a perspective lighting up vitality and love, a polarity between the unique and the universal.

From the other angle there is becoming, a perspective opening up intentionality and power, a polarity between potentiality and actuality.

Each perspective assumes the other. Together they set forth dimensions and dynamics of human centeredness.

Figure 9. **An Overview of Humanitas**

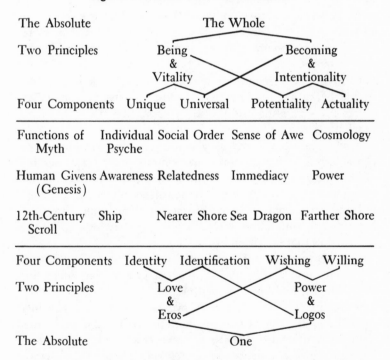

The way humanitas perceived its god(s) opened for us the way(s) people have experienced themselves. When the gods were divided, as in the Hellenistic culture, humans experienced

themselves as fractured. When the gods were ultimately undifferentiated, as in Oriental cultures, humans sought liberation
from the illusion of distinguishable selfhood. When the gods
were chaotic, as in Near Eastern cultures, humans felt themselves to be destructive and degraded. When ultimate reality
was perceived as whole, humans experienced their own potential wholeness.

The creation drama of Genesis affirms the wholeness or
oneness of life. No compromise; no qualification; no ambiguity.
The basic stuff is good. We are set within creation, as part of
creation, for the creation of creation.

From the perspective of being, individual awareness marks
one pole while human relatedness marks the other. We alter-
nate between distance and relationship, between our own
identity and our identification with others. Our ability to respond rises from within us, yet it can only be triggered by the
truly other.

I respond because another responds to me. Another responds
to me because I respond to the other. To be human under-
scores the separating and uniting of opposites, the integrating
of what's-there.

From the perspective of becoming, unbroken immediacy
characterizes one pole while autonomous power expresses the
other. We move back and forth between rest and action, between unconsciousness and consciousness, between the potential and the actual. That we are accountable comes from the
beyond. Accountability goes with power, yet is fostered by the
possibilities that lie within immediacy.

I act because I have the potential to act. I have the potential
to act because I actually act. To become human highlights
living life, the unfolding of what matters.

In Figure 9 I set down that overview. From the absolute
come the active forces of being-with-its-vitality and becoming-
with-its-intentionality. These are the powers of eros and of
logos. Each is a polarity—opposites coinciding in a dynamic
dialectic of now the one side, now the other. At the level of
culture, I show the place of the four functions of myth. At
the level of individuals, I indicate the place of the human

givens found in Genesis 2. At the level of suggestive imagery, I use the Japanese picture scroll. Identity and identification are eventually linked back with becoming, while wishing and willing find their fulfillment in being.

Maslow has separated self-actualizers into merely healthy people and transcenders. For these latter, he finds a transhuman orientation, a centering in the cosmos rather than in the individual, or even the human species itself. They go beyond self, or ego, actualization. They participate freely and fully in the mysterious awesomeness of everything that is.

For me, one of the more dramatic expressions of such a transcender is the famous imaginary portrait of the poet Li Po, painted by Liang K'ai in the early thirteenth century. Unlike the strong individualism of Western man—as seen, for instance, in Titian and to a lesser degree in Rembrandt—the Chinese appreciated individuality without emphasizing the development of personal idiosyncrasies. A fleeting glimpse would catch the essential being of a person without revealing the complete personality.

In the portrait which follows, Li Po appears to be walking on air. His head tilts in a way suggesting great vitality. His scholarly sophistication comes across as a serene reflecting on experience by participation. There is no aggressive searching to grasp reality by objective reason. Nor is there any passive immersion in the quicksand of subjective feeling. I sense dignity and direction, vitality and intentionality. The intellectual is transformed by the intuitive. The impersonal finds its fullness in the immediate. Humanitas is present without pretension. It is centered, yet transcended. It lives in a cosmos not of its own making.

Jesus as the Christ portrays traditional Western transcendence. In the crucifixion he gave up concern with Jesus of Nazareth, thereby preparing the way for the Christ of faith. In him we see a genuine human being. We come upon the authentically human in all its fullness.

The call to be oneself, finally, turns out to be the call to be more than oneself. "As the boomerang comes back to the hunter who has thrown it only if it has missed its target, in

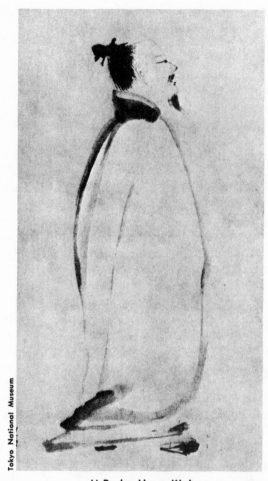

Li Po by Liang K'ai

the same way [humanitas] also returns to [itself], reflects upon [itself], and is intent upon self-actualization only if [it] has missed [its] mission and if [its] search for meaning is frustrated," so observes Viktor Frankl. To become truly human is to experience the demand to live beyond oneself in the light of true humanity.

The pull of human becoming inevitably breaks our hold on

the pressure to remain the human beings that we are. To commit oneself to values that are more than a simple maintenance of personal or social status quo is to draw the *not-yet* of potentiality into the *already* of actuality. The fulfillment of meaning always demands more than the fulfillment of me. As Eckhart saw, "The truth is that the more ourselves we are, the less self is in us." Once aware of ourselves, we become caught up in that which is more than ourselves. The Beyond comes to us in the present as the future that can never rest content with the past.

Perhaps now you can sense more fully my use of that Japanese picture scroll shown in the frontispiece. Our intuitive being throws us into life's waters out of longing for union with that which is more than ourselves. Our intellectual becoming navigates the treacherous pathway toward the site of genuine humanness. Sea dragon and ship come together in the journey toward the distant shore, having been together in the beginning on the nearer shore.

Results of Responding

To be thrown into life is to be called upon to respond. We are to make something of what is. No other organism must decide to participate in the life that is its own. Only humans must decide to be(come) what they are.

Only we experience the necessity to decide to be what we are by becoming what we are made to become.

Only we hear the question: "Where are you?" (Gen. 3:9)

Only we tremble from the threat to our being because of our becoming: "I heard the sound of the truly Other in the garden, and I was afraid, because I was naked; and I hid myself."

Only we experience anxiety accompanying awareness.

Only we resort to deceptive and defensive security operations that split our seeming from our being.

I, like so many contemporary people, am uncomfortable with the term "sin." Mistake, missing the mark, being at fault each conveys the idea of individual inadequacies. Each suggests the fact that somehow our deciding results in our being out-of-kilter. Yet that experience is precisely what "sin" expresses:

> my reason can be so unreasonable
> my emotions can be so unemotional
> my vision can be so unseeing
> my knowledge can be so unknowing
> my responses can be so unresponsive
> my becoming can be so unbecoming
> my being can be so nonbeing.

More psychologically sophisticated people prefer to reduce human puzzlement to psychological conditions. Thus, we have such clinical language as character disorders, neuroses, and psychoses. The more sensitive investigators are now claiming that within and behind psychological disturbance they are finding what can only be labeled spiritual disturbance: loss of meaning, doubts about life's goals, grief and anger over lost love, loss of courage or hope, despair over the future, dislike of oneself, realization that one's life is being wasted, etc., etc., etc.

Sin, Kierkegaard pointed out, presupposes itself. That is, we cannot really account for our state of estrangement—of being at odds with life. All we know is the fact that we *are* off-balance. The first sin is *the* sin. No additional complication essentially changes that qualitative change. The initial break, breaks immediacy. All else follows.

Because humanitas does not begin with each new baby, even though each baby marks a fresh beginning, "the sinfulness of the race acquires a history." In truth, Kierkegaard went on, "original sin is growing." We are born into a situation already off-balance. That unbalance upsets our balance. Our unbalance then adds to the total disturbance of humanity.

Anxiety floods in. We do not quite know what is happening. We sense something wrong. We realize we are entangled. We react defensively. We shift responsibility. We accuse others. We are cut off from positive meaning.

Nature has somehow produced "an unnatural state of affairs." In the process of becoming, a chasm yawns between ourselves and our environment. It is not our fault, yet we are part of its appearance. Even more, we perpetuate its presence.

There is the sea dragon. There is the ship. There is the shore from which we leapt and the shore for which we long. Each is distinguishable because all are separated. All are necessary because each is but a part.

Under favorable conditions the anxiousness motivates us to overcome the separation. Under less favorable conditions the anxiousness turns into a barrier to action. In either case we cannot *not* respond.

Hubris and Acedia

Traditionally, the garden has been used to explain humanitas' pride. The Greek word for pride is *hubris*, a kind of unlimited self-elevation. "Eat this and you shall be as god, knowing good and evil . . . you shall never die."

More recently, the garden has been used to highlight humanitas' sloth. The Greek word for sloth is *acedia*, a kind of indifference or not caring. As Harvey Cox describes it, "Sloth means being *less* than instead of *more* than [human]. Sloth describes our flaccid unwillingness to delight in the banquet of earth or to share the full measure of life's pain and responsibility. It means to abdicate in part or in whole the fullness of one's own humanity."

The issue of humanitas embraces both the hubris of straining to be more than we are and the acedia of being content with less than we are.

We demand too much;

we expect too little.

We want living without life. We prefer life without living. We expect becoming without being. We anticipate being without becoming. We yearn for power without love. We long for love without power. We separate ourselves from each other in lonely distance. We cut ourselves off from ourselves in empty relatedness. We split power from possibility in exaggerated achievement. We isolate possibility from actuality in passive nothingness.

The ship resists the sea dragon and the sea dragon fights the ship. The farther shore is forgotten in the struggle. The nearer shore is overlooked in the search.

Today, apathy constitutes much of the focus of sin. We shift the locus of initiative, involvement, and evaluation away from ourselves. Cox points out: "For Adam and Eve, apathy meant letting a snake tell them what to do. It meant abdicating what the theologians have called the *gubernatio mundi*, the exercise of dominion and control over the world. For us it means allowing others to dictate the identities with which we live out our lives."

In apathy one cares about nothing. When one does not care about anything, one has no concern—nothing random, nothing preliminary, nothing ultimate. One hides oneself in no-care or nothingness. Responsibility for what is and for what it means lies outside oneself and so outside and beyond humanity itself. As Tillich rightly saw, apathy is the only real atheism.

Unbelief and Concupiscence

Equally, the garden has been used to highlight humanitas' lack of faith. Unbelief, or better, *unfaith*, points toward a basic disorientation in life. The estrangement is not that one refuses to believe certain doctrines. The estrangement is not even the denial that God exists. For words are not reality. Unfaith lifts up the way all of us turn from a transcendent center and turn instead to ourselves as *the* center.

We lose our basic connection with the world. We cut ourselves off from our essential unity with the power of being. We refuse to trust the trustworthiness of the transpersonal power of becoming.

Unfaith invariably intertwines with *concupiscence*. Concupiscence is a Greek word for a kind of unlimited desiring. In unfaith our unlimited desiring for union with that which is beyond turns back upon ourselves. Like Narcissus we seek union only with our own reflection. There is no center other than our center, no reality other than our reality, no possibility other than our possibility, no purposes other than our purposes, no love other than our love, no hope other than our hope, no life other than our life.

We are the alpha and the omega, the beginning and the end. Yet, we experience that restless longing for participation and union. But since we shut ourselves up and cut ourselves off, that intense desiring only results in our eating ourselves up with an insatiable hunger for love or drowning ourselves in our own *self*-consciousness.

In concupiscence we try to draw the whole of reality into ourselves. Theologians such as Augustine and Luther have mistakenly restricted concupiscence to sexual desire. Such a view distorts the necessity and the dignity of bodily existence. It also denies the distortions in our thinking and our willing. What we know, how we try, what we own, what we value all give evidence of unlimited desiring and inappropriate passion.

The drive to be the center of everything ends in the experience of our ceasing to be the center of anything. Both self and world, centerdness and relatedness are destroyed. Instead of shared exuberance, there is aggressive exploitation.

No one is safe.
Nothing is sacred.
Life breaks down.

The Leap into Life

Once born we cannot return to the womb. The leap into self-awareness forever precludes a recovery of unbroken immediacy (except, of course, passing into death). "At the east of the garden" (Gen. 3:24) refers symbolically to the rising sun. We have already understood the rising sun to express dawning consciousness, human awareness. There at the threshold of selfhood, two angels guard the entrance to the womblike.

These transpersonal powers prevent our return. We cannot pull back from the anxiety of the unknown into the apathy of the known with any real safety. Even when we try, as in a psychotic break, a catatonic withdrawal, or an autistic shell,

169

we experience the ambiguity of our involvement in uninvolvement. We are responsible even for our irresponsibleness. We respond even though we respond unresponsively. We are human even when we deny our humanity.

The drama of human origin does not portray a fall, as so many have maintained. Instead, it presents a leap—a leap into life. Paradise is not lost, but sought. Wholeness is not recovered, but found. We are not to look behind to a golden age, but forward to a new city.

The Genesis 2 account of the Lord God creating humanitas from the dust of the ground and breathing into its nostrils the breath of life symbolizes our situation. Neither dust nor breath are to be taken as substances such as body-substance or soul-substance. Rather they are to be interpreted experientially as ways of being in the world: we-are-here-with-possibility. The account depicts the possibility of our maintaining *and* enhancing the humanness of human beings. It reminds us of our tendency to not-be as human as we are. It points toward our being less responsible than we can be.

As Laing puts it:

What we think is less than what we know; what we know is less than what we love; what we love is so much less than what there is. And to that precise extent we are so much less than what we are.

For the male, especially in his masculine functioning, work and its meaning becomes the focus of anxiety. His sense of worth and satisfaction derives from his work. What he does affects who he is. Whereas in the womb, being was the work —in the world, becoming constitutes the work. Now sweat and toil, frustration and disappointment, striving and straining abound. Autonomous power brings with it the anxiety of emptiness and meaninglessness.

He can fail.

He can lose his power.

He can *not-become*.

For the male, especially in his feminine functioning, existence itself becomes the focus of anxiety. His sense of acceptance and security derives from the givens of life—an environment supportive of life and conducive to humanness. What he has affects what he does. Whereas in the womb, becoming was existence—in the world, being constitutes existence. Now submission and obedience, waiting and longing, hoping and anticipating predominate. Unbroken immediacy brings with it the anxiety of fate and death.

He is limited.

He is dependent.

He can *not-be*.

In contrast, for the woman, especially in her feminine functioning, love and its meaning become the focus of anxiety. Her sense of worth and satisfaction derives from closeness and intimacy. Whom she cares about affects what she invests in. Whereas in the womb, connection was being—in the world, becoming constitutes connection. Now the difficulties of getting and growing children, the longing for intimacy, and the uncomfortableness with dependency absorb her energies. Human relatedness brings with it the anxiety of loneliness and isolation.

She can be cut off.

She can be rejected.

She can *not-belong*.

For the woman, especially in her masculine functioning, individuality becomes the focus of anxiety. Her sense of acceptance and security derives from who she is. Who she is affects what she does. Whereas in the womb, differentiating was becoming, in the world, being constitutes the differentiating. Now the struggle to be a person in her own right—standing apart, standing against, standing beside—persists. Differentiating awareness brings with it the anxiety of guilt and condemnation.

She can not stand forth.

She can submerge her identity.

She can *not-be herself*.

Like every dream, the symbolic quality of the Genesis accounts can never be reduced to a single meaning. Precisely because of their complexity these poetic myths range from

171

the most universal reaches of the cosmos to the most unique realm of the individual. They embrace the inorganic—dust of the earth—and the organic—breath of life. They anchor humanitas in creation, yet direct us toward what lies beyond.

Loss of Centeredness

One of the defining attributes of humanitas, as I keep stressing, is our insistent quest of meaning. Meaning involves the way(s) we organize our world. When humanitas is disturbed, our inner order is upset.

In the figure below you can see each aspect pulling away from its complement. Expression splits off from experience,

Figure 10. Disturbed Meaning

felt-meaning from what's-there, the outer from the inner. The center does not hold. Everything flies apart:

> disintegration of the self;
> loss of integrity.

What I have put abstractly in the figure you can see imaginatively in a painting done by a woman after taking a dose of LSD 25. She experienced the flesh as falling off her bones and her body as turning into a kit of parts. Her existence exploded into fragments. No centering secured her being. No center directed her becoming.

Our human predicament comes with that loss of center and the split in consciousness. We then set up incompatible contrasts: being versus becoming, unique versus universal, potential versus actual, the near shore versus the far shore.* We then live in an atmosphere of splits: sea dragon versus ship, eros versus logos, love versus power. We tear apart organism and environment, body and mind, subject and object, self and world, human and divine, immanent and transcendent, sin and salvation, experience and expression. Immediacy opposes autonomy; differentiation conflicts with relatedness.

Because of that predicament, the intermediate zone between each of these poles becomes filled with frightening fantasies. As Perls contended, so much energy is consumed in flooding the zone with catastrophic expectations there is little excitement left to let one be in touch with either oneself or the world.

courtesy Ronald A. Sandison

This painting, done by a woman patient following a dose of LSD 25, depicts her sensation of the flesh falling off her bones and body. The picture, a type common in psychotherapy, suggests symbolically the disintegration of the centered self.

Disintegration of the Self

Self or world?

What appears antagonistic turns out to be a matter of balance—neither too much of the self nor too much of the world. Whenever we impose too much order or too much order is imposed on us, vitality becomes rigid. Then we have only the ship's navigation. Whenever we express too much freedom or too much freedom confronts us, intentionality turns into aimlessness. Then we have only the sea dragon's maundering.

Here you see the famous Aztec calendar stone known as "Eagle Bowl." It represents a cosmic circle on which are carved symbols of the five suns. In the center, holding all together, is our present sun, Quetzalcoatl. The emblem of this sun is a human face. As such, it suggests the ordering of the

The Bettmann Archive, Inc.

Aztec Calendar Stone

universe by means of a human center. Even though we are not the center, nevertheless, we *do* center our world. Without *our* centering, for us nothing holds together. If nothing holds together, then we have broken into fragments.

174

All our understanding, finally, represents an intermingling of intuitive understanding with intellectual explanation. The intuitive participates in unifying experience and is often called mystical or religious. The intellectual searches out differences by description and definition and is usually regarded as empirical or scientific. But as Lancelot Whyte sees, they do, in truth, combine opposite aspects of that basic tendency which underlies all human experience: namely, *"the search for order in particular facts."*

Although set within a theocentric frame of reference, Eckhart's comments about the person wishing to begin a good life apply to our search for true humanity. He likened the process to a man who draws a circle:

Let him get the center in the right place and keep it so and the circumference will be good. In other words, let a man first learn to fix his heart on God and then his good deeds will have virtue; but if a man's heart is unsteady, even the great things he does will be of small advantage.

The *human* challenge is a centered wholeness. But the questions persist:

How is the navigational intention of the ship held together with the vitality of the sea dragon?

How are the far shore and the near shore connected?

How do we combine creation *of* reality with reflection *on* reality?

How does the inquiring mind complement the innocent eye?

How, in short, do we recover our human becoming and our being human? How do we discover our human being and our becoming human?

HUMAN BECOMING

TEN
One Leap Into Life

Near shore
Sea dragon
Ship
Far shore

How are these related and relatable?

>Being
>Intuition
>Intellect
>Becoming

What might the coincidence of opposites mean?

Our exploration of humanitas has found us crossing and recrossing common territory. We have viewed what we're up against from several vantage points. Let me refocus what I am about through the experience of a single individual.

I would share with you her decisive encounter with her own more genuinely human becoming. The intensity and depth of the experience carried her beyond the particular and into the universal. She herself had experienced nothing like it before, nor has she experienced anything like it since. I, however, have been privileged to participate in similar encounters. The process is ever the same, yet always surprising.

Background

The woman was twenty-six. Let's call her Claire in order to be personal, even as I eliminate identifying information. To those who knew her casually she gave the appearance of strength, brilliance, and aloofness. She had extensive training in both the fields of psychology and theology. When I first met her, I experienced her as cold and slightly hostile, direct and definitely demanding. She intellectualized every situation and attacked every authority. To her, reason was supreme; feelings were foolish. The intellect dominated the intuitive.

At the time, I was using the concept of relatedness in my teaching. The idea intrigued her because, as she said, "I feel an incapacity to commit myself to either persons or things. I want to become more aware of why I seem to avoid relations whenever they come to a certain point of closeness and commitment."

She experienced herself as a stranger and outsider, a wanderer and intruder. Even more, she felt her "self" to be a stunted "dwarf."

Our early contacts could be characterized as stormy. She made demands. I rejected them. I was "the authority." She was "the revolting victim." Eventually, we faced the question of whether we would work together in a therapeutic relationship.

She experienced that possibility as both attractive and repulsive.

"It is almost too late now," she insightfully declared, "to ask me whether I want to be involved with you. I *am* already more involved than I realized, and it will stay that way as long as you are there and look at me (with those piercing eyes). I don't seem to be quite a corpse yet, since I can and feel compelled to answer the question of therapy with you with a strong yes."

She also felt compelled to let me know how destructive her

hostility could be. She told of one therapist who had said to her, "I can't take you any longer." She reported a dream in which I had been severely injured. She tried to imagine what I expected of her—namely, that she sacrifice safety and risk anger—and could not. For her, any experience in my office would be mild compared with the reality of her life.

I found our initial sessions exhilarating and exhausting. Our minds engaged in subtle duels. Thrusts of insight and counterthrusts of avoidance. I kept telling her she could always play that game better than I. And she could.

A moment came, inevitably, when her defense dropped for an instant. In that moment she let me glimpse a beautiful, radiant, open human being. As she left, I spontaneously embraced her. I felt warm, in touch, alive as a result of that disclosure.

She reacted with disbelief. Startled, angry, frozen, she hurried from my office.

The Inner Debate

That encounter set off in her an intense internal debate. She argued with herself what the contact meant and why she had reacted so violently. In the dialogue that follows her private and undefended intuition initiates the conversation. Her public and defended intellect answers back:*

Why? Why did you punch back so hard?

I CANNOT STAND IT.

All he wanted was to show a friendly gesture, nothing to be furious about. This rage is inappropriate.

IT IS SUPERFICIAL.

What do you want? That he put all his personality, past, future, and present in this brief event?

YES.

You are unrealistic. But you don't even let him show if there were honesty behind the gesture. All he did was say some admiring compliment to you and touch you. And you almost hit him physically, but you sure made him know what you meant by words and facial expression. I bet he never dares to say something or to touch you again.

HE BETTER NOT. ALL THIS TOUCHING-FEELING-BUSINESS AROUND HERE. IT IS DISGUSTING. YOU WANT ME TO BLUSH OR TO GRATEFULLY KISS HIS HAND OR TO HIDE MY FACE SOBBINGLY AT HIS SHOULDER?

Nobody asks you for that. But how about saying simply thank you for the compliment and—if you really don't want him to touch you—making him know that in a more friendly way? He must have gotten the impression that he is worse than vermin.

HE DID NOT MEAN IT, AND I WANTED TO SHOW HIM THAT HE CAN'T GET AWAY WITH THAT—NOT IN RELATION TO ME AT LEAST.

I agree with you that any expression should show some of your real feelings.

SEE?

But what makes you think that he did not mean it? That it did not express what he really thought at that moment?

YOU KNOW VERY WELL THAT HE CANNOT MEAN IT.

Is it that you are still fixed to the image of you as a little girl, fat and clumsy and always too stern, in donated and not-quite-fitting or fashionable clothes? To the humiliating experiences in dancing school and later? Or when in your first intimate contact with a man, you were compared to a farm-horse? Do you still suspect every compliment to be either a sympathetic gift or a cynical attempt to feast on your bad need for it.

YES, I SUPPOSE. AND I HAVEN'T CHANGED MUCH SINCE THEN.

But there were also many other, extremely happy and deeply honest experiences, as you remember.

I DO REMEMBER. AND THAT IS MAYBE WHY I AM STILL ALIVE.

But you always spoiled them by pushing back, not believing, with sarcastic remarks.

YES, YOU ARE RIGHT. I'M REALLY BAD. I KNOW I PUNCH BACK THE HARDER, THE MORE VULNERABLE AND SENSITIVE A PERSON SEEMS TO BE. I'M CRUEL SOMETIMES. I'M NOT WORTH

ALL THE EFFORTS OTHER PEOPLE WASTE ON ME. I AM A
FAILURE. I WISH I HAD NEVER BEEN BORN.

Come on, now. Don't you escape with this trick again. You
want to cut off any conversation by a gesture of humility.
But I won't let you go into your old depression pit.

LEAVE ME ALONE!

You act toward me like you do toward other people.

SO WHAT?

With the difference that I won't pity you or actually be
afraid that you will kill yourself—not at this moment. I look
through your maneuvers and have an idea why you do it.

OH, I'M SO GLAD OF YOUR CONCERN. WHERE DID YOU
LEARN IT? IN PASTORAL CARE? I'M SURE YOU ALREADY
KNOW WHAT IS WRONG WITH ME. SO, GO AHEAD WITH
YOUR EXPLANATION.

Yes, I do think I have some insight.

OH, SHUT UP WITH ALL YOUR BUNK.

I think that you really . . .

WILL YOU PLEASE?!

I think that you really want very badly for someone to stand
next to you and to stay with you in spite of you. You would
be overjoyed if somebody could pass all these rigid and
hard tests that you require without shrinking back, being
hurt, or just falling back into indifference. Remember the fairy
tales where all those who dared to court the princess and
could not solve the riddles were decapitated until the castle
was surrounded by the heads of the unfortunate?

OH, ISN'T THAT TOUCHING.

Only in the stories, the father usually made up these rigid
rules. And you are making them up yourself? Are you still
waiting for your father, until he gives his blessing and says:
"Okay, daughter, I want you to be happy. You don't have to
look for me any more. You have my blessing."

MAY I ASK WHAT MADE YOU COMPARE ME TO THAT
PRINCESS?

I cannot help but interpret it that way when, for example,
you come home from the hospital [where she served as a
chaplain] with your insides turned outside because of what

you have seen and felt there, when you go around pretending
you are busy, when you turn on somebody harshly because
they have dared to read your face, when you go into
your apartment, lock the door, lean against the wall, touch
the warm wood of the door with your palms pretending it is
a friend.

THIS IS NOT TRUE!

So?

I'M TIRED. THAT IS ALL.

Tired of what?

OF NOT BEING . . . OF NOT HAVING . . .

You are right.

. . . OF BEING ALONE, OF NOT HAVING SOMEBODY TO
TURN TO.

But you close the door. You want to be alone, to suffer,
to isolate yourself, to play the hero. But I want you to go
out, you understand, because I think you are beautiful
and warm and lovable.

OH YOU BASTARD, YOU CREEP, YOU MISERABLE CREATURE
OF A PSEUDOANALYST, YOU GODDAMN LIAR . . .

Why so excited? Did I happen to touch you?

From this account you can readily sense the intensity of
Claire's conflict. Part of her recognizes her avoidance, her
defensiveness, her vulnerability. And in that recognition she
knows and accepts her tenderness and caring. Another part
of her plays the game of strength, of toughness, of not caring.
And in that denial she cuts herself off from others and herself.
Her intuition is really rational. Her intellect is really irrational.
The forces of life and death grapple in mortal combat.

A Pivotal Dream

To our next session she came, agitated and distant. She
talked around and around without touching on anything. Then,
trying to be casual and matter of fact, she reported a dream
fragment:

*I am standing on the springboard at the swimming pool
of my childhood. I am ready to jump, but suddenly the
clear water turns first into brown, then dirty and disgusting
black, mud.*

*The rectangular basin becomes bordered like a natural pool
while the mud ascends and comes closer up to me. I get
anxious, turn round to leave the springboard, but it is
already surrounded by the mud.*

*My eyes glance at the shore. I see something like hairs,
which I suddenly recognize as eyelashes. The pool is a huge
eye.*

*I awake in terror, but before that happens I catch a
glimpse of a figure standing quietly on the shore. I dimly
recognize the figure as you. My first association after waking
was the role your eyes play for me in our relationship.*

The dream seemed rather harmless, strange but not spectacular until . . . I urged her to go back into the dream and
actually jump into the mud.

"This," she remembered later, "was the turning point in
my relation to myself and the world. The difficulty of realizing
it and the intense emotion that went with it indicated that
something must be important."

The lengthy introductions at the beginning of each of her
three plunges into the mud reflected, to her, how dangerous
she experienced this encounter with her own unconscious.
Even so, "inevitably," as she said, "the wish to get to know it
was stronger than my fear of it."

The First Leap

Reluctantly and only with great effort did she agree to try
to plunge into the mud. She leaned back in the chair, closed
her eyes, and imagined herself standing once again on the
springboard. I moved into the chair next to her and offered
my hand for support. She refused.

She sprang from her chair, extremely agitated. Back and
forth she paced across my office. At last she stopped before
a narrow bookcase. It was as though the outer limits were

forcing the inward leap. She had to move away in order to dive in.

From across the room I pushed: "Now jump."

I spoke calmly yet firmly.

She jumped.

Down through the mud she sank. Down and down and down . . . A riot of images flashed by: a vault—a cave—an animal's pit. The walls were—what: stone? diamonds? earth? coal? Images, impressions, memories, previously unseen pictures, all flashed past so rapidly she could not focus. The prevailing feeling was cold, dark, blue, threat.

Eventually, a single picture emerged: a Jewish brass candelabra with seven arms.

The candles are lit. The candelabra moves towards the darkest corner on the left, the entrance of a tunnel. I follow it.

Long roots are hanging down from the ceiling and walls. I want to tap my way along the walls but realize, in horror, that the roots are really serpents. The walls are covered with squiggly worms and bugs.

Now I realize that the floor I walk on is not a usual floor, but the firm, smooth skin of an animal—a huge serpent or dragon.

The candelabra disappears behind the corner. I am paralyzed and cannot follow. I am trapped in the darkness and horrified.

In a panic she opened her eyes. She interrupted the fantasy. She was experiencing more than she could bear.

The days that followed were marked by restlessness, inability to sleep, and bodily ailments. Clearly, this initial penetration of the depths triggered anxiety.

The Second Leap

At the next session she told about the anxiety provoked by my offering to hold her hand. We talked at length of the meaning for her of emotional and physical closeness. She had to test the distance between us. Then she invited me to sit next to her. Although the space between us had grown smaller, it had not vanished. "Not because," she remarked, "of a 'real'—meaning tangible—danger but because of a real *felt* one."

She linked her growing ability to descend into the pit with her growing ability to respond physically. Less and less did her anxiety drive her to attack me or to avoid me.

Again she stood on the springboard. Again she jumped. Only this time the pictures came clearer immediately:

The pit is light by an entrance on the right side. I walk out and find myself at the swimming pool again. I feel I have to go back inside.

Between the light entrance and the dark entrance on the left is a table covered with a white cloth. In the middle lies an open book, an unlit high candle at each side. Behind the book between the candles is a small gallows with a little man in grey sheets hanging there. The man is no bigger than the book.

I bow my head. It falls off onto the book. I can see my head like it is sleeping on one side. I stretch out my hands and they fall off beside the book. All this happens painlessly and without blood. There is only the feeling of surprise and sadness, although the feeling is not very clear.

She interrupted her exploration with an aside. She could never adequately describe these impressions. For the flood was more like a multi-media presentation. She felt fortunate when an image stayed long enough to be described. Once an impression could be put into words, it stayed and, like the nucleus of a crystal, seemed to collect other impressions.

She continued:

I see a zipper that runs along my body. I unzip it and undress myself of my skin like a robe.

Thus unprotected, I turn to the entrance at the left. This time I have the greatest reluctance to enter the tunnel. It is greenish dark. After a few steps it narrows. From both sides eyes on stems grow out of the wall, stretching toward me but not looking. I cannot pass unless I touch these very disgusting eyes.

Unable to go back, I am trapped again.

Suddenly the animal under my feet moves. The walls crack open. Mud flows in and rises quickly. The eyes loosen from the walls and swim towards me. They touch me. I can hardly breathe. The mud is up to my neck.

My alternative seems to be either dying or abruptly ending the fantasy.

Because of her panic I called out to her: "Claire! Claire! Can you hear me? If you can, call my name."

"Jim! Jim!"

For the first time she called me by my first name. As she did, she reached out and took my hand. This marked another first.

Strangely, the flood is sinking. My right hand, which fell off at the entrance is restored. Now I go further. The tunnel begins to widen.

On the floor I see a big pulsating blister with a very thin skin. I go closer. I see red blood under the skin. When I look very closely, I can see the well-known candelabra which makes the blood transparent like heavy red wine.

On my right I can now see stairs going down to some dark corner. The blister is very precious but very fragile. I have to watch that I do not touch it or step on it because it would break.

You have somehow disappeared. Always you have been one step behind my right shoulder in your white shirt. I cannot see you anymore.

That second time we had penetrated further, yet not deeply enough. Time had flown by. The session was over. We turned back to the ongoing and the everyday. No interpretations had been made. No insights had been suggested. Only the experience stood out—immediate, intense, quivering.

The Third Leap

By her next visit the distance and closeness between us had joined. My personal presence no longer needed to be substantiated by physical proximity. She was still anxious and agitated, but decidedly determined and certain.

Again she jumped. Readily, though hardly eagerly. Once in the room she moved quickly to the staircase and started down:

It is extremely dark. I can only feel my way. It is narrow. I have to work my way through with some tools. Possibly a hammer.

What I feel is soft and yielding, but also in the way. Therefore I have to use a knife or something. I feel moisture on my hand. I look at it and at myself. I am covered all over with blood!

I now realize that I stand in a small room. The walls, the floor, and the ceiling are made up of heads. The heads are of friends and unknown people whose faces are distorted.

I feel horror. I scream, "I didn't know! I didn't want it!" I see some sheer skin among those heads. I pull on it. It is the body of a dead baby. I am stricken by the sudden power of this image.

Later she informed me that she was too conscious of my being there to have cried as she wanted to. She had trained herself too well in stifling her emotions. She could not let go in the presence of another person, even one like me who had become trustworthy.

Somehow, I go back to the tunnel. I see another tunnel. It runs into the "old" one from the left side at a sharp angle. Out of this part now appear three figures in long black robes with snow-white facial masks and gloves on their hands.

They strip off the gloves. I see with horror that they have claws and paws instead of hands. They take raw meat from under their gowns and in a very repelling, indecent way they gnaw on those bones, carelessly throwing them behind them. They smack their lips and burp shamelessly.

186

ONE LEAP INTO LIFE

They now discover a person on the right side wearing a white shirt. I can only see him from behind. Before I can stop it, they grab him, screw off his head and throw it away in the same careless manner. They rip off his legs and arms, leaving the pieces lying around like peeling from an orange, while they slowly walk away.

All this happens with a certain undramatic self-evidentness. Yet it only leaves me with turmoil inside. I walk to the head but do not dare to turn it over so that I can see its face.

When I finally do turn it over, it is your face. Again I am overwhelmed with sorrow and despair at this sight. But there is something like comfort in what happens because your eyes look at me kindly. You smile your warm smile. There is no catastrophe.

I urgently want to put you together again, but my hands are too huge, too clumsy, too undifferentiated for this delicate task. My hands are big like shopping bags. My fingers are like potatoes. I am sad. I do not know what to do.

Suddenly I find myself in a very strong, rushing, roaring stream. It obviously comes out of the left arm of the tunnel. It flushes me somewhere very rapidly, but I don't care. Suddenly I realize the stream comes out into the open, abruptly falling about one hundred yards.

At the bottom I see many shattered bodies and skeletons. Somebody says, "Joel 3." I can hold myself so that the stream does not drag me down, but my strength starts to leave me. I am almost ready to let go.

A vulture appears and takes me in its claws. It carries me over fissured stone deserts and empty countryside and drops me somewhere. I don't experience the fall, so there is no anxiety.

I find myself in the strangest place: flat and grey, no plant, no hill, no stone, no living being, only me. The only comfort for the eye is the dark stripe at the far horizon, far away where sky and earth meet. There is no sound, no sensation of cold or heat, even no feeling whatsoever.

Wandering around, I suddenly find something glittering,

187

*lying there. It is like a jewel. I rush near to see what it is.
It turns out to be a drop of water. To me it seems like the
most precious treasure. Of course, I cannot touch it, but I
kneel down to get a clear look. I can look through the drop
as through a peephole. I see the well-known scene: the
tunnel, the blister, the ripped-apart body.*

*Suddenly, I am there again, standing before the head,
trying to put it together. I feel again the inappropriateness
of my hands. Other hands grow out of my elbows, fine and
soft hands. With envy I watch how tenderly and carefully
they touch the costly object. But they do not belong to me.
I can only feel the other, clumsy hands.*

Here the fantasy ended.

So much experiential material; so much horror; so much
pain; so much alienation; so much struggle.

Yet no better picture could describe her journey toward relatedness and wholeness by means of awareness. For to her,
the fantasy seemed to be the coagulation of the diverse experiences that brought her closer to her integrated self. Listen
to her own reflection on this perilous venture.

Claire's Interpretation

The lack of relatedness [she informed me], among other
things, brought me into contact with you. I was not unaware
of myself and of my effect on others. I experienced myself as
unfriendly, hostile, sarcastic, and arrogant.

A friend's statement, "Somebody must really hate himself
when he stays close to you," was not really surprising, but
congruent with my own experience of myself. It was shocking
only because it did not allow room for the ambivalence I felt,
namely, the urgent wish to be able to be close, to be a loving
and a worthwhile person to know. This is one wound I resented.

The horror chamber full of chopped off heads shows that
hurt very strongly. Groping my way toward independence and
integrity, I have left many hurt people behind. Sometimes I
was reckless because I thought it was necessary in order not to

get too many wounds myself and in order not to stay a clinging vine. When realizing the results, I was more shocked,
maybe, than the particular person. To hurt another, to get
angry, is something very dangerous for me. It means loss of love
and care. But the anger and the destructiveness, even, are
sometimes too strong.

I see the three figures as deadly forces coming deep out of
the unconscious. They are strong because of the number three
and deadly because of the black color of their gowns. They
are not identifiable because of their masks. They are inhuman
because of their behavior and their strange bodies. I have to
keep a distance from them, for what they do is really horrible.
That also shows my ambivalence between aggressive and tender
feelings—there the murderous forces; here the sympathetic,
sorrowful me.

The ripped apart person is partly the real person whom I
hate to see suffer from my violence. He smiles and looks at me,
the first and only human expression I find down there in
the depths. It means to me: "I accept you."

You [she went on indicating me] did not kill me. Therefore,
there is neither reason for triumph because of the aggressive
tendencies nor for despair because of the tender tendencies.
This is an attitude only the *real* person showed toward me.
This is the gift I received.

But that ripped apart person is also a symbolic disguise of
a part of me, the tender and soft part which I have not shown
very much lately. I want this part to live. I am very sorry to see
it overpowered. I want to be able to touch others because
not to touch hurts very much. If one is able to touch, it makes
everything whole. That is what the restored hand after the
physical touch means.

I wonder what would have happened if I would have actually
touched your head? Would the clumsy hands fall off or grow
together with the tender ones? Or would they continue to
murder? When they touched the head, it fell into ashes.
[This is a later remembrance that did not appear during the
fantasy.]

But now sorrow is pervasive. I see the stream as a very self-destructive force, again coming up out of the deep unconscious. It is coupled with a certain apathy. I let myself float, but only up to the point where it gets really serious, deadly serious. If I would really let go totally, maybe I would get shattered myself.

I cannot do very much with Joel 3, to be frank. The only connection I can see is the observation that mutations in consciousness are—in individuals as well as in societies—accompanied by apocalytic visions. One could show that in the biblical sources apocalypsis indicates the "shaking of the foundations." The same indication might be true in this case, but I resent this picture. It is sentimental and exaggerated. I don't want to talk about it more.

The vulture, at other times vexing, this time helps to end the crisis. The vast landscape is a powerful picture of the loneliness one is driven into by the sorrow about living only partly, disconnected from others. When one looks more closely, then one sees lying under this loneliness the whole turmoil of ambivalence between distance and closeness, which is not resolved so that I can live with it.

The interpretation of the desert does not seem satisfactory. It seems more than an unresolved conflict—existential, like, for example, the huge serpent. Maybe I have to accept the fact that I am a person who is lonely and who has to learn to live with this fact without anxiety.

But back to the pit. There are forces of vitality mighty enough to cause an earthquake. To have seen this is another gift for me. I can stand on these forces; they carry me, though they are also repulsive as worms. There is a reliability in the regularly pulsating bloodstream, which is warmed by elements of light. This is the basis for trust in these forces. They bring me into danger when they move, yet they open up new and enriching possibilities when I risk not running away. Eros can be strong, but does not overwhelm me in passionate exaltations.

It is difficult for me to explain the other pictures. The eyes, meaning unawareness, try to hinder me from going further. It is not surprising when one thinks of what awaits me deeper in the pit. But the serpent helps.

The table seems to be an altar at which I had to sacrifice my rationality: my hands being the wish for objectivity and the skin the wish for insensitivity.

It was an audacious step for me to pursue the fantasy, to leave behind all convictions which I otherwise use to order my world. For awhile, I thought seriously I was "cracking up." I told nobody of these experiences. For awhile, I thought seriously that you—my guide—were some sort of a magician. It was true that both our unconscious forces corresponded in a fascinating, aw-ful beauty. They rhymed together, making for me new and surprising sense.

That sense eventually convinced me that there was not much magic in it. There was too much triumph and deep joy in spite of all the other feelings about my discoveries. It seems to be a foretaste of the joy and vitality awaiting me if I can unite the different forces in myself in such a harmonious way. But the sacrifice also shows that I am distorted. I need my hands— to tap my way and, above all, to touch. I am only whole when I am in touch with some*body*. But I am dependent on people who can accept that these hands are also the hands of a murderer. One person did: you! And the spirit of this gift carries me through my days.

The open book signals a new stage of awareness, but the candles are not lit yet, or not lit all the time. The two entrances symbolize the short way back to consciousness and the dark, troublesome way into unconsciousness.

Strange is the small man hanging at the gallows. I would interpret that as a religious symbol because of its place on the altar where the cross would otherwise be. Somehow this subject is touchy for me, but at the same time a new and very meaningful interpretation of the religious sources comes to me. I can see the cross not only as the symbol of death and suffering but of hope and life.

This is a breakthrough in my theological thinking and experience. The change has to do with the fact that I dared to stand the presence of your eyes. I now can relate that to the challenge to become aware. Then I jumped into the dream eye and found awareness. I went into the dark and found light!

Another thing I cannot do very much with are the colors. White is the table cloth and the shirt you wore—the light, helpful elements. But also, the faces of the three figures are white. In their black robes they certainly represent the dark and destructive forces. Blue and green in this dream are connected with threat and danger, though in other contexts they can mean coolness and growth. Here, red is the color of vitality, especially with the yellow of the brass. Grey seems to be the color of loneliness and apathy. This probably gives another meaning to the little grey man. But I stop here because I am too much in the dark with these interpretations.

A Resolving Dream

With such a wealth of inner experience, personal relatedness, and mutual sharing, our remaining sessions flowed swiftly and purposefully. Near the end of our search together she came in with an additional dream:

Today I woke with this dream, which in a beautiful way signals where I am right now and how I work on the union of polarities without destroying the tension between them.
I visit the swimming pool of my childhood after a long absence. This time I have a friend with me, whom I sort of lead around and show everything to.

Claire went on to explain to me that she had thought of this friend quite often lately. They had studied together. The friend had always been very troubled by her own physical and psychic instability. Sometimes she had been so affected that she could not study for months during which she sought to regain her balance and vitality. She took a great deal of medication to little avail.

Then the friend had been introduced to a method of meditation. Claire did not want to make that alone responsible for the friend's spectacular change. There were other factors also. But the friend herself said that she had gained incredible strength "to work and to love" by struggling with her unconscious. And the change had been there for others to see.

Claire had been pleased about the development, but strongly resented the part played by meditation. Because Claire could not find a way to communicate with the friend after that, she herself broke off the friendship, which had lasted several years.

This friend now accompanies me in the dream, a dream clear as a photograph and calm as a Sunday afternoon. Of all the details only two, maybe, are important.

We walk over the lawn under big trees. They do not allow very much space for the sun to shine through.

"Is there not too much shadow?" the friend asks.

"Yes, the trees have really grown since I was here last time. But, you know, I like it here. This is where I am at home. And also, white people cannot take too much sun with their light skin anyway. They like it here, too."

Then we walk over to the basin. It does not look in very good shape, really, and I am a little embarrassed. The basin appears to be crumbling and has not been cared for in a long time. The lawn around the basin where people are supposed to lie down looks the same way. Thistles grow wildly. Rotten grass lies around, spoiling the sight of the glittering water.

But there is a man working and I explain, "You know, the gardeners and maintenance workers have just had vacations for three weeks, but now they are back and starting their work."

By now she was "charmed by the beauty and impact with which the unconscious can formulate its message." She told me: "Unconscious and conscious can be friendly with each other as seen in the dream-relationship between my friend and me. I should write my friend that I was a coward when I ended the friendship. I know better now because I myself have encountered forces of my unconscious and am more of a person.

"Light and shadow have a coexistence," she continued, "or, even better, the shadow is accepted as something that is useful and necessary, necessary in the strange and almost humorous logic of a dream. But that shows that my white friends even have a place in this dream.

"Significant," she observed, "is the atmosphere of reconciliation. It might not be grand, but it's my home and I like it. The battle has calmed down. It's now up to the maintenance staff to keep the basin, which has to be understood as the unconscious, accessible and a pleasant place to be near, for people are meant to rest there. The basin is seen as beautiful, not as the dirty mud it was. It has been badly neglected, but now it is going to be taken care of. What a change!

"I think that in this dream symbol all other polarities are thrown together, even though they do not appear specifically: *intellect and emotion*, represented in the doubtful question 'Is there not too much shadow?' and the disarming answer, 'Maybe, but I like it'; *closeness and distance*, with a new impetus toward closeness because we 'need self-assertion to bridge separateness'—and to accept one's shadow is such a self-assertion; *negative and positive*, touched on in the oddness of the place, which causes some awkwardness, but is accepted on the whole; *love and will*, united in the maintenance workers and work; *past and future*, glimpsed in the feeling that this will be a better place to be when it is worked on."

In earlier remarks Claire had recognized the shadow as probably the very strong force of tenderness and care. Here she questions that somewhat skeptically. "Is it not a little too much sentimentality and enthusiasm?" she wondered. Then she responded, "So what? It can be used!"

Few were aware of what she was going through, yet most began reporting dramatic changes. She expressed more care. She became more relaxed. She evidenced more confidence. Her warmth enlivened. Her insights enlightened. She was a joy to be around.

As I relive this encounter, I feel as exhausted and as awed as I did during the process. Its dramatic quality, though, must not detract from its profoundly human qualities.

You may rightly ask me: What are those human qualities? You have provided a powerfully moving description of one person's transforming the human predicament into human possibilities. But can you sharpen your point more precisely? How does human becoming go with being human?

ELEVEN
Response

I have allowed Claire's experience and reflections to stand by themselves. They present an integrity, a wholeness, that ought not be confounded by what I or others say. In the final analysis, I believe that what one says about oneself—after open searching, honest feedback, and courageous reflection—stands as more decisive and valid than anything others might say.

Also, in using her experience I face the danger that it is so dramatic there seems to be little comparison with our everyday experience. Beforehand, she would have said the same. Since then, she feels similarly, tempered only by the fact that she *did* have the experience. In effect, what we have is a shaft of light penetrating the deep places of humanitas. It discloses to us forces that operate most of the time outside our awareness. By virtue of their intensity in Claire, which allowed us to see them, we can sense more surely what goes on in ordinary ways during ordinary times.

With these caveats, I lift out what I regard as salient features of humanitas. Claire provides us a focus and a filter. With her experience we can look more meaningfully at the task of our own human becoming.

The Limits of Logic

Initially, I see in Claire a picture of human imbalance and distortion. Reason came forth as exaggerated thinking; emotions as retarded feeling. She had ignored and neglected her intuition, even as she had focused on and cherished her intellect. Like the white Western world, she had come to an impasse by overemphasizing the rational at the expense of the non-rational.

But logic is limited. Life rests on a more profound and significant base than rigid rationality. There is a deeper foundation than we often acknowledge.

Nicholas of Cusa (1401?-1464) spoke of the wall of Paradise beyond which God dwelt. The door opening into that fullness, he wrote, "is guarded by the most proud spirit of Reason, and unless he be vanquished, the way in will not lie open." That door, for Cusanus, constituted the coincidence of opposites "where seeing is one with being seen, and hearing with being heard, and tasting with being tasted, and touching with being touched, and speaking with hearing, and creating with speaking."

What Claire had forgotten was the polarity to which Cusanus pointed. To see is linked with being seen. To know is bound up with being known. Our intellect depends upon our intuition; thus, the ship is carried by the sea dragon. Our intuition finds its focus in our intellect; thus, the sea dragon is guided by the ship. Exaggeration or neglect of either only shuts the door of our becoming.

For that coincidence of intellect and intuition to occur something has to happen to get us through the door. Somehow, we have to cross over the boundary by passing through the barrier. That "somehow" is known as "contact."

You recall the exalted space of Gothic architecture which I touched on above? People eventually could not tolerate the contradiction between the exaggerated height and the exaggerated length (depth). An architectural symbol of the strain appeared in the cathedral at Wells in the fourteenth century. After the tower had been raised one story, ominous signs of subsiding appeared. The careful balance went. The weight of the central tower simply became too much for the footing. The building swayed precariously.

Here you can see the ingenious device utilized to save the

Inverted arches, St. Andrew's Cathedral at Wells

structure. Stones buttressed the tower by means of spectacular
inverted arches. English church builders lost the long vista in
the nave, which they loved. However, not only did they preserve
the cathedral, they also created a charming stone pattern in
addition.

In the face of all imbalance, contact between the forces is

needed for survival, even more for fulfillment. The very stress of disequilibrium must be taken as an active response to difficulty. Just as inflammation in reaction to a physical injury has the purpose of repulsing the aggressor *and* mending whatever damage has been caused, so anxiety serves the dual purpose of alerting us to the threat to our humanitas *and* spurring us to regain our balance. Stress signals the need for a change—a shift—a refocus—in the gestalt within the person. One struggles for new life. One opens channels of previously untapped creativity.

Seeing and Being

Once alerted to threat, we can then look for it *and* look at it. It was Claire's looking that enabled her to reestablish contact with the lost forces within. When parts of life are fragmented or alienated, awareness serves as a reuniting bridge. We *intend* that we *attend to* felt-meaning that we may *see* accurately what-is.

> The perfect Way [Tao] is without difficulty,
> Save that it avoids picking and choosing. . . .
> If you want to get the plain truth,
> Be not concerned with right and wrong.

So states the opening of the oldest Zen poem.

Nothwithstanding, we always experience the boundary between predicament and possibility as anxious and ambiguous. Both our intellect and our intuition confront us with conflicting faces: a fearful one and a fascinating one. The clear water of possibility turns into the muddy water of predicament. The desire to retreat comes at the moment of diving in.

Thus, we have seen how a safe harbor could become one from which it was frightening to sail into the open sea. A harbor both shelters *and* constricts. Similarly, the color blue may be, as in the nightmare, cold and barren *or* calm and soothing. In mythology, the good mother is the water cushioning the fetus, while the terrible mother devours the person with a flood. Spontaneity and impulsivity are not easily distinguish-

198

able. Order and rigidity present similar features. In Zen it is said that "the grand round mirror of wisdom is black as pitch." And, according to an old Chinese legend, under the jaw of a black dragon lies the most precious jewel in the world.

To dive into unknown waters—to look, to see, to attend to—cannot be done casually. The threat in the descent into chaos cannot be overestimated. Even if the plunge is the way to life, it feels like the end of life. Thus, we need another to help us be present to ourselves.

We need the supporting buttress of another person. We need the demanding necessity of a situation from which we cannot escape. With experience and faith we return to the plunge more expectantly, as did Claire.

We can dive in because of the conviction that to see is to be. The way to the height passes through the depths. Life lies in the lifeless; light in the darkness; hope in the helpless. Instead of struggling to bring vitality under control, we surrender ourselves to it. We endeavor to participate in, and to become an integral part of, something that we conceive of as greater than ourselves.

In the inner world of felt-meaning we touch the outer realm of what's-there. As Laing states so succinctly: "Without the inner the outer loses its meaning, and without the outer the inner loses its substance."

Everything has both a lower and a higher meaning, even as the late classical mystics insisted:

> Heaven above, Heaven below,
> stars above, stars below,
> all that is above also is below,
> know this and rejoice.

This coincidence of contraries is the psychological law Heraclitus discovered and labeled *enantiodromia*. By that he pointed toward the regulative function of opposites, the running contrariwise so that sooner or later everything runs into its opposite. It shows itself in the dream of a ten-year-old girl in which she ascended into heaven only to find pagan dances celebrated, and she descended into hell only to find angels doing good deeds.

Escher's graphic visually conveys boundary contact and a transformation from one sphere into another. With almost mystical vision, he set forth centered continuity between frogs and fish and birds, depth and height, immanence and transcendence, finitude and freedom. A fish or a snake indicates the root of the power of liberation still contained in the prelogical. A bird symbolizes the power of transcendence. The wisdom of the deep contains no certain knowledge; instead, it carries primarily an intuition of liberation for the intellect which suffers from exaggerated self-consciousness. The transcendent function of the psyche relates the nonconscious contents to conscious purposes by means of a healing symbol. However, only the human focus unites vital force with intended

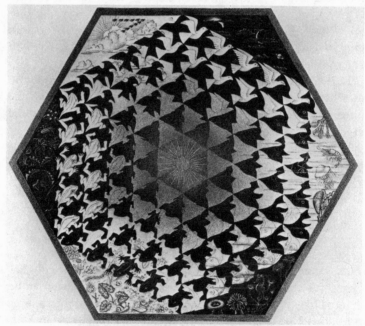

Escher Foundation—Haags Gemeentemuseum, The Hague

Verbum by M. C. Escher

form. In the center of the whole is Word, "Verbum," that which creates and organizes life for human purposes.

So Claire moved from the conscious into the unconscious. Immediately we are transported from the ordinary room into the extraordinary cave. As she grew accustomed to the cave, she discovered the instinctual base of humanitas—her own and everyone's. By focusing on the felt-meaning of her existence, Claire became more able to express what was there.

Animals usually symbolize our instinctual nature and its connection with our surroundings. More specifically, the giant serpent conveys the power moving within us, the "devouring" aspect of intimate contact. Within Christianity we find just such animal symbolism: Luke as an ox; Mark as a lion; John as an eagle; Matthew as a man. Even the Christ himself is symbolized as a lamb or a fish.

The serpentine base of our psyche symbolizes the powerful life forces—sex and love, anger and rage, power and drive, trust and fear, hurt and hope—our vitality. These are our emotions for contact. When they are roused, we are active. From the Garden where the serpent is tempting Eve (Gen. 2) to the wilderness where the children of Israel are bitten by the serpents (Num. 21:6), from Jonah in the belly of the whale, to Job's encountering the great monsters of the deep, to Daniel in the lions' den (Dan. 6:16), to Jesus with the wild beasts in the desert (Mark 1:12-13), to the great serpent dragon of the book of Revelation, we find this portrayal of the forces that threaten us from inside and out. The single beast stands for all the blind forces of creation. It indicates the *natural* power both in the inner and the outer realm.

Vitality arises from the very ground and source of our being. It is the biological substance of life. When we deny its existence, it has the power to take over the whole of our personality as though by an outside, alien force. But when we look at, attend to, stay with, and affirm it as the source and destiny of life, then it is taken in, thereby providing the power of our becoming (Num. 21:8-9). So Job (38:36 NEB) can speak of "wisdom in the depths of darkness," while Jesus exhorted us to be "wise as serpents" (Matt. 10:16).

In Hinduism we find the meditating Buddha seated on a giant snake. The snake forms the throne, surrounding Buddha with a shield of expanded hoods. The forces of nature are symbolized in this way as appreciating the unique value of the savior by protecting him and worshiping him, even before he discloses himself to people. The force of the deep—the great beast—stands for our vitality which possesses a peculiar wisdom of its own. Buddhist art abounds with wild beasts representing "the terrors of the great descent into the center of one's being."

The Chinese conceived of the world as full of every kind of supernatural animal. The most important of these was the dragon. They regarded it as a beneficent power, even though severe in its presence. Because of its constant movement, it symbolizes our extraordinary capacity for transformation and change. The dragon could reduce itself to the size of a silkworm or swell up till it filled the heavens with the golden light of the sun.

Although the dragon does not appear in Greek mythology, the vital power is not absent. It can be sensed in the presence of the snake. While the snake could be deadly, it could also be healing. The snake has remained the primary symbol of the healer since the time of Hippocrates and the cult of Asklepios.

The dragon has clearly personified both the destructive and the life-giving power of the depths. Everywhere it is linked with night, darkness, deep, water, womb, awesomeness: the state of primordial unconsciousness. "The wisdom of the serpent," observe Joseph Henderson and Maud Oakes, "which is suggested by its watchful lidless eyes, lies essentially in [humankind's] having projected into this lowly creature [its] own secret wish to obtain from the earth a knowledge [it] cannot find in waking daylight consciousness alone. This is the knowledge of death and rebirth forever withheld except at those times when some transcendent principle, emerging from the depths, makes it available to consciousness." While Freud regarded the snake as a phallic symbol, Jung thought of it as a feminine symbol. For that reason the snake and the self can be thought of as expressing the same reality in different guises—humanitas in both its vitality and its intentionality.

Once the beast is seen in the depths, we begin to experience our own substance. God of darkness turns out to be God of light. God of light is found in God of darkness. Significantly, the first works of God—the great monsters of the deep—feminine Leviathan and masculine Behemoth—at the end provide the food for the great "messianic banquet."

To see is to be.

Knowing and Becoming

As we explore that inner realm—looking and touching—it begins to stir. It moves. Now we feel its pulsating life—pulse and breath—power and meaning. Once that energy is aroused it becomes the means by which the whole personality is changed.

That is, deficient and one-sided expressions of our humanitas rise up to disrupt our limited equilibrium. They force us to take account of, and come to terms with, that which would rebalance our imbalance. They confront us with fuller manifestations of our humanity. For wholeness to emerge the shadow must be met and assimilated. What would seem to be past is present, deeply buried within us. It waits to be liberated that we might become more truly human.

But to see can never be static. To see means to know. And to know always requires intimate contact. The pool in Claire's fantasy was that which was directly seen in awareness. However, to know—i.e., stand in and under what was seen—demanded more than a plunge into the pool. It required exploring the passage. Claire had to recontact that which she had lost sight of.

Again Cusanus provided imagery of the process. God is "the power that alike enfoldeth and unfoldeth," so that one goes in and goes out of the wall or the door of coincidence alike:

I go in, passing from the creatures to Thee,
their Creator, from effects to the Cause;

I go out, passing from Thee, the Creator, to
the creature, from Cause to effects.

I go in and go out simultaneously when I
perceive how going out is one with going in,
and going in with going out.

To leap into the pool of awareness initially results in *a restriction of awareness*, an enfolding. We focus down and zero in and squeeze through and center on that which is nothing and everything, everything and nothing. But once through the barrier, once beyond the boundary, the world opens before us. We move through the room and down the passageway. From having been enfolded, we come upon an unfolding. Subsequently, we discover *an expansion of awareness*.

There is every indication that the antithesis conscious/unconscious has exhausted its usefulness. Rather than remaining two separate realms, they are now unified as aspects of one complex continuous activity. The expression and elaboration of felt-meaning always alternates with the experience of and the focus on what's-there.

As Claire came into closer and clearer contact with her being, the imagery gradually underwent transformation. The beast/serpent flowed into the more genuinely human. We come to the point where we free ourselves from the terror and immaturity of the unconscious. Sometimes that struggle for liberation has been symbolized by a hero's confrontation with a monster, as in the Japanese god Susanoco's fight with a serpent. Other times that struggle comes in an encounter with a beast, as we saw in Claire. Instead of concentrating the flow of psychic energy into the single channel of thinking, as she had in her intended unbalancing, or into feeling, as she had in her unintentioned rebalancing, every part of her personality comes alive. Precisely because her becoming remained centered in her being, her being could expand with full force in every direction.

I have been giving you a great deal of material. Let me pull it together by means of recapitulating Claire's leap into the pool of awareness.

The sequence moved in the following order: anxiety, pool, sacrifice, serpent, person, vulture. The details of that progression are shown in Figure 11.

Figure 11. The Sequence of Claire's Leap in Anxiety

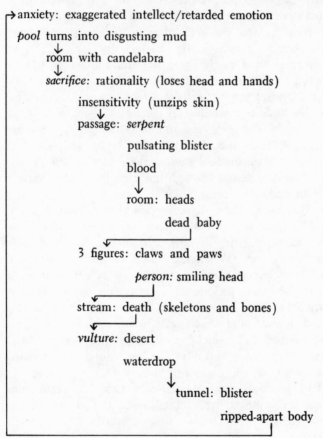

Claire came to therapy because of
    the pain of lonely isolation,
      she did not belong—

the pain of fateful death,
she was in danger of not being—

the pain of guilty condemnation,
she had not been herself—

the pain of empty meaninglessness,
she was not becoming.

She had neglected the eros of love. Like a giant serpent it lay dormant within, yet threatened destruction if approached.

She had exaggerated the logos of power. Like a great vulture it circled above, yet lived in the wastelands.

The presence of a person gave her the courage to plunge through the anxiety barrier. To do so she had to sacrifice both her objectivity and her insensitivity. Once through the gateless gate, as the Buddhists would call it, she became more aware of her being by exploring the underground passage. Having cut herself off from the vitality of her body base, she had to recontact that instinctual source. Because she had so battered it by hurting herself through hurting others, that contact proved to be a bloody process.

From the mess, three figures, part beast, part human, emerged. In their midst was a genuinely human being who continued caring despite the onslaught of her neglected, now exaggerated emotions. When the waters of death flowed, the power of transcendence appeared. It came in the form of a vulture. Rather than picking at decaying pieces of life, the bird carried her back to look again at her broken body. Her anxiety faded. She found herself again becoming.

Having looked and thereby recontacted her being, Claire then grew in her human capacity. The resolving dream contains all the elements of the presenting dream. Only this time her psyche had developed from its earlier infantile and immature instinctual depth into a later more human and mature whole. That which had been rejected was now accepted.

The sequence moved in the following order: anticipation, pool, intuitive friend, workers return, place cared for. The details of the movement are shown in Figure 12.

Claire left therapy with

a love enabling her to identify with others,
she belongs—

a faith enabling her to trust her body base,
she is—

a commitment enabling her to express
what she experienced, she is herself—

> a creativity enabling her to establish within
> herself a human center,
> she is growing meaningfully.

Figure 12. The Sequence of Claire's Recovery of Anticipation

anticipation: passionate reason/reasonable passion

pool remains clear and glittering
↓
intuitive friend: lawn
trees and shade
at home

basin: rest spot
uncared for
workers return

place cared for: intelligently
with feeling

The eros of love has been expressed. No longer serpent but intuitive woman. "Eros," as May summarizes the concept, "is the binding element par excellence." It bridges being with becoming, what's-there with felt-meaning. It enables us to carry on a continual dialogue with the inner world of persons and the outer world of nature. It carries us from the near shore of being to the far shore of becoming. In eros we find "the original creative force."

The logos of power has been experienced. No longer vulture but responsible workmen. Logos refers to the meaningful structure of life. Understanding, to draw on May again, comes from the structure of language, which itself depends upon the structure of human relationships. As creation began with the differentiating Word, so creativity continues with the distinguishable person.

In place of death and decay, Claire finds growth and renewal. The place of her person is now cared for thoughtfully and tenderly. Intellect and intuition are reunited—the coincidence of opposites. When integrated, the feminine force becomes the vitality of consciousness, while the masculine force becomes the intentionality of the nonconscious. Similarly, the feminine provides male consciousness with relationship and relatedness, while the masculine gives female consciousness a capacity for reflecting, deliberating, and knowing. Eros pulls toward the far shore of being from the near shore of becoming. Logos guides toward the far shore of becoming from the near shore of being.

Human becoming experiences itself in being human; being human expresses itself in human becoming.

To follow philosopher Susan Langer's ideas, the ability to perceive form is intimately linked with human rationality. In contrast to the ability of animals to adapt themselves to the world, humanitas' ability to reason enables us to adapt the world to ourselves. The serpent links us with life. The ship directs that life in terms of human purposes.

In the end, the decisive focus is not the immediately unavailable vitality of the underground. That is only the beginning. Because of our intuition, we leap into the waters of life. But the leap serves the purpose of carrying our ship. In the end, the decisive focus is the transcendent intentionality of reaching the far shore of our being-in-becoming.

The first stage begins with the *impersonal*—the sea dragon. Then comes the decisive transformation in the intentionality of the *personal*—the ship. Only consciousness that stands on and is carried by the prelogical can take an authentic posture toward the underground. "The daemonic," to use May's construct for human vitality, "thus pushes us toward the logos." The more we come to terms with our daemonic powers, the more we find ourselves conceiving and living by a universal structure of reality. "This movement toward the logos is *trans*personal." We seek true humanity in a new humanness.

We lose our minds and recover our senses. We draw on resources not our own. While beyond dualism, differentiation remains. We are present as ourselves; we participate as part of the whole. We know both the nonlogic of the logical and the logic of the prelogical.

Buber made the point that "to become a person means to become someone who responds to what happens from a center of inwardness." A center and a responding are the keys.

As we see, so we are.

As we know, so we act.

Nicholas referred to that wall or gate of invisible vision beyond which God was to be found as "at one and the same time all things and nothing," both generative power and a living mirror, "the coincidence of shining and reflection, of cause and effect alike," Absolute Power and Absolute Sight.

> To see is to be;
> to be is to see.
>
> To know is to do;
> to do is to know.

Transforming the Elements

Focus again on the figure/ground interaction of the gestalt. Here you can see another example besides the earlier one of chalice and faces. What do you see?

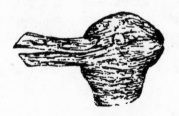

Duck or Rabbit?

If you focus on the right half of the drawing, you will see a rabbit. There is a line that suggests a mouth. You are only dimly aware of the ears trailing out to the left.

If you focus on the left half of the drawing, you will see a duck. There are extensions that suggest a beak. You are only dimly aware of the back of the head on the right.

You cannot see both a duck's beak and a rabbit's ears simultaneously. You can, however, switch from one to the other very rapidly. But to see a duck you must neglect seeing a rabbit's mouth. To see a rabbit you must neglect seeing a duck's beak.

Now there is nothing significant psychologically in whether you see a duck or a rabbit. But if you can see only the rabbit or only the duck that does suggest consequences for the way you respond. You have lost certain possibilities of understanding because of a single way of seeing.

The parts of the picture of the rabbit are exactly the same as the parts of the picture of the duck—except for one decisive fact: the gestalt itself. Different parts are focused figure. Different parts are diffused ground. Black, that once was perceived as bad by all, can now be seen as beautiful by many. The pool, that once was perceived as muddy, can now be seen as clear. We increasingly are learning that people's symptoms express what we regard as health as much as they show what we take as illness.

In the Malayan culture whenever anyone tells of a dream of falling, one is asked: "Where did you fall to and what did you discover?" In other words, the intention is to transform the fear of falling into the joy of flying. So, the fluttery anxiousness of butterflies—being overwhelmed by the many —can be transformed into the graceful, integrated certainty of the butterfly—becoming the wholly one. All the elements are present whether we experience butterflies or butterfly. In the gestalt of fear, we collapse. In a gestalt of grace, we connect.

Drawing on different symbolism and using different language, Jacob Boehme (1575-1624) pointed to the same reality:

That which in the dark world is a pang, is in the light-world a pleasing delight; and what in the dark is a stinging and enmity, is in the light an uplifting joy. And that which in the dark is a fear, terror and trembling, is in the light a shout of joy, a ringing forth and singing. . . .

The dark world is therefore the ground and origin of the light-world.

Such configurations are but another way of pointing toward *metanoia* — change — transformation — turning about — repentance. We are freed from the past to live toward the future by being able in the present to reconstruct all our constructions of life and death. Animosity changes into animation. What once came across as hostility now comes through as liveliness.

Boehme believed that once we break through the gates of hell, we find ourselves in "the inmost birth of the Godhead." There we are "embraced with Love as a bridegroom embraces his dear bride." This is but a figurative way of pointing toward what psychiatrist Andras Angyal claimed as "the discovery of *the healthy roots of the neurotic trends,* i.e., finding health right inside the neurosis."

Transformation of the unhealthy gestalt into a healthy one requires exclusive attention to the center, the focus of creative change. As Claire exposed herself to the serpentine forces of the unconscious, so must we. In doing so, we must not identify ourselves with them nor run from them. Either response defeats the possibility of change. We are to transform passive nouns—such as a *bind,* meaning "trapped"—into active verbs —such as *bind,* meaning "to link." Through contact we experience the pieces of our inner world and bring them into a pattern in our conscious life. We hold together the sea dragon and the ship; *we* bind the near shore and the far shore.

"The principle of conscious life," insisted Jung, "is: *Nihil est in intellectu, quod non prius fuerit in sensu.*" Nothing is in the intellect which is not first found in the senses. The unconscious operates with a degree of autonomy. It draws upon the illustrative possibilities of what's-there in the sensible world. It makes clear felt-meaning in the concrete images.

Thus, we become that light which we truly are.

TWELVE
Expectation

There is no single way of seeing.

What I see as chaotic you may view as spontaneous. What I see as order you may regard as rigidity. What I take as desirable you may find detestable.

What we see depends not only on what's-there but even more on its felt-meaning.

Claude Monet (1840-1926) was the leader of French Impressionism. He often painted the same scene again and again, varying each picture primarily in terms of the time of day and the season of the year. In an exhibition in 1891, he hung no less than fifteen canvasses, each depicting a haystack painted at a different hour and a different season. Monet's concern was not with rural landscapes. Rather, he was exploring the way light, in its varied aspects, altered landscapes.

Similarly, in exploring humanitas I have portrayed it in a variety of ways. Again and again I have directed your attention to its mixed character. There has been the positive-with-limitations and the negative-with-possibilities.

Escher's graphic on "Relativity" sharpens the experience I am pressing. Look at the staircases. If no one is present, they are simply there—suchness, if you will. Put people in, and we see opposites and contrasts. Depending upon angle and direction, people move in various ways. If I ask "who is going in the right direction?" we would find ourselves en-

Relativity by M. C. Escher

tangled in a fruitless argument. If you saw only the man going down and I saw only the man going up, we would be locked into limited visions. We would be orienting what's-there from separate and exclusive viewpoints. We would be organizing felt-meaning in contradictory ways.

How varied the attempts to understand humanitas. Some emphasize the direction of the ship; others the dynamics of the sea dragon. Some stress the vitality in the near shore of being; others the intentionality in the far shore of becoming. Each points toward ways of dealing with our human predicament. All disclose our insistent quest for meaning.

Meaning, as I have indicated, involves the way we order and express our experience. We take pieces and put them into a pattern. We find fragments and create a whole. We use details to make a design. But the pattern and the whole and the design are never *the* pattern nor *the* whole nor *the* design. These are only approximations. Seemingly, there are an infinite number of patterns and wholes and designs.

What I see as the figure of the gestalt you may regard as the ground. What I take to be the ground you may see as the figure. Because of that we must expect differences.

How We See

I have been pressing you to intensify your involvements, as I try to intensify mine. I have been drawing upon the ways we see situations—perceptions—as a tool for understanding and acting. For how and what we see largely determine what happens to us. We tend to see in terms of wholes—pictures, patterns, configurations, designs, constellations. What we recognize influences how we respond.

As we see, so we act.

We have found fractures in our experience and expression. Poles — dichotomies — separations — splits — opposites — divisions—name it as you will, the reality's the same. One part sees fluidity, another stability. One part organizes for freedom, another for order. One part creates chaos, another cosmos. There is the sea dragon; there is the ship. We leave the near shore to seek the far shore. We reject the far shore to cling to the near shore.

Styles of Responding

That basic split is reflected in contrasting styles of responding. Simplicity and complexity of perception correspond to simplicity and complexity in personality. Symmetry and balance versus asymmetry and restlessness.*

One large part of humanitas prefers simplicity. It tends to ignore differences and to resist instability. The configuration of characteristics includes: "social conformity, respect for custom and ceremony, friendliness toward tradition,

214

somewhat categorical moral judgment, an undeviating patriotism, and suppression of such troublesome new forces as inventions that would temporarily cause unemployment."

Lest you inadvertently infer a homogeneous group preferring simplicity, let me juxtapose contrasting groups that reflect this preference. Obviously, on the surface "law and order" people—middle Americans—may be listed under this style. But what would you do with those who leave the complexity of collapsing culture in the face of future shock for the simplicity of communal living in an agrarian setting? They are friendly toward the order of nature. They reject the tyranny of technology. They affirm simple (nonphony) loyalty to one another. They show an antiorder simplicity even as the others disclose an ordered simplicity.

I regard a preference for simplicity as neither desirable nor undesirable. It simply is. Such people orient themselves, organize what they find, and act on what that means with *a focused clarity*.

In contrast, another large part of humanitas prefers complexity. It tends to bring out differences and to accept instability. The configuration of characteristics includes: "artistic interests, unconventionality, political radicalism, high valuation of creativity, . . . and a liking for change."

Again, do not infer a homogeneous group preferring complexity. Clearly, at a casual glance, "freedom and spontaneity" people—marginal Americans—may be listed under this style. But what would you do with those who encourage diverse cultural traditions within establishment settings? They are friendly toward the process of history. They reject the arbitrariness of authority. They affirm the multiple loyalties of several worlds. They manifest an antifreedom diversity even as the others reveal a freedom complexity.

I regard a preference for complexity as neither desirable nor undesirable. It simply is. Such people orient themselves, organize what they find, and act upon what that means with *an open searching*.

Both simplicity and complexity have been shown to be associated with a high degree of personal and group effectiveness. They have also been found to be associated with a high degree of personal and group ineffectiveness.

In terms of *positive impact*, preference for simplicity goes with stability and balance, likableness and straightforwardness. Preference for complexity is found with variety and richness, intensity and expansiveness. The former finds expression in an easy optimism. The latter comes out in lifting pessimism to the level of the tragic, producing participation in the human scene.

In terms of *negative impact*, preference for simplicity is associated with fanatical rejection and repression of all that threatens disorder and disequilibrium. Preference for complexity correlates with frantic acceptance and reinforcement of all that offers the novel and the strange.

In terms of *pathological impact*, preference for simplicity produces stereotyped reactions, rigid and compulsive morality, and hatred of aggressive and erotic emotions. Complexity results in disorganized behavior, bitter cynicism, and hostile depreciation of everything.

The simplicity preference is effective in situations where inner cohesiveness matters. That is, where a friendly orientation to structure is required. On the other hand, the simplicity preference tends to be ineffective in situations where outer correspondence matters. That is, it rejects whatever threatens disorder and so misses what it has overlooked or ignored.

The complexity preference is effective in situations where outer connection matters. That is, where an integration and synthesis of diverse forces are required. On the other hand, the complexity preference tends to be ineffective in situations where inner coherence matters. That is, because it goes along with many forces, it tends to surrender to chaos and to reject organization.

These contrasting approaches to seeing reality are primarily a matter of perceptual preference. We choose what we will attend to. Embedded in the world are both the stable and the unstable, both the predictable and the unpredictable, both order and chaos.

But even the simplicity/complexity distinction obscures the subtlety, the richness, the variedness in what we see and how we see. For the way we see the world and what we see in the world are very selective and often distorted. We prefer to see visions and to ignore sights.

A Totality

You see, we see in terms of the meanings we bring, the data we find, the angle from which we look, and the interaction between the brought/the vantage point/and the found. What we perceive is always a totality. It is never an isolated episode. Perhaps that is why the Zen tradition pictures Bodhidharma with wide-penetrating eyes. Our perceived world is at once so much more and so much less than what is potentially present in our physical environment.

We know now that no single way of seeing a situation can give us its essential character. In medieval times, relationships of persons as well as things were fixed. Just as an observer could look at a private patrician fortress in Bologna in the thirteenth century and embrace it at a single glance, so an observer could look at an individual and know his place in society and his view of society.

Today, the complexity of space and time are such that no single focus can convey the richness and variedness of any person or object or situation. Modern physics has found that space—which we once thought of as solid, stable, static, absolute—must now be thought of as relative to a moving point of reference. Today the essence of space is, as Sigfried Giedion has demonstrated, "its many-sidedness, the infinite potentiality for relations within it. Exhaustive description of an area from one point of reference is accordingly, impossible; its character changes with the point from which it is viewed."

Below you see two views of Donatello's famous statue of John the Evangelist. On the left you see it as it is in the museum: ordinary, unimpressive, conventional, static. On the right you see it as it was intended to be seen on the facade

Alinari—Scala, New York/Florence

Two views of Donatello's statue of St. John the Evangelist

of the cathedral: imposing, inspiring, awesome, dynamic. Humanitas can be seen both as mediocre and as magnificent.

Where we stand affects what we see.

What we see, obviously, can never fully encompass what's-there. We interpret what's-there in such varied ways. What seems to be the same objectively, always contains the contrast between what-is and the way we experience it.

In the Freedom Summer of 1964 in Mississippi, the civil rights activists responded differently to thirst and to drinking fountains. The whites did not drink as a matter of principle. They would not be part of a social structure that deliberately dehumanized some. The blacks, on the other hand, did drink as a matter of principle. They intruded into a social structure so as to rehumanize it.

What we see, thus, depends in part on *what we bring*— our background, our experience, our expectations, our hopes, our fears, our conflicts, our confidence.

Yet it is *what we find* that influences how we act. If we see the world as strange and uncomfortable, we move away from it and want little to do with it. So the pool in Claire's dream turns into disgusting mud to be rejected or resisted. If we see the world as friendly and exciting, we move closer and want more experience with it. So the pool becomes a place of rest and renewal.

As I have touched on above, the way we see the world is always a gestalt—the relationship of the figure to the ground. That which is out in front is sharp and focused. It has contour, texture, distinctiveness. That which is behind is diffused and unfocused. It is vague and unclear, yet it provides the atmosphere, the setting, the frame of reference.

What we see, in short, is always the result of that figure/ground dynamic.

In an unhealthy gestalt we are disturbed, confused, bored, compulsive, impulsive, fixated, frenzied, strained, self-conscious, "not with it." The pool of awareness is fraught with anxiety. We either stare at one part with a fierce intensity for fear of losing it, or we look frantically from part to part in a desperate attempt to find a pattern. The familiar feels elusive; the unfamiliar frightening.

In a too-fixed figure, we lock into one, and only one, way of seeing a situation.

Immediately after World War II, to cite one example, a half-dozen professionals gathered in Berkeley, California. As psychologists, they wanted to shift their attention from preoccupation with pathology to concern with the positive. In trying to define "what is present when health is present," they arrived at a consensus on the healthy personality. What they failed to see were the limitations in their affirmations. For the virtues they saw applied only to: the temperate zone, men rather than women, middle-age rather than adolescence, and whites. In brief, each "saw his own image in what he judged to be good."

Persons who fix too firmly upon closeness and affiliation usually exhibit bland, often naive, and certainly uninsightful behavior. Their relationships are dominated by external values and approval from others. They misread social reality by overlooking in themselves hostility and/or power. They avoid the undertow of depression by a strained overoptimism that everything's all right when it isn't.

In contrast, persons who fix too firmly upon distance and dominance usually reveal decided misperception of weakness in others. They regard others as too passive and too hostile. Not only do they look down on others, but their very contemptuousness allows them to exploit weakness in others for their own self-centered gains.

In a too-chaotic ground, we are unable to focus on any single aspect of the situation. We experience being bombarded by anything and everything. All is random; all is racing. Nothing stays put. Nothing stands still. Nothing means anything. Boom—boom—boom—now this—now that—what next—oh no —oh yes—not that—yes that—how come—can't be—too much —too much—too much—too . . .

In contrast, in a healthy gestalt we are interested, attentive, concerned, excited. We shift our focus from part to part easily, freely, smoothly. The figure is sharp and clear; the ground is vibrant and contrasting. There is a freshness in the familiar and an excitement in the unfamiliar. New configurations present new insights. More possibilities become available.

With her resolving dream Claire could, *and* wanted to, show her friend her home. All was familiar yet fresh, shadowy yet desirable. She saw the various forces at work. She assessed where they were and understood what they were doing. Through integrating the several parts of herself, she could be what she knew by becoming what was possible.

In her earlier fantasy we could see her rigidity in the fixed room, the multiple heads, and the narrow passageway. Now we see a flexible intellect in the thoughtful care of the workmen. In her earlier fantasy we could sense her chaos in the bloody breakthrough of the wall, the pulsating blister, the figures ripping up a body and chewing on raw meat. Now we sense an ordered intuition in the charm and richness of the shade and the shadows. As she could take those isolated and exaggerated fragments of feeling and thinking back into herself, the bizarre turned into quiet beauty. She became whole again—at one with herself and her world.*

EXPECTATION

What We Know

If I were to stop here, I would mislead you. For I would be conveying the impression that life is finally and permanently centered and complete.

Claire's resolving dream was a decisive turning point in her becoming. After that people experienced her as warm, lively, insightful, caring. Yet she still had times when her feminine intuition would recede into the menacing serpent. She could not avoid her masculine intellect rising into the scavenger vulture. When her center would give, the parts would split off. Yet they could and would come together again. The vacation break would pass; the caretaking could continue.

In the book of Revelation (20:1-3 NEB) we read:

> Then I saw an angel coming down from heaven with the key of the abyss and a great chain in his hands. He seized the dragon, that serpent of old, the Devil or Satan, and chained him up for a thousand years; he threw him into the abyss, shutting and sealing it over him, so that he might seduce the nations no more till the thousand years were over. After that he must be let loose for a short while.

The vision reminds us that there is no permanent wholeness. Perfect harmony eludes us. No ultimate resolution is possible. This is a symbolic way of suggesting that the structures of our becoming can never contain the spirit of our being. Every structure eventually grows unstable after it has reached its optimum complexity. Then it dies by coming apart in order that the elements can begin another similar cycle.

Piercing the Negative and Tending the Positive

I hope I have brought you to the point of seeing the necessity of the coincidence of contraries. Whenever there is too much light (clarity), then we find ourselves in the dark (confusion). With too much sun we go blind. Whenever there is too much darkness (confusion), then we come upon light (clarity). When the daylight goes, the stars can be seen. As Nicholas himself put it: "Otherness in unity is without otherness be-

221

cause it is unity. . . . The opposition of opposites is an opposition without opposition."

When we are organized in terms of an unhealthy gestalt—as Claire was in her presenting dream—we find the truly human to be brittle and fragile. Then we must, as Kierkegaard saw, pierce through every negativity. For life has increasingly narrowed until there is little or no room in which to move around, much less in which to feel at home. The light of what-is must be carried into the pit of what-is-not–yet-is.

We start at the periphery and explore the complexity that lies in the midst.

In order to recenter in a healthy gestalt, Claire had to know and had to express the serpentine. She had to let go of her control. She had to allow her comprehension to recede into the background. She then had to pull out from the ground lost fragments of love and of power. She could not avoid the painful. For what seemed to be past was present, deeply present, buried within her being.

The unhealthy gestalt demands a breaking-up of the configuration. We are to dive into the mud. Through such an act we refocus the chaos. We come into the room and then explore the passageways. We pierce what-is-not–yet-is. Or, as the Sanskrit word *samadhi* implies, we put things together, joining the meditator with that on which one meditates. We recover the contrasts.

A healthy gestalt—as was Claire's resolving dream—enhances the truly human. She gained a larger area in which she could feel at home. She enjoyed more human contact. To care for her life and to converse with others resulted in more liveliness and meaning for her.

We start with the centered self and enjoy our several worlds.

In order to maintain that healthy gestalt, however, Claire had to see and to affirm the shade and the feminine as well as the sun and the masculine. A healthy gestalt needs constant attention. We are to tend the positive. We are to cultivate the parts. We are to maintain the contrasts. In the end, though, we experience the unity, living at the heart of reality.

In dealing with that treasure buried in the most intimate

part of our being, Eliade makes the same point. He shows that only *after* a perilous and pious journey in a distant region can the meaning that guides one be understood. And the one who reveals that meaning must be a stranger.

Using Everything

For our human becoming every part of us is necessary. No part can be excluded. The stranger is our other. Concretely, that means everything is related and relatable. We are to utilize every facet of ourselves for our humanity.

In our drive for achievement, we Westerners have over-identified with our heads or, at best, with our hearts. Orientals, in their drive for at-one-ment, have overidentified with their bellies, cultivating the feeling of the center of gravity in the *hara*. The *hara* refers specifically to the stomach and abdomen with the associated functions of digestion, absorption, and elimination. Western emphasis on the head symbolizes human intentionality—the ship and the far shore. Eastern emphasis on the *hara* symbolizes human vitality—the sea dragon and the near shore.

Both the intentionality of our becoming and the vitality of our being are required for full humanness. We will never touch the shores of genuine humanity without the coincidence of dragon and ship.

In that earlier dream of the forty-year-old woman, the pieces of the collapsing tower turned into the parts of the new build-ing. In Claire's dreams, the serpent turned into the woman friend and the refreshing shade. The cruel claws and the circling vulture turned into the touching hands and the responsible workmen. Every part plays a part.

In the Chinese language "man" is symbolized by a pair of legs. Thus we see 人. Humanitas stands upon the earth. A head indicates greatness and conveys the idea of integration. Wholeness is symbolized by a complete figure: a body, legs, outstretched arms, and, fittingly, a head. Thus we see 大. The intuitive senses give us our base of being. The guiding intellect shapes the greatness of our becoming.

Our sensing informs us that something exists. Our thinking instructs us what that something is. Our feeling lets us know whether that something is agreeable or not. And our intuiting gives us perspective as to the origin of that something—from whence it comes—and its destiny—whence it is headed.*

To be(come) a whole person one experiences a freeing sense of security, as the Christian life has been described. One can live with a kind of inner autonomy. Even in the face of threat or uncertainty one need not distort or manipulate what's-there. One avoids making it feel different from what it is.

One, thus, is like a mirror. A mirror allows every object to be reflected equally. It is not able to receive some input and to ignore other input. It neither adds to nor subtracts from what's-there. It plays no favorites. It is incapable of discrimination. Felt-meaning corresponds with what's-there, and what's-there appears in felt-meaning. Wants and needs overlap.

We can be glad that the predominantly intellectual West is experiencing the disgrace of its successes. For that means as a culture and as individuals we stand on the threshold—springboard—of being able to experience the grace of our failures—the room and the underground passages. The ignored, the overlooked, the repressed, the excluded elements of humanitas are once again asserting themselves, generating an urgency and a potency that hold promise of a more human future. The limitation of our overworked intellect is preparing the way for the liberation of our undercultivated intuition.*

Thus, we center in more on deepening one another's "courage to live." Such deepening demands heightened involvement, experiencing, if you will, our less manageable and less abstract vitalities. We undo our exaggerated concentration on the details of getting around. We give up our strained attempts to grab hold of the means of making it. We let go of the automatic habits of living.

To use everything requires us to identify with both the figure and the ground of our gestalt.

We identify with the figure or parts by descending into the inner world. We leap into the pool of uncertainty. There we experience ourselves in the room and the passages and with the serpents and the bodies and the figures and the vulture and the desert. We reintegrate the fragments. We take back what we have pushed away. *We become* the vital parts.

Equally, we identify with the background, or the "set," by ascending into the outer world. We wander around the pool of clarity and certainty. Here we express ourselves through the woman and the workmen and the garden and the sun and the shade. We refresh the whole. We let go what we have hung on to. *We are* the intended whole.

By means of a nondemanding, nonaggressive, nonassaultive, nonjudgmental attitude, we observe what goes on around us and within us, as it is, for what it is. We neither accept nor reject thoughts, images, sensations, perceptions. Like a small child, we grow conscious of small clues—sights and sounds, particles and particulars, bits and pieces. We respond afresh to stimuli we previously ignored or blocked from awareness.

In other words, we recover where we are, what we see, and what goes on. From such efforts to know reality comes a deep sense of awe and wonder, beauty and humbleness. "Look lovingly on some object," counsels a four-thousand-year-old Sanskrit teaching. "Do not go on to another object. Here, in the middle of this object—*the blessing.*"

William Blake (1757-1827) attacked the timidly conventional and self-righteous establishment of his time. His strategy, however, was to accept the language of conventional morality while reversing its values. Initially, evil is associated with the body in hell and good with the soul in heaven.

Blake came to the proposition, startling to many, that heaven and hell must marry. The real good is not simply a freedom from restraint, but a marriage of the contrary extremes: desire and restraint, energy and reason, hell's promptings and heaven's limitations. Without these contraries there could be no progression in *human* existence.

No Ultimate "No"

Ultimately, we can use everything for our human becoming because of a basic conviction. In genuine humanitas there is no "no," only "yes" (2 Cor. 1:19-20). I have been operating implicitly on that assumption throughout the book. Let me now make it explicit.

In 1910, Freud wrote a brief review of a pamphlet by philologist Karl Abel entitled "The Antithetical Sense of Primal Words." Freud began by repeating a point he had made in *The Interpretation of Dreams:* "The word 'No' does not seem to exist for a dream. Dreams show a special tendency to reduce two opposites to a unity or to represent them as one thing."

Freud owed his initial understanding of this dream pattern of disregarding negation and expressing contraries by identical means of representation to Abel's work. Abel pointed out that in the Egyptian language there were a number of words "with two meanings, one of which says the exact opposite of the other." Examples of these antithetical meanings were compound words like "oldyoung," "farnear," "bindloose," and "outsideinside."

The strangeness can be immediately dispersed when we remember that ideas come about through comparison and contrast. To create is to divide. To conceive is to differentiate. "Man has not been able to acquire even his oldest and simplest conceptions," wrote Abel, "otherwise than in contrast with their opposite; he only gradually learnt to separate the two sides of the antithesis and think of the one without conscious comparison with the other."

Here are some of the examples Freud listed:

Latin *altus*: high/deep
    sacer: holy/accursed
German *Boden*: ground-floor/attic
English *cleave*: hold to/divide

The same phenomenon was noted in the way Egyptian words could *"reverse their sound as well as their sense.* Let us suppose the word 'good' was Egyptian;" speculated Freud, "then it could mean 'bad' as well as 'good,' and be pronounced *doog* as well as *good.*"

We come upon a similar pattern in a classic Zen *koan*

226

[story, situation, problem]: "A monk asked Master Chao Chou, 'Does a dog have the Buddha nature?' Chao Chou answered, 'Wu!' (meaning 'No!')." In interpreting this, G. C. C. Chang claims that the Zen student working on the *koan* "should not think of *both* the question and the answer. Instead, he should put all his mind into the single word *wu*."

To put all one's energies into the single word *wu*, of course, is to go beyond the split between question and answer, subject and object. In addition, the word *wu*, as used in this example, is pronounced according to the second tone. That contrasts with the same word pronounced according to the fourth tone. The *wu* of the second tone means "nothingness"; that of the fourth tone, "enlightenment."

Thus, *if we ask a question, we are to turn it into a statement.* That is affirming the possibilities of the negative. "Are you there?" becomes "You are there."

In the anxious situation we need an enfolding focus. We are to plunge through the barrier that separates us from what's-there. You-are-there.

Thus, *if we make a statement, we are to turn it into a question.* That is questioning the limitations in the positive. "You are here." becomes "Are you here?"

In the exciting situation we need an unfolding search. We are to explore the places which express the felt-meaning of what's-there. Are-you-there?

Within the question and around the statement lies Reality.

Meister Eckhart expressed this experience in mystical language:

To get at the core of God at his greatest, one must first get into the core of himself at his least, . . . for all that God can do is focused there.

Then, in another fragment, Eckhart affirmed the everlasting "Yes":

The divine One is a negation of negations. . . . What does "One" mean? Something to which nothing is to be added. . . . Every creature contains a negation: one denies that it is the other. . . .

but God contains the denial of denials. He is that One who denies of every *other* that it is anything except himself.

The negation of negation means fullness of being. The mystical method uses the negative to avoid describing what cannot be described. But every "no" takes its life from the "yes" it negates. Every "yes" takes its life from the "no" it denies. The one in the many and the many in the one. The treasure that we finally see in the seemingly empty house we have been exploring is the true image of humanitas. I am not the distorted image of me; I am the genuine image of God—as are you.

We experience the demand to give account to ourselves of ourselves and of the meaning of our existence. We find meaning by creating and enhancing values. Rather than remaining within ourselves or returning to ourselves, we invest ourselves in that which is more than and beyond what's-there. We move from what is to what matters, from conserving to creating, from indicative to imperative. The ultimate goal of *human* pursuits is *"intentionality* directed toward *fulfillment."*

All is usable in our human becoming. Everything is related and relatable.* The near shore and the far shore are two views of one Reality. The sea dragon and the ship are two aspects of one process. And since everything holds together, we, too, can hold together, for there *is* wholeness—Oneness—All.

References

Without endless footnotes I would be unable to convey the breadth of my indebtedness to others. To list these, however, would interrupt the flow of what I am saying. So, I live with the sacrifice of scholarly nuances and accountability for the sake of getting *my* concerns across.

What references I do have are indicated by pages. This eliminates footnote numbers which could prove distracting in ordinary reading. Wherever a specific reference appears in the text, I have referred to its source for the reader who wants such information immediately. Occasionally a special note is added for a more technical discussion. This is shown by an * in the text.

ONE	*What I Am About*
pp. 18-19	Campbell, 1949, 388-90.
p. 19	Dumoulin, 1969, 41, 76; Kapleau, 1967, 335, 345; Suzuki, 1961, 298; Okudaira, 1962, 100, 101, 122, 139.
p. 28	Reps, 1961, 31-32.
p. 28	Everything I say is predicated on what the German philosopher Fichte (1956, 79) called the accompanying "I" conciousness. That is, every third-person statement, such as, "man is a mess" or "life is meaningful," looks and sounds like an objective statement. Actually, all statements —even ones like "the temperature reading is . . ."—depend finally upon the first person statement, "I am of the opinion that . . ."
TWO	*What Does Humanitas Mean?*
p. 29	Legge, 1891, II, 56.1, 100.
p. 30	Keller, 1961, 239.
p. 31	Polanyi, 1964, 87-88.

p. 31	Quoted in Kepler, 1948, 1969.
p. 31	Bretall, 1951, 354.
pp. 33-34	Saarinen, 1959.
p. 34	Kuh, 1965, 28, 30.
p. 35	Frankl, 1963.
p. 36	David Diop quoted in Fanon, 1968, 136.
p. 36	Clark, 1967, 6, 1, 33-34.
pp. 38-39	Saarinen, 1959.
p. 40	Themis, 1969.
pp. 40-42	*New York Times News of the Week in Review*, Sept. 12, 1971, E8; *Democrat and Chronicle*, Rochester, N.Y., Sept. 12, 1971, 2A; Sept. 13, 1971, 2A; *Newsweek*, Sept. 27, 1971, 31.

THREE	*What Do Humans Desire?*
p. 45	Polanyi, 1969, 15-16.
p. 45	Gendlin, 1962, 15, 27-29, 230, 33, 5.
pp. 45-48	Flavell, 1963, 47-48.
p. 46	Harlow, *et al.*, 1950; Harlow, 1953; Berelson and Steiner, 1964, 249; White, 1959.
p. 46-47	Berlyne, 1958*a*, 1958*b*; Berelson and Steiner, 1964, 245-46.
p. 48	Toffler, 1970, 269, 63.
p. 49	Reich, 1971, 2-3, 176.
p. 49	Sanders, 1970.
p. 50	Polanyi, 1964, 300; Maslow, 1969.
pp. 50-51	For a more thorough exposition of these levels of formal learning see Bruner, 1961, 1965, 1966.
pp. 52-53	F. H. Allport, 1965, 22, 39.
p. 54	Murray, 1962; Maslow, 1954; Sullivan, 1953; Glasser, 1972; Harlow, 1953; White, 1959; Buhler, 1959; Berelson and Steiner 1964, 258.
pp. 54-55	Cited in McClelland, 1955, 135.
p. 55	Packard, 1957, 14, 13, 37.
p. 55	Reich, 1971, 4.
p. 55	Maslow; this diagram first appeared in Maslow's article "Toward a Humanistic Biology," *American Psychologist*, 24 (August, 1969), 724-35; and is used by permission of the journal and of Mrs. Maslow.
p. 56	Quoted in Berelson and Steiner, 1964, 238.
p. 56	Leary, 1957, 117-18.
p. 57	Fromm, 1968, 65-70; 1947.
p. 57	Quoted in Berelson and Steiner, 1964, 238.
pp. 58-59	Clark, 1967, 63.
p. 59	Rokeach, 1960, 400; Auden, 1947, 38.
p. 59	Maslow, 1969.

FOUR	*Where Do We Look?*
p. 61	Wickes, 1968, 120-21.
pp. 61-62	Maslow, 1962, 43, 45, 46.

REFERENCES

p. 62   I am indebted to Dr. Caroline Hoffberg for insight into the
           card and its interpretation.
p. 64   Jourard, 1964, 16.
p. 65   Bonhoeffer, 1962, 28.
p. 65   Progoff, 1959, 13.
p. 66   Quoted in Kelsey, 1968, 63-64; night, 1952, 40.
p. 66   Freud, 1960, 71.
p. 67   Cleaver, 1968, 13-16.
p. 68   Freud, 1960, 31, 28, 36, 20.
p. 68   Tauber and Green, 1959, 65.
p. 69   Jung, 1969.
p. 69   Campbell, 1960, 350.
p. 70   Puech, *et al.*, 1959, 3.
pp. 70-71 Calvin, 1962, 37.
p. 71   Kierkegaard, 1954, 211; Lowrie, 1951, 203.
p. 71   Quoted in Progoff, 1959, 34.
pp. 71-72 Tillich, 1968, 63, 111-12.
p. 72   G. Allport, 1955.
p. 72   Exodus 23:9, Leviticus 19:33-34; Philemon 15-16; Matthew
           25:31-46.
p. 72   May, 1953.
pp. 79-80 cf. Kierkegaard, 1954, 162, for the source of the paraphrase.

FIVE   *Where Are You?*
pp. 81-82 Schutz, 1967, 107-14.
p. 83   Murphy, 1958, 23.
p. 83   Kapleau, 1967, 213.
pp. 83-84 Perls, 1969, 70-71; Fagan and Shepherd, 1971, 28-29.
p. 85   Perls, *et al.*, 1951, 75.
p. 85   Watts, 1957, 28.
p. 85   Kapleau, 1967, 10.
pp. 86-89 Zevi, 1957, 87, 82, 107, 114, 115, 242.
pp. 90-91 Perls, 1969, 49; Fagan and Shepherd, 1971, 25.
p. 91   Perls, *et al.*, 1951, 40.
p. 91   Watts, 1957, 19-20.
p. 92   Fagan and Shepherd, 1971, 143.
pp. 93-94 Perls, *et. al.*, 1951, 43, 45, 55, 45-46.
p. 95   *Ibid.*, 47.
p. 96   Reps, 1961, 160.
pp. 96-97 Combs and Snygg, 1959, 25.
pp. 97-98 Solley and Murphy, 1960, 263-64.
p. 99   Reps, 1961, 166, #36.

SIX   *Some Human Tools*
p. 100   Rogers, 1961, 26.
p. 101   Cassirer, cited in Jacobi, 1959, 80.
p. 101   Jacobi, 1959, 75.
p. 101   Whyte, 1962, 59.
p. 101   Burling, 153, 95.
pp. 101-2 Jung, 1960*a*, 346; original italics omitted.

p. 102   Holt, 1964.
pp. 102-3   Hackin, *et. al.*, 1963, 28.
p. 103   May, 1960; quoted in Jacobi, 1959, 77-78.
pp. 104-5   Eliade, 1959, 98-99.
p. 105   Jacobi, 1959, 91. In writing of myths, Mark Schorer has concluded: "Myths are the instrument by which we continually struggle to make our existence intelligible to ourselves. A myth is a large controlling image that gives philosophical meaning to the facts of ordinary life; that is, which has organizing value for experience." Quoted in Watts, 1969, 3. Grimal, 1965, 9.
p. 105   Quoted in Nims, 1963, 62.
p. 106   Polanyi, 1964; Giedion, 1967, 5-6.
p. 106   Watts, 1969, 4-5.
p. 106   Campbell, 1965, 518-23.
p. 107   Eliade, 1967b, 14.
p. 108   MacKenzie, 1965, 26-61; Grunebaum and Caillois, 1966.
p. 108   Quoted in Kelsey, 1968, 276, 8, 142-44.
pp. 108-9   MacKenzie, 1965, 107.
p. 109   Whyte, 1962, 70. Recent experimental research on sleeping and dreaming (MacKenzie, 1965, 321; Jones, 1970, 24-42; Bremer, 1966; Dement, 1966) has clearly demonstrated how crucial the sheer fact of being able to dream is. Physical and psychic functioning can be seriously impaired if a person is not allowed to dream. Dreaming presents a distinct and biologically determined rhythm, as necessary and as natural as breathing. It is related to the cycle of sleep and wakefulness observed even in small infants. While the imagery is a psychological characteristic, the dream is accompanied and identifiable by the electroencephalographic (EEG) tracings of electric impulses within the brain, the onset of rapid eye movement (REM), increased blood pressure, decreased muscle tonus, increased variability in arousal thresholds, and in males a cycle of penile erection.

In assessing "the new psychology of dreaming," Jones, (1970, 24-31) reexamines the evidence that distinguishes sleep from wakefulness.

The findings clearly differentiate four stages of sleep, with the first one, and that closest to wakefulness, being the rapid eye movement (REM) stage in which we ordinarily dream. This period is activated by "a noncortical system which is one of the lowest on the phylogenetic scale—the pontile-limbic system. It is a basic feature of mammalian life, all mammals so far studied showing clear evidence of it, and all nonmammals so far studied showing little or no evidence of it." It rhythmically occurs about every hour and a half through the night, lasting increasingly longer with each occurrence. It has been variously called the paradoxical phase of sleep, activated sleep, dreaming sleep, the D-state, or REM sleep.

REFERENCES

In the three nonrapid eye movement (NREM) stages, there was originally thought to be no discernible mental activity and certainly no dreaming. More careful research design and interpretation have uncovered the fact that the "mind" never "rests." Contrary to generally accepted theory, it is always active!

In the period from relaxed wakefulness to unequivocal sleep, four successive stages have been observed. When examined electroencephalographically, sleep onset shows a pattern of (alpha) a-EEG waking REMs, a-EEG with slow eye movement (SEM), stage one descending, and stage two descending. When looked at psychologically, sleep onset shows a pattern of three successive ego states. Initially, there is the relatively intact ego (I), followed in descending stage one by a relatively destructuralized ego state (D), and during descending stage two, because of the progressive reappearance of what Freud called "secondary process" pattern content, a relatively restructuralized ego (R).

Investigators now divide ego function into two parts. On the one hand, the ego maintains secondary process, on the other, it maintains contact with the external world. Thus, as a person withdraws into sleep there is the loss of contact with outer reality, accompanied by regressive and disorganized psychic activity or what Freud called "primary process." Once the withdrawal has been completed, there is the paradoxical return to nonregressive content even though there is a complete loss of contact with reality. The psychological sequence, then, is I-D-R.

During our waking phase the cognitive process that we associate with reason is dominant. This constitutes secondary process. In stages two through four of sleep (NREM) secondary process again appears. Jones labels this "thinking sleep." In the intermediate dimension between the most outer and the most inner dimensions lies Freud's primary process which Jones calls "dreaming sleep." Thus, dreams include the psychological qualities of experience typical both of wakefulness and of thinking sleep, yet with their own idiosyncratic imprint.

p. 109	Fagan and Shepherd, 1971, 204.
p. 110	Foulkes, 1969, 129; Tauber and Green, 1959, 171; Jung, 1966, 330; Jones, 1970, 187.
p. 110	Westman, 1961, 63-64; Jung, 1964, 53.
pp. 110-11	Quoted in Progoff, 1970, 186-88, 195.
p. 111	Dement, 1966, 87-93.
pp. 111-12	Stewart, 1969.
p. 112	Fagan and Shepherd, 1971, 212; also see Perls, 1969, 67-71 for a more extended discussion.
pp. 112-13	Hall, 1959, 16-27; Jaffé, 1964, 264.
p. 113	Perls, 1969, 101-6.

pp. 113-14   Hall, 1959; MacKenzie, 1965, 236.
p. 115   Jung, 1966, 153.
p. 115   May, 1960, 45.
p. 116   Jung, 1964, 102.

SEVEN   *More Focused Insights*
pp. 117-18   V. E. Devadutt, personal communication; Jaffé, 1964, 240-45; De Laszlo, 1958, 319; Jung, 1960a, 343, 365; Von Franz, 1964, 307; Hughes, 1968, 88; Sze, 1956, I, 16; Giedion, 1967, 873; Perry, 1970, vii-viii; Naranjo and Ornstein, 1971, 56, 19.
p. 118   Hughes, 1968, 88, 98, 94-95; Jaffé, 1964, 246-49.
pp. 118-19   Jung, 1960a, 367-68; Adler, 1961, 95.
pp. 119-20   Tillich, 1963, 111, 67.
p. 120   Stoudt, 1968, 112.
p. 120   Buckley, 1967, 25-26.
pp. 122-24   Wain, 1959.
p. 124   Quoted in Maritain, 1953, 19; Tillich, 1963, 232-35.
p. 124   Tillich, 1952, 81.
pp. 124-27   Sze, 1956, II, 20, 55, 101.
p. 127   Tillich, 1963, 268.
p. 128   Buckley, 1967, 25-26.
p. 129   Giedion, 1964, 522, 438-39, 436-37, 522; Schachtel, 1966, 37.
p. 129   Kuh, 1969, 13-14.
p. 130   Mayer and Harris, 1970, 50.
p. 130   May, 1969, 182, 211-12, 218.
p. 131   Tillich, 1952, 81.
pp. 131-32   Scully, 1962, 7, 44-46, 63-64.
p. 133   Tillich, 1963, 41-44.
p. 133   Grimal, 1965, 275.
p. 133   Neumann, 1962, 8; Sze, 1956, I, 27.
pp. 133-34   Arnheim, 1966, 234; originally published by the University of California Press; reprinted by permission of The Regents of the University of California.

EIGHT   *What Makes Humans Human?*
p. 138   Loomis, 1960.
p. 138   Jung, 1962, 311; Long, 1963, 220.
pp. 139-40   Guthrie, 1951, 73-87, 145-82, 183-204.
pp. 140-42   Watts, 1969, 70-102; Henderson and Oakes, 1971, 84-89.
pp. 142-43   Perry, 1970, 75-80; Campbell, 1962, 107, 111; Campbell, 1965, 74-87; Eliade, 1967a, 98-108.
p. 144   Campbell, 1965, 105; Anderson, 1957, 169; Westman, 1961, 81-82.
p. 145   We do not have in these accounts, Von Rad (1961, 72-73) maintains, "a rubble heap of individual recensions but . . . a whole with a consistent train of thought."
p. 145   Von Rad, 1961, 48-49.

p. 145   Anderson (1967, 38): "From the Exodus, Israel looked back to the creation, confessing that the God who was active at the beginning of her history was likewise active at the beginning of the world's history."

pp. 145-46   Cassirer (1955, 94-104) has shown that among almost every people, "the process of creation merges with the dawning of the light." The real "object" of creation mythology, consequently, may be regarded as the dawning of consciousness, showing itself as the bursting forth of light out of the darkness of unconsciousness. With the victory of light came "the origin of the world and the world order."

With the coming of light the whole pattern of culture followed. Religious, juridical, economic, social, and political life grew precise and differentiated. Every phenomenon of the marked-off, the bounded, the limited, the designated evolved from the sacral ordering of space. As the cosmos was divided by the lines from east to west and north to south, so was the earth divided. The state, the community, the individual all acquired a definite space, an individuality, a specified existence. From the arrangement of the Roman house, to the layout of Roman military camps, to the spatial symbolism of the Christian church, to the construction of cities, to the building of the world, we find reflected the original intuitive meaning of space. Beginning with the opposition between light and dark, the world is classified and arranged in a constant pattern of opposites and contrasts (Neumann, 1962, 104, 6, 107-8).

p. 146   Von Rad, 1961, 75.

p. 146   Kierkegaard, 1944, 26-27.

p. 147   Neumann, 1962, 15; Neumann, 1955; MacKenzie, 1965, 204.

p. 148   Tillich, 1957, 38.

p. 148   "In his innocence," Kierkegaard (1944, 37-39) suggested, "man is not determined as spirit but is soulishly determined in immediate unity with his natural condition. Spirit is dreaming in man." In such a state, "man is not merely an animal, for if at any time of his life he was merely an animal, he would never become a man. So then the spirit is present, but in a state of immediacy, a dream state."

p. 149   Kierkegaard, 1954, 182-207.

p. 150   Von Rad (1961, 78-79, 80-81), quoting Westman, observes that " 'language itself is an originating, creative, interpretative something, in which arrangement, rearrangement, and regulation must properly occur.' " Man reaches into the confusion of the world; emphasizing, depreciating, assembling, " 'he brings together what belongs together. That which lies piled up in the confusion of the world does not at the start possess its own form; but rather, what is here distinguished with discrimination receives its own form only as it comes together in the analysis.' . . . This naming is thus both an act of copying and an act of appropriative ordering, by which [humanitas] intellectually objectifies the creatures for [itself]."

p. 150   Westman, 1961, 83.
pp. 150-51   Ogden, 1967.
p. 151   Cox, 1969, 12.
p. 151   "Knowledge of good and evil," Von Rad (1961, 79) states, "means . . . omniscience in the widest sense of the word . . . never . . . purely intellectual knowing, but rather an 'experiencing,' a 'becoming acquainted with.' "
pp. 151-52   Von Rad, 1961, 85.
p. 152   Harrelson (1964, 48) sees the symbol and awareness of nakedness as touching upon "a good deal more than the dawn of self-consciousness." For him, nakedness shows up "the broken relationship which obtains between man and woman when the two of them have overstepped the bounds appointed by God." Not only do they stand over against each other, a gulf separating those who are "one flesh" (Gen. 2:24), but even more that separation now obtains between them and God himself.
p. 152   Gendlin, 1962, 15, 230.
p. 152   Quoted in May, 1950, 48.
p. 152   Gendlin (1962, 5) insists that "meaning is *formed* in the interaction of experiencing and something that functions symbolically. Feeling without symbolization is blind; symbolization without feeling is empty." Or again, as Ricoeur (1965, 17) puts it: "The understanding without intuition is empty, intuition without concepts is blind."
p. 153   Ricoeur, 1965, 32, 60; Polanyi, 1964
p. 153   Jones, 1970, 66.
p. 154   Von Rad, 1961, 87.
p. 155   Loomis, 1960, 17.
p. 156   Westman, 1961, 83.
p. 156   Buber, 1965, 110-20.
p. 157   Harrelson, 1964, 47.
p. 157   Jung, 1926.
pp. 157-58   Neumann, 1962, 10-11; 1955, 114-15.
p. 158   Henderson and Oakes, 1971, 134.
p. 158   Jaffé, 1964, 246; Jung quoted in Jacobi, 1959, 129.
p. 158   Kierkegaard, 1944, 3, 5, 92, 40; also see May, 1950, 37.

NINE   *What Are We Up Against?*
pp. 163-64   Maslow, 1971, 280-95.
p. 164   Rowley, 1970, 16, 31, 39.
p. 164   Frankl, 1966; 1956, xvii.
p. 165   Blakney, 1957, 17.
p. 166   Maslow, 1971, 31.
p. 166   Kierkegaard, 1944, 28-31, 56-57, 47.
pp. 167-69   Tillich, 1957, 51-68.

REFERENCES

pp. 167-68   Cox, 1969, xiv-xviii.
p. 170   Macquarrie, 1965, 87.
p. 170   Laing, 1967, 14.
p. 172   MacKenzie, 1965, 306.
p. 172   G. Allport (1955) distinguished two main philosophical traditions in understanding the human predicament (also see Rychlak, 1968; Coan, 1968).

On the one side are those who view humanitas in the Lockean tradition, as a blank tablet, a passive and reactive organism, that has little or nothing intrinsically enabling it to orient, organize, initiate, and evaluate. *The ultimate locus of what matters lies outside.* The position can be traced through associationism, environmentalism, behaviorism, positivism, and operationism. Those who hold such a view tend to press for external authority and control.

On the other side are those who view humanitas in the Leibnizian tradition as a purposive active organism in which the substance of reality resides completely. *The ultimate locus of what matters lies inside.* The position can be found in introspectionism, phenomenology, existentialism, and gestalt psychology. Those who hold such a view tend to press for internal authority and autonomy.

In the phenomenological approach, highlighting experience, the focus is precept-oriented: unity and immediacy, wholism and relationism, revelation, perception, the dialectic. In the psychophysiological approach, highlighting the observable, the focus is object-oriented: elementalism and objectivism, reason, sensation, the demonstrative. As William H. Ittleson (1962, 671) concluded from this: "the *reductio ad absurdum* of the first view is reached by the solopsist, who believes that there is nothing outside of his own head; of the latter view by the behaviorist, who believes that there is nothing inside of his."

p. 173   Perls, *et al.*, 1951; Perls, 1969, 8, 125-27.
p. 174   Henderson and Oakes, 1971, 95-99.
p. 175   Whyte, 1962, 13; italics in original.
p. 175   Blakney, 1957, 240.
p. 175   Gombrich, 1969, 395.

TEN   *A Leap into Life*
p. 178   The inner debate, on the surface level, is really Claire working with herself. On a deeper level it represents *our* working together, with her undefended intuition utilizing me as a therapist to strengthen and clarify itself against her entrenched intellect.

ELEVEN   *Response*
p. 195   Cusa, 1928, 44, 46-47.
pp. 196-97   Kessel, 1964, 182.

p. 198   Selye, 1956, 101; May, 1969, 170.
p. 198   Quoted in Watts, 1957, 115.
pp. 198-99   Neumann, 1962, 7; Kapleau, 1967, 111; Chang, 1970, 229.
p. 199   Laing, 1967, 33.
pp. 199-200   Jung, 1962, 50; 1960b, 82; 1964, 70.
pp. 200-201   Escher, 1971; Henderson and Oakes, 1971, 43.
p. 201   Jung, 1964, 206, 207, 125, 238.
p. 201   Buttrick, 1962, III, 481-82; Westman, 1961, 121.
p. 201   May, 1969, 123.
p. 202   Zimmer, 1955, 64-65; Adler, 1961, 242; Johnston, 1971, 86.
p. 202   Sze, 1956, I, 82-83.
p. 202   Kerényi, 1959.
pp. 202-3   Jacobi, 1959, 146ff; Henderson and Oakes, 1971, 40.
p. 203   Boehme, 1958, xxvi-xxvii.
p. 203   Gen. 1:28; Job 40:15-24; 41:1-34; I Enoch 60:7-9; II
              Baruch 29:3-4; also see Anderson, 1967, 40-41.
pp. 203-4   Cusa, 1928, 53.
p. 204   Whyte, 1962, 182-83.
p. 204   Jung, 1964, 119.
pp. 207-8   May, 1969, 78-88, 156, 176.
p. 208   Jung, 1968, 16.
p. 208   Quoted in Schachtel, 1966, 91.
pp. 208-9   Jung, 1962, 187; May, 1969, 177.
p. 209   Quoted in Friedman, 1960, 61.
p. 209   Cusa, 1928, 54-55.
pp. 209-10   Gombrich, 1969, 5.
p. 210   Bugental, 1965, 55.
p. 210   Stewart, 1969, 162-63.
pp. 210-11   Boehme, 1958, 38-39.
p. 211   May, 1969, 134.
p. 211   Quoted in Stoudt, 1968, 58; Angyal, 1965, 267, 111.
p. 211   Jung, 1960a, 385.
p. 211   Merton, 1967, 27.

TWELVE   Expectation
p. 212   Kuh, 1965, 16, 11-15.
pp. 214-16   Barron, 1968, 180-99. An attitude questionnaire was de-
              veloped to test personality differences between independents
              and yielders. The samples included undergraduate students
              in Pennsylvania colleges and Ph.D. students in Berkeley,
              California.
p. 217   Combs and Snygg, 1959, 24.
p. 217   Giedion, 1967, 852-53, 435-36.
pp. 217-18   Gardner, 1959, 17-18.
p. 218   Belfrage, 1966, 134.
p. 219   Perls, et al., 1951.
p. 219   Barron, 1968, 1-6.
pp. 219-20   Leary, 1957, 304-40.
p. 220   The Rorschack inkblot test provides a powerful tool for
              assessing the health or unhealth of thought and action. The

REFERENCES

instrument taps thought by the testee's response to and use
of form. Emotion is tapped by the response to and use of
color. Form is constructive insofar as it gives order and
structure to the uncertain inkblots. Form becomes destructive whenever it takes on too much prominence. That is,
when it grows too rigid, too schematic, or too stereotyped.
Such destructiveness appears when the testee's responses do
"not allow for flexibility, fluctuation and for openness to
the charm, richness, and impact of color" (Schachtel, 1966,
87).

p. 221	Selye, 1956, 246.
pp. 221-22	Cusa, 1928, 61.
p. 222	Chang, 1970, 202-3.
pp. 222-23	Eliade, 1967b, 244-45.
p. 223	Howe, 1964.
p. 223	Naranjo and Ornstein, 1971, 67; Kapleau, 1967, 67.
p. 223	Sze, 1956, I, 9.
p. 224	Jung, 1964, 61.

p. 224   To be a good scientist, apparently, one has to be a careful
conservative *and* a wild radical, simultaneously. For "the
hallmark of the creative enterprise," contends Macworth
(1965), "is that there should be effective surprise because
only minds with structured expectancies and interests can
distinguish real trends from trivial improbabilities."

p. 224   Duncombe, 1969.

p. 224   At last we are seeing a convergence of the empirical-experi-
mental approach of the West and the empirical-experiental
approach of the East (Naranjo and Ornstein, 1971, 211-
32). Research in alpha rhythms in the brain is confirming
the necessary collaboration of these two modes of knowledge. It has been found that alpha rhythms taken from
electrodes at the rear of the head are different from those
at the front or the side of the head. To complicate matters
more, waves from the right and left hemispheres are not
always identical. What appears to be the case is that the
two hemispheres function differently. The left hemisphere
seems the source of the verbal, the rational, and the analytical. The right hemisphere seems the source of the nonverbal,
the subjective, and the emotional.

p. 225	Reps, 1961, 166, #37.
p. 225	Norton, 1968, Blake, plate 3.
p. 226	Freud, 1958, 55-62.
p. 227	Chang, 1970, 71-72, 224.
pp. 227-28	Blakney, 1957, 246, 247, 329.
p. 228	Fromm, 1947, 41; Buhler, 1969.

p. 228   Looking back on his twelve years of work on *The Masks of
God*, Campbell (1970a, xx) reports the main result: confirmation of "the unity of the race of man, not only in its
biology but also in its spiritual history." The same motifs
keep reappearing in new relationships.

239

Bibliography

Adler, Gerhard. *The Living Symbol: A Case Study in the Process of Individuation.* New York: Pantheon Books, Bollingen Series, Vol. 63, 1961.

Allport, Floyd H. *Theories of Perception and the Concept of Structure: A Review and Critical Analysis with an Introduction to a Dynamic-Structural Theory of Behavior.* New York: John Wiley & Sons, 1955.

Allport, Gordon W. *Becoming: Basic Considerations for a Psychology of Personality.* New Haven: Yale University Press, 1955.

Anderson, Bernard. *Creation Versus Chaos: The Reinterpretation of Mythical Symbolism in the Bible.* New York: Association Press, 1967.

_____. *Understanding the Old Testament.* Englewood Cliffs, N.J.: Prentice-Hall, 1957. 2nd ed. 1967.

Angyal, Andras. *Neurosis and Treatment: A Holistic Theory.* Edited by E. Hanfmann and R. M. Jones. New York: John Wiley & Sons, 1965.

Arnheim, Rudolph. *Toward a Psychology of Art: Collected Essays.* Los Angeles: University of California Press, 1966.

Auden, W. H. *The Age of Anxiety.* New York: Random House, 1947.

Barron, Frank. *Creativity and Personal Freedom.* Rev. ed. Princeton: D. Van Nostrand, 1968.

Belfrage, Sally. *Freedom Summer.* Greenwich, Conn.: Fawcett Publications, [1965] 1966.

Berelson, Bernard, and Steiner, Gary A. *Human Behavior: An Inventory of Scientific Findings.* New York: Harcourt, Brace & World, 1964.

BIBLIOGRAPHY

Berlyne, Daniel E., "The Influence of Complexity and Novelty in Visual Figures on Orienting Responses," *Journal Experimental Psychology* 55(1958, *a*), 289-96.

_____. "The Influence of the Albedo and Complexity of Stimuli on Visual Fixation in the Human Infant," *British Journal of Psychology* 49(1958, *b*), 315-18.

Blakney, Raymond B., Ed. *Meister Eckhart: A Modern Translation.* New York: Harper Torchbooks, 1957.

Boehme, Jacob. *Six Theosophic Points and Other Writings.* With an introductory essay "Unground and Freedom" by Nicholas Berdyeav. Ann Arbor: University of Michigan Press, 1958.

Bonhoeffer, Dietrich. *Letters and Papers From Prison.* Edited by Eberhard Bethge. Translated by Reginald H. Fuller. New York: The Macmillan Company, 1962.

Bremer, Frederic. "The Neurophysiological Problem of Sleep." In G. E. Von Grunebaum and R. Caillois, Eds. *The Dream and Human Societies.* Pp. 53-75.

Bretall, Robert, Ed. *A Kierkegaard Anthology.* Princeton: Princeton University Press, 1951.

Bruner, Jerome S. *On Knowing: Essays for the Left Hand.* Cambridge, Mass.: Belknap Press, [1962] 1963.

_____. *The Process of Education.* Cambridge, Mass.: Harvard University Press, 1961.

_____. *Toward a Theory of Instruction.* Cambridge, Mass.: Belknap Press, 1966.

_____. The Growth of Mind. *American Psychologist* 20 (Dec., 1965), 1007-17.

Buber, Martin. *The Knowledge of Man: Selected Essays.* Edited with an introductory essay by Maurice Friedman. Translated by Maurice Friedman and Ronald Gregor Smith. New York: Harper Torchbooks, [1965].

Buckley, Walter F. *Sociology and Modern Systems Theory.* Englewood Cliffs, N.J.: Prentice-Hall, 1967.

Bungental, J. F. T. *The Search for Authenticity: An Existential-Analytic Approach to Psychotherapy.* New York: Holt, Rinehart & Winston, 1965.

Buhler, Charlotte. "Humanistic Psychology as an Educational Program." *American Psychologist* 24 (Aug., 1969), 736-42.

_____. "Theoretical Observations About Life's Basic Tendencies." *American Journal of Psychotherapy* 13 (1959), 561-81.

Burling, Judith, and Burling, Arthur H. *Chinese Art.* New York: Bonanza Books, [1953].

Buttrick, George H., Ed. *The Interpreter's Dictionary of the Bible.* 4 vols. Nashville: Abingdon Press, 1962.

Calvin, John. *Institutes on the Christian Religion*, Vol. 1. Translated by Henry Beveridge. Grand Rapids, Michigan: Eerdmans Publishing Co., 1962.

Campbell, Joseph. *The Hero with a Thousand Faces*. Princeton: Princeton University Press, Bollingen Books, Vol. 17, [1949] 1965.

————. *The Masks of God: Creative Mythology*, Vol. 4. New York: Viking Press, [1968] 1970(a).

————. *The Masks of God: Occidental Mythology*, Vol. 3. New York: Sheed & Ward, 1965.

————. *The Masks of God: Oriental Mythology*, Vol. 2, New York: Viking Press, 1962.

————. *The Masks of God: Primitive Mythology*, Vol. 1. New York: Sheed & Ward, 1960.

————, Ed. *Myths, Dreams and Religion*. New York: E. P. Dutton, 1970(b).

Cassirer, Ernst. *The Philosophy of Symbolic Forms*, Vol. 2. *Mythical Forms*. Translated by Ralph Manheim. New Haven: Yale University Press, 1955.

Chang, Garma C. C. *The Practice of Zen*. New York: Harper Perennia Library, 1970.

Clark, Kenneth B. *Dark Ghetto: Dilemma of Social Power*. Foreword by Gunnar Myrdal. New York: Harper Torchbooks, [1965] 1967.

Cleaver, Eldridge. *Soul on Ice*. Introduction by Maxwell Geismer. New York: Delta Books, 1968.

Coan, Richard W. "Dimensions of Psychological Theory." *American Psychologist* 23 (Oct., 1968), 715-22.

Combs, Arthur W., and Snygg, Donald. *Individual Behavior: A Perceptual Approach to Behavior*. Rev. ed. New York: Harper & Brothers, 1959.

Cox, Harvey. *On Not Leaving It to the Snake*. New York: Macmillan Paperbacks, [1968] 1969.

Cusa, Nicholas. *The Vision of God*. Translated by Emma Gurney Salter. Introduction by Evelyn Underhill. New York: E. P. Dutton, 1928.

De Laszlo, Violet S., Ed. *Psyche and Symbol: A Selection from the Writings of C. G. Jung*. Garden City, N.Y.: Doubleday Anchor Books, 1958.

Dement, William C. "The Psychophysiology of Dreaming." In G. E. Von Grunebaum and R. Caillois, Eds. *The Dream and Human Societies*. Pp. 77-107.

Dollard, John. *Caste and Class in a Southern Town*. 2nd ed. New York: Harper & Brothers, 1949.

Dumoulin, Heinrich. *A History of Zen Buddhism*. Translated by

BIBLIOGRAPHY

Paul Peachey. Boston: Beacon Press, [1963] 1969.

Duncombe, David C. *The Shape of the Christian Life.* Nashville: Abingdon Press, 1969.

Eliade, Mircea. *From Primitives to Zen: A Thematic Sourcebook of the History of Religions.* New York: Harper & Row, 1967(a).
————. "Methodological Remarks on the Study of Religious Symbolism." In M. Eliade and J. M. Kitagawa, Eds. *History of Religions: Essays in Methodology.* Chicago: University of Chicago Press, 1959.
————. *Myths, Dreams, and Mysteries: The Encounter Between Contemporary Faiths and Archaic Realities.* Translated by Philip Mairet. New York: Harper Torchbooks, 1967(b).

Escher, M. C. *The Graphic Works of M. C. Escher.* Translated from the Dutch by J. E. Brigham. Rev. ed. New York: Ballantine Books, 1971. I am indebted to Jeffrey Dimmit for bringing this work to my attention.

Fagan, Joen, and Shepherd, Irma Lee, Eds. *Gestalt Therapy Now: Theory, Techniques, Applications.* New York: Harper Colophon Books, [1970] 1971.

Fanon, Frantz. *Black Skin, White Mask.* Translated by Charles Lam Markmann. New York: Grove Press, [1967] 1968.

Fichte, J. G. *The Vocation of Man.* Edited by R. M. Chisholm. Indianapolis: Liberal Arts Press, 1956.

Flavell, John H. *The Developmental Psychology of Jean Piaget.* With a Foreword by Jean Piaget. Princeton: D. Van Nostrand, 1963.

Foulkes, David. "Theories of Dream Formation and Recent Studies of Sleep Consciousness." In C. T. Tart, Ed. *Altered States of Consciousness.* Pp. 117-31.

Frankl, Viktor E. *The Doctor and The Soul: An Introduction to Logotherapy.* New York: Alfred A. Knopf, 1956.
————. *Man's Search for Meaning: An Introduction to Logotherapy.* New York: Washington Square Press, 1963.
————. "Self-Transcendence as a Human Phenomenon." *Journal of Humanistic Psychology* (Fall, 1966), 97-106.

Freud, Sigmund. *The Ego and the Id.* Translated by Joan Riviere. Revised and newly edited by James Strachey. New York: W. W. Norton & Co., 1960.
————. *On Creativity and the Unconscious.* Selected with Introduction and Annotations by Benjamin Nelson. New York: Harper Torchbooks, 1958.

Friedman, Maurice S. *Martin Buber: The Life of Dialogue.* New York: Harper Torchbooks, 1960.

Fromm, Erich. *Man for Himself*: *An Inquiry into the Psychology of Ethics*. New York: Rinehart, 1947.
_____. *The Revolution of Hope*: *Toward a Humanized Technology*. New York: Bantam Books, [1968].

Gardner, Helen. *Art Through the Ages*. 4th edition revised under the editorship of Sumner McK. Crosby. New York: Harcourt, Brace & Co., 1959.
Gendlin, Eugene T. *Experiencing and the Creation of Meaning*. *A Philosophical and Psychological Approach to the Subjective*. Glencoe, Ill.: The Free Press, 1962.
Giedion, Sigfried. *The Eternal Present: The Beginnings of Architecture*. A contribution on Consistency and Change. New York: Pantheon Books, Bollingen Series, Vol. 35, 1964.
_____. *Space, Time and Architecture: The Growth of a New Tradition*. 5th ed., rev. Cambridge, Mass.: Harvard University Press, 1967.
Glasser, William. *The Identity Society*. New York: Harper & Row, 1972.
Gombrich, E. H. *Art and Illusion: A Study in the Psychology of Pictorial Representation*. Princeton: Princeton University Press, Bollingen Series, Vol. 35, part 5, [1961] 1969.
Grimal, Pierre, Ed. *Larousse World Mythology*. New York: G. P. Putnam's Sons, 1965.
Grunebaum, G. E. Von, and Callois R., eds. *The Dream and Human Societies*. Berkeley: University of California, 1966.
Guthrie, W. K. C. *The Greeks and Their Gods*. Boston: Beacon Press, [1951] 1968.

Hackin, J.; Huart, Clément; Linossier, Raymonde; DeWilman-Grabowska, H.; Marchal, Charles-Henri; Maspero, Henri; and Eliseev, Serge. *Asiatic Mythology*: A detailed description and explanation of the mythologies of all the great nations of Asia. Introduction by Paul-Louis Couchoud. New York: Thomas Y. Crowell, 1963.
Hall, Calvin S. *The Meaning of Dreams*. New York: Dell Books, [1953] 1959.
Harlow, Harry F. "Mice, Monkeys, Men and Motives." *Psychological Review* 60 (1953), 23-32.
Harlow, Harry F.; Harlow, Margaret K.; and Meyer, Donald R. "Learning Motivated by a Manipulation Drive." *Journal of Experimental Psychology* 40 (1950), 228-34.
Harrelson, Walter. *Interpreting the Old Testament*. New York: Holt, Rinehart and Winston, 1964.
Henderson, Joseph L., and Oakes, Maud. *The Wisdom of the*

BIBLIOGRAPHY

Serpent: The Myths of Death, Rebirth and Resurrection. New York: P. F. Collier, [1964] 1971.

Holt, Robert R. "Imagery: The Return of the Ostracized." *American Psychologist* 19 (1964), 254-64.

Howe, Reuel. "The Nature of Pastoral Supervision." Address at Fall Conference on Clinical Pastoral Education, Oct. 14, 1964.

Hughes, Robert. *Heaven and Hell in Western Art.* New York: Stein & Day, 1968.

Ittelson, William H. "Perception and Transactional Psychology." In Sigmund Koch, Ed., *Psychology: The Study of a Science.* Vol. 4. New York: McGraw-Hill Book Company, 1962, 660-704.

Jacobi, Jolande. *Complex/Archetype/Symbol in the Psychology of C. G. Jung.* Translated by Ralph Manheim. Princeton: Princeton University Press, Bollingen Series, Vol. 62, 1959.

Jaffé, Aniela. "Symbolism in the Visual Arts." In C. G. Jung, Ed., *Man and His Symbols.* Pp. 230-71.

Johnston, William. *Christian Zen.* New York: Harper & Row, 1971.

Jones, Richard M. *The New Psychology of Dreaming.* New York: Grune & Stratton, 1970.

Jourard, Sidney M. *The Transparent Self.* Princeton: D. Van Nostrand, 1964.

Jourard, Sidney M., and Overlade, Dan C. *Disclosing Man to Himself.* Princeton: D. Van Nostrand, 1968.

Jung, Carl G. *Aion: Researches into the Phenomenology of the Self.* Vol. 9, part 2. Translated by R. F. C. Hull. 2nd ed. Princeton: Princeton University Press, 1968.

―――――. *The Archetypes and the Collective Unconscious.* Vol. 9, part 1. Translated by R. F. C. Hull, 2nd ed. Princeton: Princeton University Press, 1969.

―――――. "Dream Symbols of the Individuation Process." In *Spiritual Disciplines*: Papers from the Eranos Yearbooks. Edited by Joseph Campbell. New York: Pantheon, Bollingen Series. Vol. 30, part 4. 1960(a), 341-423.

―――――, Ed. *Man and His Symbols.* London: Aldus Books in association with W. H. Allen, 1964.

―――――. *Memories, Dreams, Reflections.* Recorded and edited by Aniela Jaffé. Translated by Richard and Clara Winston. New York: Pantheon Books, 1963.

―――――. *Mysterium Coniunctionis: An Inquiry into the Separation and Synthesis of Psychic Opposites in Alchemy.* Translated by R. F. C. Hull. New York: Pantheon Books, Bollingen Series, Vol. 14, 1963.

―――――. *The Practice of Psychotherapy.* 2nd ed., rev. Translated by R. F. C. Hull. New York: Pantheon Books, Bollingen Series, Vol. 16, 1966.

――――. *Psychological Types: The Psychology of Individuation.* Translated by H. Godwin Baynes. New York: Harcourt, Brace & Co., 1926.

――――. *Symbols of Transformation: An Analysis of the Prelude to a Case of Schizophrenia.* Vol. 1. Translated by R. F. C. Hull. New York: Harper Torchbooks, 1962.

――――. *Two Essays on Analytical Psychology.* Translated by R. F. C. Hull. New York: Meridian Books, 1960(b).

Kapleau, Philip. *The Three Pillars of Zen: Teaching, Practice, Enlightenment.* Foreword by Huston Smith. Boston: Beacon Press, 1967.

Keller, Helen. *The Story of My Life.* New York: The Macmillan Co., 1961.

Kelsey, Morton T. *Dreams: The Dark Speech of the Spirit.* Garden City, N.Y.: Doubleday & Co., 1968.

Kepler, Thomas, Compiler. *The Fellowship of the Saints.* Nashville: Abingdon-Cokesbury Press, 1948.

Kerényi, C. *Asklepios: Archetypal Images of the Physician's Existence.* Translated by Ralph Manheim. New York: Pantheon Books, Bollingen Series, Vol. 65, part 3, 1959.

Kessel, Dmitri. *Splendors of Christendom.* Switzerland: Edita Lausanne, 1964.

Kierkegaard, Soren A. *The Concept of Dread.* Translated with Introduction and notes by Walter Lowrie. Princeton: Princeton University Press, 1944.

――――. *Fear and Trembling/The Sickness Unto Death.* Translated with Introduction and notes by Walter Lowrie. Garden City, N.Y.: Doubleday Anchor Books, [1954].

Knight, John. *The Story of My Psychoanalysis.* New York: Pocket Books, [1950] 1952.

Kuh, Katherine. *Break-up: The Core of Modern Art.* Greenwich, Conn.: New York Graphic Society, 1965.

――――. "The Mystifying Maya." *Saturday Review of Literature* (June 28, 1969), 11-17.

Laing, Ronald D. *The Politics of Experience.* New York: Pantheon Books, 1967.

Leary, Timothy. *Interpersonal Diagnosis of Personality.* New York: Ronald Press, 1957.

Legge, James, Tr. *The Sacred Books of China: The Texts of Taoism.* Vol. 39. Oxford: The Clarendon Press, 1891.

Long, Charles H. *Alpha: The Myths of Creation.* New York: George Braziller, 1963.

246

BIBLIOGRAPHY

Loomis, Earl J., Jr. *The Self in Pilgrimage*. New York: Harper & Brothers, 1960.
Lowrie, Walter. *A Short Life of Kierkegaard*. Princeton: Princeton University Press, [1942] 1951.

McClelland, David C., Ed. *Studies in Motivation*. New York: Appleton-Crofts, 1955.
MacKenzie, Norman. *Dreams and Dreaming*. New York: Vanguard Press, 1965.
Macquarrie, John. *An Existentialist Theology: A Comparison of Heidegger and Bultmann*. New York: Harper Torchbooks, 1965.
Macworth, Norman H. "Originality." *American Psychologist* 20 (1965), 51-66.
Maritain, Jacques. *Creative Intuition in Art and Poetry*. New York: Pantheon Books, Bollingen Series, Vol. 35, part 1, 1953.
Maslow, Abraham H. *The Farther Reaches of Human Nature*. New York: Viking Press, 1971.
————. *Motivation and Personality*. New York: Harper & Row, 1954.
————. "Toward a Humanistic Biology," *American Psychologist* 24 (Aug., 1969), 724-35.
————. *Toward a Psychology of Being*. Princeton: D. Van Nostrand, 1962.
May, Rollo. *Love and Will*. New York: W. W. Norton & Co., 1969.
————. *Man's Search for Himself*. New York: W. W. Norton & Co., 1953.
————. *The Meaning of Anxiety*. New York: Ronald Press, 1950.
————, Ed. *Symbolism in Religion and Literature*. With Introduction. New York: George Braziller, 1960.
Mayer, Jean, and Harris, T. George. "A Conversation: Affluence, the Fifth Horseman of the Apocalypse." *Psychology Today* 3 (Jan. 1970), 43-50, 58.
Merton, Thomas. *Mystics and Zen Masters*. New York: Delta, 1967.
Murphy, Gardner. *Human Potentialities*. New York: Basic Books, 1958.
Murray, Henry A. *Explorations in Personality*. New York: Science Editions, [1938] 1962.

Naranjo, Claudio, and Ornstein, Robert E. *On the Psychology of Meditation*. New York: Viking Press, 1971.
Neumann, Erich. *The Great Mother: An Analysis of the Archetype*. Translated by Ralph Manheim. Princeton: Princeton University Press, Bollingen Series, Vol. 47, [1955] 1972.
————. *The Origins and History of Consciousness*. Vol. 1. Trans-

lated by R. F. C. Hull. New York: Harper Torchbooks, 1962.
Nims, John Frederick. "The Classicism of Robert Frost," *Saturday Review*, Feb. 23, 1963, p. 62.
Norton Anthology of English Literature. Vol. 2. New York: W. W. Norton & Co., 1968. I am indebted to Mary Dean for this reference.

Ogden, C. K. *Opposition: A Linguistic and Psychological Analysis*. With Introduction by I. A. Richards. Bloomington: Indiana University Press, 1967.
Okudaira, Hideo. *Emaki: Japanese Picture Scrolls*. Tokyo: Charles E. Tuttle Co., 1962.
Orlinsky, Harry M., Ed. *Notes on the New Translation of the Torah*. Philadelphia: The Jewish Publication Society, 5730-1969. I am indebted to James Astman for this reference.

Packard, Vance. *The Hidden Persuaders*. New York: David McKay Co., 1957.
Perls, Frederick S. *Gestalt Therapy Verbatim*. Compiled and edited by John O. Stevens. Lafayette, Calif.: Real People's Press, 1969.
Perls, Frederick S.; Hefferline, Ralph F.; and Goodman, Paul. *Gestalt Therapy: Excitement and Growth in the Human Personality*. New York; Julian Press, [1951].
Perry, John Weir. *Lord of the Four Quarters: Myths of the Royal Father*. Foreword by Alan W. Watts. New York: George Braziller, [1965]1970.
Polanyi, Michael. *Personal Knowledge: Towards a Post-Critical Philosophy*. New York: Harper Torchbooks, [1958] 1964.
————. *The Tacit Dimension*. Garden City, N.Y.: Doubleday Anchor Books, 1967.
Progoff, Ira. *Depth Psychology and Modern Man*. New York: Julian Press, 1959.
————. "Waking Dream and Living Myth." In Joseph Campbell, Ed., *Myths, Dreams, and Religion*. Pp. 176-95.
Puech, Henri-Charles; Guillamont, A.; Quispel, G.; Till, W.; and Masih, Yassah 'Abd Al; Eds. and trs. *Gospel According to Thomas*. New York: Harper & Brothers, 1959.

Reich, Charles A. *The Greening of America*. New York: Bantam Books, [1970] 1971.
Reps, Paul, Ed. *Zen Flesh, Zen Bones: A Collection of Zen and Pre-Zen Writings*. Garden City, N.Y.: Doubleday Anchor Books, [1957] 1961.
Ricoeur, Paul. *Fallible Man. Translated* by Charles Kelbley. Chicago: Henry Regnery Co., 1965.

BIBLIOGRAPHY

Rogers, Carl R. *On Becoming A Person*. Boston: Houghton Mifflin, 1961.

Rokeach, Milton. *The Open and Closed Mind*. New York: Basic Books, 1960.

Rowley, George. *Principles of Chinese Painting*. Princeton: Princeton University Press, [1959] 1970.

Rychlak, Joseph F. *A Philosophy of Science for Personality Theory*. Boston: Houghton-Mifflin, 1968.

Saarinen, Aline B. "New Images of Man—Are They?" *New York Times Magazine* (Sept. 27, 1959), 18-20.

Sanders, Marion K. "The Professional Radical, 1970: Saul Alinsky/ A Conversation." *Harper's* (Jan., 1970), 35-42.

Schachtel, Ernest. *Experiential Foundations of Rorschach's Test*. New York: Basic Books, 1966.

Schutz, William C. *Joy: Expanding Human Awareness*. New York: Grove Press, 1967.

Scully, Vincent. *The Earth, The Temple and The Gods: Greek Sacred Architecture*. New Haven: Yale University Press, 1962.

Selye, Hans. *The Stress of Life*. New York: McGraw-Hill Book Co., 1956.

Solley, Charles M., and Murphy, Gardner. *Development of the Perceptual World*. New York: Basic Books, 1960.

Stewart, Milton. "Dream Theory in Malaya." In C. T. Tart, Ed. *Altered States of Consciousness*. Pp. 159-67.

Stoudt, John Joseph. *Jacob Boehme: His Life and Thought*. New York: The Seabury Press, 1968.

Sullivan, Harry Stack. *The Interpersonal Theory of Psychiatry*. New York: W. W. Norton & Co., 1953.

Suzuki, Daisetz T. *Essays in Zen Buddhism*. First Series. New York: Grove Press, 1961.

Sze, Mai-mai. *The Tao of Painting: A Study of the Ritual Disposition of Chinese Painting*. Princeton: Princeton University Press, Bollingen Series, [1956] 1963.

Tart, Charles T., Ed. *Altered States of Consciousness: A Book of Readings*. New York: John Wiley & Sons, 1969.

Tauber, Edward S., and Green, Maurice R. *Prelogical Experience: An Inquiry into Dreams and Other Creative Processes*. New York: Basic Books, 1959.

Themis, B. A. "Man Is Only Human." *Christianity and Crisis* (Apr. 28, 1969).

Tillich, Paul. *The Courage To Be*. New Haven: Yale University Press, 1952.

―――――. *A History of Christian Thought*. Edited by Carl E. Braaten. London: SCM Press, 1968.

————. *Systematic Theology: Existence and the Christ.* Vol. 2. Chicago: University of Chicago Press, 1957.

————. *Systematic Theology: Life and the Spirit; History and the Kingdom of God.* Vol. 3. Chicago: University of Chicago Press, 1963.

Toffler, Alvin. *Future Shock.* New York: Random House, 1970.

Von Franz, M. L. "Conclusion: Science and the Unconscious." In C. G. Jung, Ed., *Man and His Symbols.* Pp. 304-10.

Von Grunebaum, G. E., and Caillois, Roger, Eds. *The Dream and Human Societies.* Berkeley: University of California Press, 1966.

Von Rad, Gerhard. *Genesis: A Commentary.* Translated by J. H. Marks. Philadelphia: The Westminster Press, 1961.

Wain, Louis. "Schizophrenic Cat Paintings." *World Health* 11 (May-June, 1959). Guttmann-Maclay Collection.

Watts, Alan W. *The Two Hands of God: The Myths of Polarity.* New York: P. F. Collier, 1969.

————. *The Way of Zen.* New York: Vintage Books, 1957.

Westman, H. *The Springs of Creativity.* With an Introduction to Part Three by Sir Herbert Read. New York: Atheneum, 1961.

Wheelwright, Philip, Tr. *Heraclitus.* New York: Atheneum, 1964.

White, Robert. "Motivation Reconsidered: The Concept of Competence." *Psychological Review* (1959), 297-333.

Whyte, Lancelot Law. *The Unconscious Before Freud.* Foreword by Edith Sitwell. London: Social Science Paperbacks, Tavistock Publications, [1959] 1962.

Wickes, Francis G. *The Inner World of Childhood: A Study in Analytical Psychology.* Introduction by Carl G. Jung. New York: Signet Books, 1968.

Zevi, Bruno. *Architecture As Space: How to Look at Architecture.* Translated by Milton Gendel and edited by Joseph A. Barry. New York: Horizon Press, 1957.

Zimmer, Heinrich. *The Art of Indian Asia: Its Mythology and Transformations.* Completed and edited by Joseph Campbell, with photographs by Eliot Elisofon and others. Vol. 1. Princeton: Princeton University Press, Bollingen Series, Vol. 39, [1955] 1960.

Index of Subjects

251

INDEX OF SUBJECTS

Macworth, Norman, 239
Maeterlinck, Maurice,
102-3
Mandala, 118
Marduk, 143-44
Mark (evangelist), 201
Marriage, 35, 36
Masculine principle, 156,
157-58, 170-71, 208
Maslow, Abraham, 50,
59, 61-62, 163-64
Matthew (evangelist),
201
May, Rollo, 27, 130,
207-9
Maya, 142
Mayan temple, 129
Mayer, Jean, 130
Meaning: 39, 139, 147,
160, 203; creation of,
145, 152, 236; levels of,
82-83, 106, 199; mo-
ment by moment, 32;
multiple, 104, 110; or-
ganization of, 96-97,
172; sense of, 57, 98-
99, 117; significant,
57; world of, 101. *See
also* Language
Meaninglessness, 34, 35
Meaning trip, the, 18,
213-14, 228
Meditation, 83, 192-93
Metanoia, 211. *See*
Transformation
Mirror, 85, 91, 151, 209,
224
Monet, Claude, 212
Monkeys, 46
Moses, 98
Mother, 198. *See also*
Infant
Muhammad, 108
Munch, Edvard, 34
Murphy, Gardner, 71, 83
*Mustard Seed Garden
Manual of Painting,
The*, (Li Yü), 126-27
Mystery, 45, 101, 116,
117, 138
Mysticism, 71, 199, 200,
227-28
Myth: 101-7, 108-9, 111,
139, 198, 202, 232;
creation, 138-44, 235

Name, 155, 185. *See also*
Language
Narcissus, 168-69
Nature, 166-67
Near Eastern religion,
143-44, 162
Needs: 52-59, 160; orien-
tation and devotion,
57, 119. *See also* Desire

Negative, the, 38, 42,
221-22, 227-28
Nietzsche, Frederick, 48
Nirvana, 142
"No," 225-28. *See* "Yes"
No-Exit Relationship,
72-79

Oakes, Maud, 202
Ogden, C. K., 150-51
Opposites, 92, 93-94, 96,
114-15, 119, 162, 214,
225, 226. *See also* Co-
incidence of opposites;
Opposition
Opposition, 150-51, 221-
22
Order, 215, 235. *See also*
Marduk
Organization, 106-7, 129,
138, 212-13
Oriental. *See* the East
Origen, 71
Originality, 124-25

Participation, 31-32, 39,
44, 61, 111, 114, 199,
209
Pathological, the, 66-67,
68-69, 216
Paul (apostle), 24
Pentecost, 98
Perception, 52-53, 57-58,
83, 97-98, 129, 150-51,
160, 208, 209-10, 212-
20, 225
Perls, Frederick S., 27,
83-84, 90-91, 93-94,
109, 112, 113, 121, 173
Persona, 115
Personal: 109, 127;
depths, 67-69, 100; re-
sponse, 101, 104, 110.
See also Participation;
space, 86; subjective,
50; time, 89-90; world,
94, 112-13, 152-53
Perspective, 104, 128-29,
210-11, 216, 218, 219,
225, 227
Plato, 66
Po-chang, 142
Polarities: 51, 172-73,
192, 208, 223; being/
becoming, 32, 59, 61,
82, 134-35, 161, 167,
168, 176, 208; being/
seeming, 52-54, 62-64;
central/peripheral
vision, 85, 102; felt-
meaning/what's-there,
47-48, 53-54, 55, 56-
57, 58, 59, 89, 99, 100,
103, 104, 110, 114,
116, 118, 138, 147, 152,

Polarities—*Cont'd*
172, 199, 201, 204,
207, 211, 224, 227; in-
tuition/intellect, 116,
176, 181, 196, 198,
207; potentiality/
actuality, 127-33, 162,
165; reality/appear-
ance, 53-54; sea
dragon/ship, 19-21, 59,
100, 102, 116, 134-35,
137, 160, 165, 167,
168, 173-74, 176, 196,
208, 211, 213, 223, 228;
unconscious/conscious
18, 193, 204, 214;
universal/unique, 19,
120-27; vitality/inten-
tionality, 134-35, 164,
173-74, 202-3, 208, 223
(*see also* Sea dragon/
ship); wish/will, 128,
131; yin/yang, 133-34.
See also Coincidence
of opposites
Positive, the, 38, 221-22,
227-28
Potentiality. *See* Polarities, potentiality/
actuality
Power, 149-51, 162, 167,
170, 201, 203, 206,
207-8, 209. *See also*
Intentionality
Powerless, 49, 130, 153
Prelogical, 68, 103, 109,
116, 209
Presence, lack of, 84
Pride. *See* Hubris
Progoff, Ira, 111
Projection, 62-64, 111
Psychic compensation,
principle of, 115
Psychoanalysis, 66
Psychotherapy, 64, 177-
78, 205-7

Race, the crisis of, 27,
57-59, 98, 218. *See also*
Black experience
Rapid eye movement
(REM), 111, 232-33
Rasmussen, Knud J., 69
Reality: 106-7, 164, 175;
religious, 104, 222;
transcendent, 23, 69,
71, 105, 116, 120; ulti-
mate, 162, 227. *See
also* God
Reason. *See* Thought
Reich, Charles, 43, 55
Relatedness, 26-27, 70,
156-58, 177, 223-25
Religion: 174-75; com-
parative, 104-5;

INDEX OF SUBJECTS

Index of Scripture